ASSESSMENT OF HUMAN MOTIVES

ASSESSMENT OF

SPONSORED BY

DEPARTMENT OF PSYCHOLOGY

SYRACUSE UNIVERSITY

EDITED BY

GARDNER LINDZEY

UNIVERSITY OF MINNESOTA

HUMAN MOTIVES

Gordon W. Allport

Raymond B. Cattell

Leon Festinger

Irving L. Janis

George A. Kelly

George S. Klein

Gardner Lindzey

Henry A. Murray

Roy Schafer

HOLT, RINEHART AND WINSTON

New York - Chicago - San Francisco
Toronto - London

CONTENTS

Preface

This volume is intended to provide an introduction to the thought and investigation of a number of distinguished psychologists who have contributed to the assessment and understanding of human motivation. The array of conceptions, prescriptions, and findings to follow is likely to be of particular interest to individuals within the fields of personality and clinical psychology. The fruitfulness of these ideas is not completely limited to these areas, however, for motivational concepts occupy a central role in many domains of psychology. Thus, the psychologist concerned solely with problems of perception or learning, as well as the social psychologist, may find much that is stimulating or that resonates with his own work in the contributions contained in this volume.

Although the contributors represent a healthy diversity of interest and theoretical conviction, they share a common concern with respect to problems that have implications for how to go about assessing human motives. Prior to the preparation of their papers the contributors were given a set of issues relevant to the assessment of motives, with the suggestion that they might care to deal with some or all of these issues in their presentation. These issues are identified and discussed very briefly in the first chapter, and an attempt is made to establish the position of the contributors in regard to these specific questions. This procedure encouraged a further unity in the total presentation.

Perhaps a word should be said concerning our use of the term assessment in the title of this book. This word has come to be used by many psychologists as a means of referring to measurement in the most permissive sense, i.e., measurement that utilizes instruments possessing few of the metric properties that are ideally desirable. For our purposes, then, the term assessment is a means of emphasizing the importance of measurement, at the same time making clear that avenues of study utilizing relatively crude and undeveloped methods of data collection or measurement are not to be excluded. Our decision to focus upon problems of assessment stems from a conviction that past decades of speculation concerning motivational properties of the human organism are likely to result in future progress only when the terms that have been so effortlessly employed in theoretical discussion are given some reasonably precise means of empirical translation. Actually, as the reader will note in the pages to follow, there is no scarcity of theoretical formulation in spite of our deliberate emphasis upon assessment.

With the exception of the first chapter, the papers comprising this volume were presented at a conference which was held at Syracuse University during the spring of 1957. Financial support for the conference was provided by a grant from the United States Public Health Service. I am deeply grateful to the members of the Department of Psychology at Syracuse University who participated in arranging the conference and selecting the participants. Particularly active in this planning stage were Sanford Dean, Joseph Masling, and Jerome Schiller.

Gardner Lindzey

Minneapolis
June, 1958

ASSESSMENT OF HUMAN MOTIVES

GARDNER LINDZEY

University of Minnesota

1 *The assessment of human motives*

This chapter represents no more than a slight appetizer intended to whet the reader's appetite for the feast to follow. Consequently, its aims are few and simple. First, I plan to comment briefly upon the general status of motivational assessment within psychology. Second, I intend to consider the over-all importance for psychology of inquiry concerned with matters of method or procedure. Third, I shall outline very briefly the nature of the chapters to follow. In conclusion, I shall discuss a series of key issues relevant to the assessment of motives with special reference to the position of the various contributors to this volume.

No area of psychology has been subjected to a more prolonged and less systematic scrutiny than has the domain of motivation. It has been more than half a century since Freud and McDougall lamented the tendency of the structuralist psychology of their era to overlook or minimize the importance of motivational variables. In the intervening years many distinguished psychologists have centered much of their attention upon this class of variables but with remarkably little in the way of tangible and widely accepted gain. As Allport demonstrates in a subsequent chapter, although thousands of motivational variables have been propounded during the brief history of psychology, none has secured prolonged and widespread acceptance. In fact, for almost every set of motivational variables there has been a counterproposal to the effect that the last thing in the world that psychologists should be interested in is compiling lists of motives. Theorists who conceive of behavior as primarily motivated by benign and socially approved motives may be paired with theorists who see the chief impellents of behavior as primitive and unacceptable urges. For those who believe learned or socially acquired motives are of predominant importance there is opposition in the form of theorists convinced that the physiologically grounded and largely innate drives are of primary importance. Some have emphasized the abstract or logical status of motivational constructs, while others have stressed the physical reality and concrete existence of motives.

The conceptual nature of motivational variables has remained so murky that even the clear distinction of these variables from other classes of concepts employed in psychological theory is yet to be accomplished. The identification of motivational concepts as representing one type of disposition concept has, of course, been pointed out, and likewise the kinship between reduction sentences and motivational concepts. However, the formal imprecision of psychological theories prevents such logical analyses from contributing much to an understanding of the nature of these concepts. Among the most illuminating contributions in this area are papers by Koch (1941a, 1941b), perhaps psychology's most astute methodologist, and this sophisticated observer was led to conclude, after surveying the status of empirical findings bearing upon motivation, that we had not yet reached a stage where we could reasonably even aspire to general systematic theory (Koch, 1951). Thus, whether we examine the field of motivation from the point of view of theory, meta-theory, or empirical findings, much remains to be accomplished.

While McDougall, Freud, the Instinct Theorists and Simple and Sovereign Formulators such as Bentham, Hobbes, LeBon, and Tarde have all contributed heavily to current conceptions of human motivation, only within the past two decades have psychologists shown a deep concern with the problems of *assessing* motives. Most of the early theorists were content to identify the mainsprings of human behavior; they showed little concern over individual differences in the strength or existence of these motives and over problems of inferring or establishing these individual differences. Psychologists who were concerned early with assessing motivation tended to focus their interests upon infra-human subjects and thus had little to say of value to the person interested in human motives. It may be safely concluded that the first forty years of this century belong, so far as measurement is concerned, to the cognitive, *not* the conative, sphere of human behavior. Intelligence and the various special abilities and achievements received the bulk of psychologists' attention during this era, and there have been handsome dividends from these concerted efforts.

World War I, with the development of the Army Alpha and the Army Beta tests of intelligence, is commonly considered to have provided the most important impetus for the mental testing movement which sprang to prominence in the years following the war, building upon the foundations provided by Binet, Terman, and Spearman. What the first war did for the development of techniques for assessing intellectual functioning was almost exactly duplicated by World War II in the area of motivation. The development of questionnaires designed to identify the psychologically unfit, the extensive use of projective techniques both in special selection programs and in connection with the diagnosis and treatment of psychiatric patients, the increased familiarity with major and minor problems of mental disorder on the part of both psychologists and the general public, the dawning awareness of the power and pervasive impact of hidden sources of motivation upon the important domains of behavior—all of these factors growing out of the war contributed to an increased concern over the process whereby one could confidently identify the major sources of motivation which determine individual behavior.

The shift in focus for psychologists from the cognitive to the conative or motivational is nicely reflected in the fact that during the past decade and a half the Rorschach Test and unconscious motivation have become as widely known and discussed by the general public as were the intelligence test and IQ some twenty-five years earlier. Within psychology the growing interest in personality and clinical research, coupled with the acceptance of some professional responsibility for helping to meet mental health needs, led to a major change in the composition of most psychology departments. The field of clinical psychology, which had little identifiable existence prior to 1940, became by 1950 one of the major fields of graduate study in psychology. With only a few exceptions, the major universities not only established such programs but watched them grow in size to a point where they equaled or surpassed the traditional areas of specialty within psychology. Inasmuch as the clinical psychologist is primarily concerned with matters of motivation, whether he deals with pathology or normal development, the burgeoning of this field is both a reflection of the increased interest in human motivation and its assessment, and at the same time a demonstration of the need for further development in this area. The interested reader will find a fuller account of many of these events in a recent paper by Murray (1956).

There are many in psychology who have grave reservations concerning the wisdom and long-range defensibility of psychology's expansion on the clinical frontier. These reservations usually center about the question of whether application should be promoted prior to the development of a basic science with its attendant theories and instruments. In coping with this objection it is obvious that the more rigorously and sensitively we can measure or assess human motives, the firmer the ground on which clinical psychology rests. One might say that the entire specialty —diagnostic, therapeutic, and investigative—rests upon the assumption that human motives can be measured successfully. Thus, the more convincing the evidence that can be supplied to support this assumption, the more tenable is the position of clinical psychology.

In general, then, an interest in motivation has long been characteristic of psychologists, but only in recent years has there been a serious effort to provide an adequate means of measuring human motives. Further, this present interest in motivational assessment represents one of the major developments of the past several decades in psychology and is reflected in a prodigious amount of contemporary activity.

INTERDEPENDENCE OF THEORY AND METHOD

Contemporary psychologists display for the most part a boundless respect for the importance of systematic theory. I would be tempted to say they are overawed by theory if it were not for the fact that theory is potentially such a powerful tool that perhaps it is impossible to overestimate its significance. In any event, this worship at the altar of theory has led many psychologists to develop a derogatory attitude toward the individual who engages in mere method or procedural research. In the eyes of many, the person who contributes to the solution of a problem of measurement or method is a technician struggling with a tiny fragment of the broad problem of behavior, lacking the lofty vision necessary to deal creatively with an encompassing theoretical view of human behavior. This common attitude suggests that in the area of motivation we must admire and applaud the theoretical contributions of Freud, Hull, and Lewin, while the contributions of Thurstone or Rorschach must be considered of secondary importance. Such a view would necessarily imply the relative triviality of our present enterprise, because we have chosen to focus upon the assessment or measurement end of the theory-method continuum.

There are many grounds for disagreeing with this contention. One may even argue that psychological theory at our present stage of development has *less* to contribute to the generation of research and the extension of psychological knowledge than has the careful study of specific empirical phenomena or particular methods (cf. Koch, 1951; Skinner, 1956). According to this view, the relative importance suggested in the last paragraph should be reversed, and theoretically derived research given a lower billing than that which begins closer to the actual data being examined. A more moderate position suggests that systematic theory has, in fact, a unique importance upon the psychological scene but goes on to insist that theoretical advance is inextricably linked to procedural or measuremental developments. It is this view which we choose to advocate here.

Just how important is method or procedure in contributing to theoretical advance? In view of what has just been said, one might reason that the general importance of the topic of our conference stands or falls with the answer to this question. Obviously, the answer will depend upon the chief functions that we believe a theory should fulfill. Let us simply assume that a theory should serve the dual functions of unifying or making congruent known empirical findings, and suggesting new empirical relations to be explored or verified. While both of these are important, most persons would agree that the generation of research, liberally defined, is the prime contribution of a theory, and it is upon this function that we shall dwell.

Given this relatively innocuous view of what theory should do, let us examine the role of measurement in connection with one of the most important existing psychological theories—psychoanalysis. This theory is chosen, not with the expectation that the role of method or procedure is unusually important here, but rather because of the theory's manifest importance in the area of psychology with which this volume is concerned. A similar kind of analysis could be carried out for any psychological theory which would, I am sure, arrive at the same conclusions. A much more elegant and detailed analysis, conducted by Koch (1954) with reference to Hull's reinforcement theory, clearly reveals the essential role of measurement in attempts to interpret a theory empirically.

PSYCHOANALYTIC RESEARCH: ILLUSTRATION OF
THE IMPORTANCE OF INSTRUMENTATION

There is no need to underscore the point that Freud's intellectual contributions rank with those of the foremost scholars of our time. His impact upon the thinking world can be compared realistically only with Darwin and Marx among scholars of the past century. Indeed, it is difficult to find a field of human knowledge this side of the physical sciences that has not been influenced by Freud's formulations. If we put aside the question of good or bad and ask only, "How much?" there can be no doubt that the contribution of psychoanalytic theory to modern thought has been profound.

What of the research that the theory has stimulated? Here, too, we must arrive at a positive verdict insofar as we are concerned solely with quantity. A mere fifteen years ago a reasonably complete survey of the systematic research relevant to psychoanalysis was reported in a monograph that was less than an inch thick (Sears, 1943). A comparable survey today which approached comprehensiveness would be closer to a yard than an inch in thickness.

Granted the large number of such studies, what can be said concerning their quality? Now, quality of research is a very difficult thing to assess, and it is almost true that there is no such thing as an investigation that is beyond criticism. Further, so long as there is criticism that can be raised against a study, there will be some people to say that this study is valueless or of relatively little value. As evidence of this, there are entire psychological journals filled with investigations that distinguished psychologists would judge to be, without exception, worthless. Of course, there are other journals that these psychologists would defend as reporting worth-while investigations which in turn would be criticized by another set of reputable psychologists as containing only speculation or fantasy. Evaluation of research depends upon numerous implicit and explicit assumptions, some theoretical and others having to do with convictions concerning the research process, the cumulation of knowledge, and the logic of science. Further, there is the undeniable role of irrational factors, personal bias, and self-interest. These individual differences in estimating the merit of research are relevant to our present discussion because I am about to suggest that the vast bulk of investigation pertaining to psychoanalytic theory falls into two different categories, distinguished primarily by the individuals who approve of the research in each category.

The first of the categories consists of what might be called *clinical research* or *uncontrolled observational studies*. Here we classify all the inquiries that are based upon material derived from actual clinical cases, with no attempt to introduce experimental controls or to assess the role of chance factors. Most prominent among these studies are, of course, the investigations reported by Freud himself, for example, the case of Little Hans, the case of Dora, Schreber, the Rat Man, and the Wolf Man. In addition to these, however, there is a cumulation of fifty years of literature in which more or less able, and more or less sensitive, investigators have suggested that in their experience with patients they have found confirmation for earlier findings, new findings, contradictory findings, illustration of old concepts, and suggestions of new concepts. These studies are not uniformly of the same quality, but the best of them are considered by the clinical analyst to represent the evidential basis for psychoanalytic theory and generalization. Thus, to the clinical analyst, any good example of this type of study would be acceptable as providing important evidence bearing upon psychoanalytic theory.

What is the reaction to these studies of the investigator who has been carefully trained in laboratory technique, statistical inference, empirical control, and experimental design? What of the person who knows the boundless deceit of the human organism when it is a matter of testing empirically his own ideas and preconceptions? Virtually without exception these individuals consider such studies to possess no merit so far as providing evidence is concerned. They might concede them some role in the discovery phase of investigation but certainly not in the testing or confirmation of ideas. These studies tell us largely what their authors wanted to observe, say our critics, and they fail to meet the most elementary standards of adequate empirical control.

Given this research, which is acceptable to the analyst but completely unacceptable to the well-trained investigator, one naturally asks whether there are not some studies that are considered worth while or important by this hypothetical investigator? If we assume that he does not simply write off, or dismiss, this entire area of investigation, the answer to this question is clearly "Yes!" Investigations tending to meet his exacting standards have been summarized on several occasions, by Sears (1943), and Hilgard (1952), among others. In general, these studies consist of *research* in which the investigator has worked outside of a clinical setting *in* some kind of *experimental or controlled circumstance*. While these inquiries naturally show considerable variation, they are similar in attempting to hold constant all but one or a small number of relevant variables, in introducing at least minimum quantification, and in performing some type of statistical analysis.

Typical of these investigations are the many studies of "repression" using electric shock or taboo words, the studies of regression or fixation using children playing with toys or rats running through mazes, the studies of projection involving self-ratings and ratings of others, and the studies of displacement employing sparring white rats or attitude scales. While most well-trained psychologists have many objections to these studies individually, they would nevertheless contend that insofar as there is any *evidence* relevant to psychoanalytic theory it is provided by this class of investigation.

There is no need to speculate about the reaction of the clinician to such studies—it is typically one of acute nausea! He contends, with more than a small degree of justification, that these studies may have some independent merit but that they certainly do not bear directly upon psychoanalytic theory, for the investigators have introduced alien measures in an irrelevant setting, and frequently with only a vague grasp of the nature of the theory they purport to test. It is indisputable that the operations or observations embodied in such studies have only the vaguest or most obscure relation to the data with which psychoanalytic theory has typically dealt.

Here we are, then, with a vast amount of research that has occupied the time and energy of hundreds and hundreds of investigators during the past three or four decades, and we find almost none of it pleasing to both of the interested professional groups. At this point, let us ask the question of why it is that so few studies are mutually satisfactory to clinician and experimenter alike. Or more broadly, what are the factors that have made it difficult to translate the clinical wisdom of psychoanalysis into attainable research goals. At risk of oversimplification, permit me to suggest that the major difficulties here have to do with four factors: (1) *the formal inadequacies of psychoanalytic theory*, (2) *the importance of genetic propositions within psychoanalysis*, (3) *the mutual reluctance of most well-trained investigators and clinicians to work outside their customary areas*, and (4) *the absence of adequate techniques or methods for measuring variables pertinent to psychoanalytic theory*. A word about each of these.

There are many *formal shortcomings* to psychoanalysis as a body of theory, and these shortcomings pose a striking problem for the person who wishes to use the theory as a means of generating ideas for investigation. It is clear that initially there is a lack of satisfactory *coordinating definitions* for the empirical concepts of the theory. That is, there is no provision for the necessary steps whereby the theoretical statements can be translated into the world of reality or observation. Just what is the empirical referent of oral fixation, castration anxiety, primary narcissism, or genital adjustment? The literature contains many statements that are relevant to the empirical translation of these concepts, but these statements are by no means adequately explicit, nor are they even completely consistent among themselves. Furthermore, most of the discussions are concerned with relating psychoanalytic concepts to events in the psychoanalytic interview and consequently are of little use in the attempt to apply the theory to other domains of behavior. Even more fundamental is the objection to psychoanalysis on the grounds that the *axiomatic base* or the core assumptions of the theory are not explicitly indicated. The point where theory leaves off and testable derivation begins is by no means clear. What appears analytic or assumed to one observer is an empirical statement open to test for a second observer. Furthermore, the *syntax* of the theory, the internal rules whereby the elements or concepts of the theory are related, is highly inadequate. Without an explicit grammar or syntax, and a clearly demarked set of underlying assumptions, it is inevitably very difficult to manipulate the theory in such a way as to generate empirical statements to be investigated. It is true that the very ambiguity and vagueness introduced by these flaws make the theory ideal from the point of view of after-the-fact incorporation of known or observed findings. This a dubious virtue, however, for the person interested in investigation.

The second difficulty we have referred to is posed by the *heavy emphasis in psychoanalysis upon relations that span a long period of time*. The so-called genetic propositions that refer to the relation between events taking place early in the life of the individual and events taking place in adulthood present a peculiar dilemma for the investigator. These long-term relations pose such difficult problems in empirical control at the level of human behavior that almost no well-designed and controlled studies have been carried out bearing upon these propositions. The history of longitudinal or growth studies of child development makes clear that such investigations lead quickly to bulging files but seldom result in clear-cut or definitive empirical findings. It is true that some interesting studies have been carried out with lower animals, but in order to place much faith in these, one must accept wholeheartedly a number of rather tenuous assumptions concerning the continuity of man with rat, dog, and mouse. Fortunately, there *are* propositions to be derived from psychoanalysis that have to do with contemporary events or simultaneously existing variables, and some of these have been investigated.

A rather unique factor that tends to interfere with satisfactory investigation in this area has to do with the fact that *the socialization process involved in developing skillful and dedicated clinicians and investigators* tends to inhibit or hamper the crossing over of these two professional lines. The majority of persons well-trained in investigation would not be caught dead in such a messy area as psychoanalytic research. That is, the person who has internalized the norms of a subgroup

that prizes rigorous and precise investigation is going to be pretty unhappy with most of the problems that present themselves in this area,
for they are simply not susceptible to elegant handling at present. In
similar vein, the individual who is well socialized as a clinician is likely
to be seriously embarrassed if his colleagues catch him fracturing the
daylights out of the natural givenness of clinical phenomena, as most
research necessitates. To take an elaborately described, complex and
poignant, clinical case and reduce it to a single score on one or a small
number of variables seems so brutally abstract as to offend any sensitive
observer. Thus all the natural rewards, as well as the pressures from
fellow colleagues, encourage the clinician to continue thinking in terms
of case histories, and the well-trained investigator to remain in the laboratory dealing with problems that have little or no relevance to psychoanalysis. I should make clear that this conservative tendency is not
simply a matter of passive conformity to approved standards, for it is
related most importantly to the fact that in the process of becoming
sensitive clinicians and skillful experimenters each group develops internal values and conceptions of what is important or significant that
simply rule out the data and approach of the other.

Finally, we turn to the difficulty with which we are most concerned
here, *the absence of adequate measuring devices for intercepting or
assessing variables of special relevance to psychoanalytic theory.* It is
clear that most of the variables that are central to psychoanalysis, such
as oedipal conflict, anal fixation, identification, narcissism, projection,
and sublimation, are a far cry from the variables upon which the psychologist has traditionally focused. Thus it should come as no surprise
to find that the methods the psychologist has emphasized seem relatively inappropriate for assessing variables of major interest to the
psychoanalyst. The bulk of psychoanalytic observation and the root of
most generalization in this area consist of responses from the world of
imagery—dreams, free associations, remote memories, and psychotic
ramblings. These responses are made under circumstances that depart
dramatically from those characterizing everyday report or normal day-
to-day conduct. The responses also differ greatly from those involved in
customary psychometric procedures, for the latter usually require that
the subject respond with a maximum of accuracy and within a very
limited range of response possibilities. The hallmark of the psycho-

metrician or expert in psychological measurement is repeatability, precision, and avoidance of ambiguity. The clinician is more concerned with richness of response and the significance and meaningfulness of his data. The raw material of the psychoanalyst, when compared to the raw material of the psychometrician, is relatively disorderly, chaotic, irrational, profuse, asocial, and emotion-charged. In general, the questionnaire and rating-scale approaches, which traditionally have been favored by the psychologist, seem inappropriate to the task of measuring variables central to psychoanalytic theory, and this inadequacy appears an understandable consequence of the rather different kinds of observational data with which the two traditions have dealt. Consequently, the individual interested in testing derivations from psychoanalytic theory has often found himself choosing between relevance and rigor, for those instruments with the most desirable measurement properties are precisely those which appear to have least appropriateness for assessing psychoanalytic variables.

At this point all that has been said is that there is a considerable gulf between psychoanalytic formulation and adequate investigation; further, we have suggested some of the factors that have operated to preserve, if not to widen, this gulf. What needs to be added is the observation that the most serious and limiting of the four factors we have considered is the measurement shortcoming. If there were adequate techniques to permit the sensitive and replicable assessment of variables of central theoretical importance, we could confidently expect that the formal imprecision of the theory would gradually give way to increased clarification and specification. Moreover, the attractiveness of the field for individuals trained in laboratory science would be appreciably enhanced if there were satisfactory measuring tools. Even the longitudinal study of relevant propositions would be facilitated if we could confidently assess dimensions of central importance to psychoanalysis.

To summarize, we have examined the impact of a tremendously influential psychological theory and have found a pronounced deficit in relevant empirical findings that are widely accepted. Moreover, this low incidence of significant and verifiable findings seems largely attributable to the absence of measuring instruments adequate to assess psychoanalytic variables. Thus, if we grant the theory an important status on the contemporary scene, we are forced to concede the central importance of efforts to develop instruments that will permit the theory to be efficiently translated into the world of reality. Until this procedural stage has been satisfactorily negotiated it is impossible to carry out coordinated empirical investigations that can be considered valid reflections of the theory.

If we return to the question with which we began this discussion, "How important is the contribution of method to theoretical development?" the answer appears to be "Very important indeed!" A concern with the *assessment* of motives is fully as crucial as a concern with the *theory* of motives; in fact, the two are not to be clearly separated. Advance in one area automatically presupposes advance in the other.

The fact that we have anchored our discussion of theory and method in a discussion of psychoanalytic research is particularly appropriate in view of the nature of several of the chapters to follow. While a number of the chapters have relevance to what we have been discussing, it is Irving Janis' paper that deals most directly with the problem of method and psychoanalytic theory, and much of what has been said above is elaborated and reinforced by the content of Professor Janis' chapter. Further, his work, as well as that of Klein and Schafer, has done much to diminish some of the difficulties to which we have alluded.

A PREVIEW OF WHAT IS TO FOLLOW

Before considering some of the similarities and differences between our contributors in their approach to the assessment of human motives it may be helpful to the reader if we pause and indicate very briefly something about what is to be found in each of the subsequent chapters.

In the following chapter the reader will find a bold new approach to the formulation of human personality. George Kelly in one stroke has solved all the problems confronting the individual concerned with motivational assessment, for he recommends eliminating such concepts from the psychologist's theoretical storehouse. His approach to behavior appears to emphasize cognitive variables, although he himself would assert that it eliminates the necessity for the conventional distinction between cognitive, conative, and affective variables. He suggests that the *personal constructs* used by the individual to order or bring meaning to his phenomenal world provide the key by means of which his behavior can be understood and studied systematically. Moreover, Professor Kelly speaks out strongly against several classical errors which he feels have too long obstructed the thinking of psychologists. The first of these is the tendency to look always to the object of a word for its possible significance rather than to the subject or the person speaking the word. The second misconception has to do with relying upon the "principle of the excluded middle," with its implication that a proposition concerning a given object or person must be either true or false, never irrelevant. These novel ideas are given concrete anchoring in a detailed discussion of the therapeutic process.

The next chapter also involves a cognitive approach to human motivation. In this treatment, however, Leon Festinger develops systematically the importance of cognitive dissonance (simultaneous acceptance of incompatible beliefs) as a variable with important motivational implications. Not only does the state of cognitive dissonance produce efforts to reduce or eliminate the dissonance, but Festinger also suggests the likelihood of individual differences in susceptibility to cognitive dissonance. Thus he formulates a new motivating condition or factor, provides some fascinating empirical evidence (both naturalistic and experimental) to support predictions derived from his formulations, and ends on the suggestion that the variable is worth further inquiry as a potential measure of individual differences relevant to the understanding of human motivation.

In George Klein's chapter we find still another cognitive approach to the problem of human motivation, but one that is quite different from either of the preceding chapters. Klein is deeply concerned with the measurement and study of what he calls cognitive attitudes or, more broadly, cognitive styles. These styles refer to the characteristic way or manner in which the individual goes about thinking, perceiving, and ordering his cognitive world, and have implications for the manner in which the individual will express or actualize drive states. Klein has also developed objective techniques for assessing individual differences along these important ego dimensions. In an important sense his work can be considered to represent an experimental ego psychology which involves an intriguing synthesis of the holism of gestalt and personalistic psychology, the clinical sophistication of psychoanalysis, and the objectivity of sensory psychology.

Even more specifically concerned with psychoanalysis and the ego processes is Roy Schafer's chapter. Here is a clear and detailed discussion of regression in the service of the ego, showing how a concept once anchored in psychopathology has been elaborated to serve an important function in accounting for normal and supranormal behavior. Not only does Schafer bring the reader up to date on many of the recent developments in ego psychology; he also approaches the difficult task of specifying objective criteria which will permit one to use the concept of ego-controlled regressive activity in an efficient and replicable manner in clinical practice and investigation. Moreover, he demonstrates convincingly the extent to which such a process influences response to traditional devices for assessing motives and thus can represent either a source of error or a diagnostic lever, depending upon the sophistication of the test interpreter. Finally, he points to the fact that adaptive regression may even play a role in the productive activity of the test interpreter or student of human behavior himself.

Still within the main stream of influence of psychoanalytic theory is Irving Janis' paper, which indicates how the psychoanalytic interview or case study can be used as an important research tool. Janis points to the serious flaws that have existed in the research literature of psychoanalysis in the past, and emphasizes the pressing importance of a wedding between individual, clinical investigation and the norms and standards developed in experimental or laboratory research. He suggests some of the potential gains for psychology of investigation utilizing the psychoanalytic interview, and strongly advocates an extension of this method to deal with problems other than those specifically concerned with psychopathology.

Henry Murray's chapter roams over the entire range of problems encountered in motivational assessment, reports some new and exciting findings from his own work, and leaves the reader with a variety of new ideas. In particular, Professor Murray deals in an illuminating manner with some of the central problems involved in making dispositional inferences from thematic projective technique protocols. At the same time, he presents an important new concept (ascensionism) which is as relevant to contemporary culture as it is to the diagnosis of motives. Finally, he expresses active concern over the almost exclusive fixation of American psychologists upon the negative and instrumental side of human motivation.

In marked contrast to the chapters we have just described is Raymond Cattell's ambitious program for the identification and measurement of the major components of human motivation. His approach, which is labeled an objective and structured avenue to the study of motives, leans most directly upon the use of multiform, objective measures derived from diverse areas of response that appear theoretically congruent. The results provided by these measures are then subjected to factor analysis. His chapter shows many of the fruits of this approach in the form of specific variables or factors, and, in addition, he outlines points of contact between his own findings and the formulations and observations of a number of other important theorists.

In the final chapter, Gordon Allport approaches the old and difficult problem of what units should be employed in the study of human motivation. He suggests that, just as the adoption of inappropriate units of analysis held back developments in the life sciences for many centuries, so, too, psychology may soon be impeded if its search for serviceable units is not successful. In spite of the short history of psychology we have had a multitude of different motivational units that have been given a try, and, as Allport points out, none has proved definitively successful. In the process of outlining and classifying the types of units traditionally employed by psychologists, Allport deals directly with a number of central issues in this area and manages once again to argue persuasively for an approach to motivation that places the single individual with all his uniqueness at the center of the investigative stage.

MAJOR ISSUES IN THE ASSESSMENT OF HUMAN MOTIVES

Psychologists are not noted for unanimity and mutual support when it comes to central theoretical and empirical issues. Nor does the behavior of leading psychologists in regard to assessing human motives provide an exception to this generalization. Rarely do two investigators operate with just the same assumptions concerning what is the most fruitful approach to understanding and measuring motivation. The grounds for disagreement are not endless, however, and most of these individual differences can be seen as derivatives of one or more of the following basic issues.

How Important Are Conscious as Opposed to Unconscious Motives in Understanding Human Behavior? It is well known that some persons approach the study of human behavior with the conviction that all that is vitally important and of greatest significance is most deeply buried and least accessible. Such a viewpoint is a logical derivative of Freud's psychoanalytic theory, with its consistent emphasis upon unconscious factors as the major determinants of the most central elements of human behavior. The famous analogy between conscious and unconscious motivation and the iceberg, with its relatively slight mass above water and its primary bulk below the surface, provides a dramatic model of this view of behavior. The extreme alternative to this position suggests that there is no such thing as unconscious motivation and that consequently all behavior can be accounted for in terms of relatively rational motives of which the individual is aware. Such a position has almost vanished from the contemporary scene, and in its place we find a number of viewpoints which accept the existence of unconscious determinants but maintain that these motives operate only under exceptional circumstances (mental disorder, extreme stress) when customary modes of behavior have failed the individual. Another contemporary point of view implies that the apparent importance of unconscious motives can be accounted for by the subtle operation of other more basic psychological processes, so that there is no need to invoke an unconscious state or a process of repression.

We find considerable variation among our contributors on this issue. The variation can partially, but by no means altogether, be accounted for by the degree to which psychoanalysis has had impact upon the individual participant's thinking. Professor Kelly does not employ the concepts of conscious and unconscious but admits that a person is more fully aware of some personal constructs than of others. Furthermore, he considers that a relative lack of awareness of the personal constructs guiding an individual's life would be most likely to occur under the impact of anxiety and in time of stress. Leon Festinger, like Kelly, focuses most of his paper upon cognitive factors; consequently, he shows little interest in the distinction between conscious and unconscious motivation. On the other hand, there seems to be nothing in his account to imply that the process of dissonance reduction must take place consciously. Consequently, his position seems congruent with an acceptance of the dual importance of conscious and unconscious motives, even though he does not emphasize this distinction.

Although George Klein is primarily concerned in his chapter with matters of cognitive style rather than motive, it is clear that his position is close to psychoanalysis in accepting the deep and enduring importance of unconscious motives. Schafer and Janis resemble Klein in this respect, and it is worth noting that all three have been exposed to psychoanalytic training and are interested in the extension and application of psychoanalytic theory. Cattell accepts the existence and importance of unconscious motives, although the results of his research suggest two principal second-order factors that correspond more closely to "integrated interests versus unintegrated interests" than to "conscious versus unconscious." Murray, somewhat surprisingly, in view of the extent to which he has been associated with psychoanalysis, gives a rather balanced picture of the dual importance of both conscious and unconscious motives. Allport, too, seems more moderate in his acceptance of the importance of both classes of motives than he has at times in the past, although he still feels that the importance of unconscious factors is often overemphasized.

It is clear that none of the contributors denies the existence of unconscious determinants of behavior, or even implies that their study is consistently unrewarding. Still, there is considerable difference in emphasis upon these factors, with Schafer and Janis, in their present discussion, showing the deepest interest in these processes and Allport showing the least interest.

What Is the Relative Importance of Direct as Opposed to Indirect Techniques for Assessing Human Motives? A great deal of the variation in response to this question can be accounted for purely in terms of the person's position with regard to the first question. Insofar as indirect techniques, which are typified by the projective techniques, have usually been considered, if not the "royal road to the unconscious," at least a road that is better paved and more adequately mapped than other roads presently available, it is natural that those primarily interested in unconscious motivation would be interested in this class of techniques. Consistently the individual who is centering upon conscious forms of motivation is likely to consider direct techniques a more rewarding approach to assessing motives.

Perhaps a word should be said concerning the distinction between direct and indirect methods of assessing motives. Although these terms enjoy considerable current vogue and refer to clusters of instruments that are roughly distinguishable, there is actually a good deal of confusion concerning just what are the differentiating features of these instruments. Consequently, there is some overlap in techniques which would be classified under these two headings by different psychologists. In some instances the directness of the approach may be equated to the degree of inference that is required on the part of the interpreter, or it may refer to the overtness or manifestness of the response upon which the interpretation is based, or it may refer to the extent to which the purpose of the test is visible and clearly understood by the subject and observer alike. Fortunately, these different referents of the word "indirect" are all positively correlated so that we can obtain moderately good consensus concerning what is meant by the term without arriving at a more fundamental agreement concerning the defining properties of these two types of tests. For present purposes it is sufficient to oppose projective techniques, dream interpretation, and various kinds of clinical interviewing techniques (as illustrative of indirect techniques) to structured questionnaires, ratings of overt behavior, and self-ratings (as representative of direct techniques).

Our participants again show variation that ranges from indifference to the question, at one extreme, to a feeling that the kinds of information revealed by projective technique, psychoanalytic interview, or dream are clearly of greater importance than the information that can be obtained through questionnaire or self-appraisal techniques. Those who feel that there is a balanced contribution to be made by these two approaches represent a third point of view.

George Kelly again expresses some discomfort with the terms employed but indicates that in his own work he finds it fruitful occasionally to employ the subject's word at face value, while on other occasions he feels that it is better to interpret this behavior in the context of other information concerning the subject. However, he questions whether the latter approach is any less direct than the former. Raymond Cattell also is somewhat unhappy with this distinction. His findings imply, he suggests, that direct techniques (questionnaires or self-surveys, which Cattell calls opinionnaires) account for no more than 10 per cent of the variance in most significant domains of behavior, while his structured and objective measures of behavior account for a considerably higher proportion of the variance. Given this finding, he asks quite reasonably, are not his structured measures, which would scarcely be classified as direct, more direct in their capacity to penetrate to important motives than are the traditional questionnaires? Thus Cattell and Kelly seem to have arrived at a similar position on this issue from very different vantages. Neither Klein nor Schafer seems to assign any significant role to direct or structured measures of motives, and Schafer specifically indicates his conviction that questionnaire or survey techniques are much less likely to produce interesting and significant findings than are the more time-consuming and challenging clinical tools. Allport, Murray, and Janis indicate their belief in the importance of a dual consideration of both types of measures. Allport couples his plea for balance with the suggestion that recent years have seen a too exclusive concern with projective techniques, with too little attention paid to other approaches to measuring motives. Murray's clear and emphatic defense of direct approaches to human motivation may again come as a surprise to many, in view of the fact that he has been so closely linked with important developments in projective testing. In general, the authors present a rather balanced picture in their evaluation of direct and indirect techniques, with perhaps a slight preference for indirect measures.

Is It Essential, in Assessing Motives, to Provide Some Appraisal of the Ego Processes, Directive Mechanisms, or Cognitive Controls That Intervene between the Motive and Its Expression? Traditionally, attempts to employ motivational variables predictively assumed that the prediction was automatic when the investigator had secured an adequate index of the strength of the individual's motive and had also mapped his psychological ecology well enough to know what was relevant to this motive in the surrounding world. Recent developments in cognitive-perceptual research, together with a growing interest in those mechanisms which control and shape instinctual expression, have made the task of the individual who would predict from motivational variables considerably more difficult. Now he must not only appraise the strength or intensity of the relevant motivational variables and plot the psychological environment but also concern himself with individual differences in mode of expression, cognitive style, controlling mechanisms, or ego processes. Thus, according to this doctrine, different individuals in the same situation, and with the same motivational structure, will behave quite differently, depending upon the characteristic manner in which they control or direct the expression of their motivational urges.

None of our contributors denies the importance of ego processes or controlling mechanisms, although George Kelly is again somewhat uncomfortable in the face of this terminology. Actually, insofar as the issue is relevant to his position, he would consider the controlling mechanisms to be closely related to his personal constructs, and thus far *more* important to assess than any set of motivational variables. Of the remaining speakers, George Klein and Roy Schafer may be considered not only to have emphasized the importance of ego processes but actually to have devoted most of their papers to the demonstration of why it is essential that the investigator not overlook such factors. Klein's work makes clear that, depending upon the individual's characteristic cognitive attitude or style, the expression of his motivational states will show considerable variation. Schafer deals saliently with a particular ego operation, regression in the service of the ego, which has important implications not only for the general adjustment of the individual but even for the understanding of what given responses to tests of motivation may signify. Both authors agree that attempts to employ motivational measures in the absence of knowledge of the kind of intermediary variable they discuss is a hazardous and imprecise process. The research of Cattell has led to the isolation of a self-sentiment factor that importantly influences the operation of most or all motives. This self-sentiment can readily be conceived of as an intermediary cognitive process. Allport clearly implies that the most useful kind of motivational assessment involves specification of cognitive and attitudinal elements, together with specification of the motive. Thus a majority of the present authors appears to accept or emphasize the importance of including cognitive factors or ego processes in any attempt to assess motives.

In Assessing Human Motives, How Important Is It to Specify the Situational Context within Which the Motives Operate? One of the many disputes which psychologists have found themselves engaged in with members of other disciplines has centered about the question of the generality of behavioral tendencies. Many representatives of disciplines devoted to the study of sociocultural factors (anthropology and sociology) have been concerned lest the psychologist create a picture of man that views his behavior as too exclusively impelled from within. These hearty environmentalists consider the impact of external and situational factors to be at least as important as enduring, internal, and personal impellents of behavior. An excellent discussion of many of the arguments that have been made concerning this issue is to be found in Allport's (1937) general treatise on personality.

Logically enough, it is Allport, among our contributors, who deals most extensively with this issue in the present volume. He provides an excellent outline of the persuasiveness of the argument advanced by those who are so committed to situationalism that they consider it hopeless to attempt to understand and predict behavior from within. Allport himself does not appear discouraged by the gloominess of the outlook of the situationalists. In fact, he concludes that attention to the situation within which motives will operate is desirable and necessary but that there is certainly no need to give up the quest for true motivational units simply because some of the variation in behavior is determined by another class of variables. For George Kelly, knowledge of the situation is crucial in order to establish the relevance of whatever psychological variable is employed, and probably no other author in the series would disagree with this stand. Janis specifically advocates increased concern with the situational factors that operate in the present to determine the activation and expression of motives. As a group, our contributors seem only moderately interested in the situational context of motivational expressions, and they are clearly unconvinced by the argument that behavior is so largely determined by situational factors that the study of motivational factors is a fruitless enterprise.

How Necessary Is Knowledge of the Past in the Assessment of Contemporary Motivation? Here we find ourselves faced with one of psychology's classic conflicts—genetic versus ahistorical representation, Lewin's contemporaneous-field theory versus Freud's historical-psychoanalytic theory, determinism of the past versus autonomy of the present. Fortunately, the present context is ideal for producing illumination rather than the sterile polemics which often have been associated with this issue in the past. The positive feature of the present setting is its emphasis upon measurement, which anchors the discussion where it should commence. No respectable theorist has ever supported the notion that an interest in the past is essential as such. Freud and others defended an interest in the past as a means of arriving at an understanding of development and as a source of information about contemporary motivation. Thus, if we are able to understand present motives exhaustively without recourse to the past, and if we are interested solely in the present operation of these motives, then there is indeed no need to reach back into the history of the organism. This point of view is probably acceptable to all of the participants in this conference, even though some, such as Allport and Festinger, have been associated in the past with positions that were identified as contemporaneous or ahistorical, while others, such as Murray, Klein, Schafer, and Janis, have been heavily influenced by psychoanalysis.

The important issue here is the functional dependence or freedom of present motives from past events, and this issue does not seem to have intruded itself heavily into the discussion of our participants, although it is not hard to infer individual differences on this score. It seems likely that Allport, Festinger, and perhaps Kelly are less impressed with the ineradicable influence of the past than are the remaining speakers. Even on this question current developments in psychoanalytic theory, with their increased emphasis upon ego processes, nicely exemplified by Schafer's paper dealing with a single important ego process, have led to considerable reduction in the classic differences between pschoanalytic theorists and other psychological theorists. In other words, the difference between a position such as that exemplified by Allport (1937), with his concept of functional autonomy, and classical psychoanalysis has been considerably reduced through the increased role assigned by psychoanalytic theorists to relatively autonomous structures in the adult personality.

At This Time Is the Area of Motivation More in Need of Developing Precise and Highly Objective Measures of Known Motives or Identifying Significant New Motivational Variables? Here we find an opposition between trail blazing and consolidation. The essential question is whether we now possess sufficient insight into human motivation, and the variables to be used in representing it, to warrant the belief that our efforts can best be spent in devising means of assessing accurately these variables. Or are we still so far from an adequate formulation that we would be foolish to stop now and focus our attention upon what has already been identified or proposed? While psychology as a whole may have experienced a reasonable proportion of persons concerned with creating, as opposed to those concerned with testing, ideas it seems likely that the area of motivation has had less than its share of consolidators. That is, most individuals working in this area of psychology have been either partly or wholly concerned with formulating variables, and there have been precious few who appeared willing to see what could be done with the conceptions already in hand. Obviously, such a state of affairs is due in part to the relatively primitive state of theoretical formulation in this area.

What of our present contributors? We clearly have a heavy representation of scholars who have contributed new and important variables to the psychological scene. Murray, whose extensive formulations are best viewed in *Explorations in Personality* (1938), has contributed as many psychological variables to the contemporary scene as any psychologist. Allport's conceptions and Cattell's also have been formulated in novel theoretical terms and have had considerable impact upon other psychologists. George Klein is presently concerned with expounding a limited number of original variables. George Kelly, too, has contributed new variables, although he would scarcely consider them motivational; in fact, when faced with the above question, his response was a succinct "Neither." Festinger also is concerned with expounding a new and, for him, uniquely important motivational variable.

Have these same contributors shown the same degree of concern for the problems of measuring or assessing the motives that already exist or which they have formulated? Yes! Their efforts represent a healthy contrast to the general picture painted above of this area. Two of the authors, Janis and Schafer, are working extensively with variables that have already been identified and conceded central theoretical importance, and most of the remainder seem deeply involved in the measurement process. Murray for many years has been concerned with developing techniques or devices that will permit one to intercept the variables which he considers of central importance. Cattell, employing the powerful weapon of factor analysis, not only identifies or establishes the new variables which he is proposing, but through the same operation he derives at least a beginning metric for these same motivational variables. Further, he has diligently attempted to refine and develop the initial measures which have been produced by his factor analyses. Thus our authors seem to provide a healthy blending of interest in creation or new formulation with concern for operational specification and careful, critical study.

In Attempting to Understand Human Motivation Is It Advisable at Present to Focus upon One or a Small Number of Motivational Variables, or Should an Effort be Made to Appraise a Wide Array of Variables? Do Multivariate Techniques of Analysis Have an Indispensable Contribution to Offer to the Study of Human Motivation? The history of motivation theory reveals individuals who have chosen to conceive of human behavior as stemming primarily from a single master motive, or from a pair or trinity of motives, and it also reveals theorists who insist that the number of motives is too great ever to submit to cataloguing. Between these two extremes are theorists who insist that motives are large in number but not too numerous to prohibit classification and measurement.

Establishing a person's position with regard to the number of motives that actually determine human behavior does not necessarily reveal his conviction with regard to how many motives should be studied at a given time. There are those who accept the existence and importance of multiple motives but for reasons of strategy consider it essential to begin the investigation of motivation by concentrating upon a small number of motives to be carefully investigated under well-controlled circumstances. Others believe that the very essence of human motivation lies in the interaction between, and simultaneous operation of, motives and that an attempt to study a single motive or only a small number of motives is bound to be fruitless.

A special question related to the matter of multiplicity of motives has to do with whether the investigator considers it essential to employ multivariate techniques of analysis. Classical experimental investigation has focused upon the relation between two variables, ideally susceptible to the labels of independent and dependent, and has developed powerful analytic techniques for extracting a maximum of information from such designs. More recently, heralded by Spearman's and Thurstone's technique of factor analysis, there has developed a small cluster of techniques (e.g., Lazarsfeld, 1950, 1954; Rao, 1948, 1952) that permit, or indeed encourage, the investigator to pursue a number of simultaneously interacting variables. Thus, assuming the demands of quantification have been met, the clinician's frequent plea for devices that will permit him to study many variables simultaneously seems to be fulfilled. It is true that computational problems mount rapidly with such an approach, but with the advances that have been made during the past decade in high-speed computation this does not seem an insuperable handicap.

Among our present contributors we have a number who are firmly committed to the essentiality of studying motives multiformly. Allport, Murray, and Cattell stand in the forefront of contemporary psychologists in their insistence that man's individuality is not to be encompassed fruitfully by one, two, or a small number of motivational variables. It should be noted that Allport in his present paper expresses some alarm over the popularity of shotgun approaches to the study of behavior; so sheer number of variables alone is not sufficient to satisfy him. Kelly, too, although he rejects motives, seems insistent upon the importance of multiplicity in the concepts used to represent human behavior. Only Festinger, Schafer, and Klein seem, in their papers, to be content to focus upon one or a small number of variables, and it is not clear that they would insist upon this strategy as the most defensible. Actually, both Klein and Schafer employ the full range of psychoanalytic variables in their own work. Thus some of the contributors are explicit in their insistence upon the importance of studying motivation with the aid of many variables, while others fail to deal with the issue explicitly but have chosen in their present treatment to limit their focus to one or a small number of variables.

When it comes to the use of multivariate analysis, the case is clear. Here it is Cattell versus the field! Only Cattell has employed such techniques centrally in his program of research, and only he seems convinced that such devices occupy an essential role in the establishment of further understanding of human motivation. This statement does not mean that all of the others are opposed to such devices but only that they do not see this approach to the study and exploration of human motives as offering a uniquely powerful vantage. Even Allport, who deals specifically and critically with factor analysis, is willing to concede some role to this technique in personality research.

What Is The Relative Importance of Detailed Studies of Individual Cases, Compared to Carefully Controlled Experimental Research and Large-Scale Investigations? The psychometric and clinical traditions are nowhere more squarely confronted than on this question. If one is interested primarily in precision and mensuration, then repeated observations are essential. If one is interested in veridicality and accuracy of individual representation, then a large number of cases is very likely to defeat the intent of the investigator. Thus only when there is repeated observation for the single individual is this conflict even in principle resolvable. The issue is clearly related to the preceding discussion, for as the number of variables ascends it is highly probable that the number of subjects will descend.

Among our contributors are there any who would object to the casual scrutiny of large numbers of subjects? Most would! Only Cattell and Festinger in their own work have often employed large numbers of subjects, and even they have coupled this practice with other research that has been focused upon small numbers of subjects. Murray and Allport have both pioneered in their emphasis upon the importance of detailed studies of individual cases. Allport, in his chapter, points specifically to the surprising neglect among contemporary psychologists of studies employing a sample of events or responses provided by an individual subject. Klein shares a heavy personalistic emphasis with Allport and is deeply committed to the importance of intensive study of small numbers of subjects. Schafer, who has published two volumes with case histories illustrating the application of psychological tests (Schafer,

1948, 1954), has all the usual clinician's convictions concerning the importance of intensive study of individual cases. In his chapter he speaks out strongly concerning the dangers of prematurely seeking objectivity and quantification at the cost of detailed knowledge of individual subjects. Janis devotes most of his paper to the advocacy of a research approach that focuses upon the single case, with the goal of using intensive, individual study to illuminate motivational processes that may be involved in complex phenomena observed in connection with large-scale studies. Thus our select group seems rather heavily in favor of personalistic or individualistic approaches to the study of human motives, with an attendant emphasis upon the intensive study of a small number of subjects.

Is There a Unique and Important Contribution to the Understanding of Human Motives That Can Be Made at Present through the Medium of Comparative or Lower-Animal Studies Which Cannot Be Duplicated by Means of Investigations Utilizing Human Subjects? There seems little doubt that comparative psychology has had considerable influence upon our present conceptions of human motivation. The work of Warden, Neal Miller, Beach, Hebb, Levy, Lorenz, and others has contributed heavily to what is known and believed concerning human motives. Not only is it possible to carry out types of investigations with lower animals that cannot be conducted with human subjects, e.g., studies of the genetic process, effects of cortical damage, long-range developmental studies, but also the relative simplicity of some of the infrahuman species has permitted certain issues to be seen more clearly with lower animals than with human subjects. Finally, just as it is sometimes possible to study another culture more objectively than our own, so too it may be that it is easier to approach another species without the binding preconception or prejudice that operates inevitably in the study of human beings. The fruits of comparative psychology can, of course, contribute at the level of human subjects only hypothesis, or ideas, because the frailties of cross-species generalization are well known, and it is commonly accepted that findings demonstrated for another species must be shown empirically to have specific utility or application to the human animal.

None of our present contributors has employed animal investigations extensively in his own research, and none seems particularly interested in the potential contribution of such investigation to an understanding of human motivation. Only Kelly responds specifically to this question, and he indicates doubt that there is any special contribution to be made by comparative studies. In other contexts both Murray and Allport have indicated reservations concerning the extent to which conceptions of human motivation seem to have been guided and formed by knowledge of motives at the infrahuman level. In general, then, among the present authors there seems no support for, or interest in, animal studies of motivation.

Clearly there are other issues or assumptive differences that could be cited as distinguishing individuals interested in the assessment of motives. However, the nine issues we have discussed are reasonably comprehensive and provide an adequate framework from which to view and compare the contributions included in this volume.

The chapters to follow present a rich and provocative array of viewpoints. They reveal many common convictions shared by workers in this area, but at the same time they frankly depict the diversity and flat disagreement that still characterize this domain of psychology. Taken as a whole, they present a valid cross section of contemporary thought and activity bearing upon one of psychology's central problems—the assessment and understanding of human motivation.

REFERENCES

Allport, G. W. *Personality: a psychological interpretation.* New York: Holt, 1937.
Hilgard, E. R. Experimental approaches to psychoanalysis. In E. Pumpian-Mindlin (ed.), *Psychoanalysis as science.* Stanford, Calif.: Stanford University Press, 1952. Pp. 3-45.
Koch, S. The logical character of the motivation concept: I. *Psychol. Rev.,* 1941a, 48, 15-38.
———. The logical character of the motivation concept: II. *Psychol. Rev.,* 1941b, 4, 127-154.
———. The current status of motivational psychology. *Psychol. Rev.,* 1951, 3, 147-154.
———. Clark L. Hull. In W. K. Estes *et al., Modern learning theory.* New York: Appleton-Century-Crofts, 1954. Pp. 1-176.

Lazarsfeld, P. F. The logic and mathematical foundation of latent structure analysis. In S. A. Stouffer *et al., Measurement and prediction.* Princeton, N.J.: Princeton University Press, 1950. Pp. 362-412.

————. A conceptual approach to latent structure analysis. In P. F. Lazarsfeld (ed.), *Mathematical thinking in the social sciences.* Glencoe, Ill.: Free Press, 1954. Pp. 349-387.

Murray, H. A., *et al. Explorations in personality.* New York: Oxford University Press, 1938.

————. Foreword. In G. G. Stern, M. I. Stein, and B. S. Bloom, *Methods in personality assessment.* Glencoe, Ill.: Free Press, 1956. Pp. 9-20.

Rao, C. R. Utilization of multiple measurements in problems of biological classification. *J. roy. Stat. Soc.,* Ser. B, 1948, 10, 159-203.

————. *Advanced statistical methods in biometric research.* New York: Wiley, 1952.

Schafer, R. *Clinical application of psychological tests.* New York: Int. Univ. Press, 1948.

————. *Psychoanalytic interpretation in Rorschach testing.* New York: Grune & Stratton, 1954.

Sears, R. R. *Survey of objective studies of psychoanalytic concepts.* New York: Social Science Res. Council, Bull. No. 51, 1943.

Skinner, B. F. A case history in scientific method. *Amer. Psychologist,* 1956, 11, 221-233.

GEORGE A. KELLY

Ohio State University

2 *Man's construction of his alternatives*

This paper, throughout, deals with half-truths only. Nothing that it contains is, or is intended to be, wholly true. The theoretical statements propounded are no more than partially accurate constructions of events which, in turn, are no more than partially perceived. Moreover, what we propose, even in its truer aspects, will eventually be overthrown and displaced by something with more truth in it. Indeed, our theory is frankly designed to contribute effectively to its own eventual overthrow and displacement.

Half-Truths vs. Infallibility. We think this is a good way for psychologists to theorize. When a scientist propounds a theory he has two choices: he can claim that what he says has been dictated to him by the real nature of things, or he can take sole responsibility for what he says and claim only that he has offered one man's hopeful construction of the realities of nature. In the first instance he makes a claim to objectivity in behalf of his theory, the scientist's equivalent of a claim to infallibility. In the second instance he offers only the hope that he may have hit upon some partial truth that may serve as a clue to inventing something better and he invites others to follow this clue to see what they can make of it. In this latter instance he does not hold up his theoretical proposal to be judged so much in terms of whether or not it is the truth at last—for he assumes from the outset that ultimate truth is not so readily at hand—but in terms of whether his proposition seems to lead toward and give way to fresh propositions, propositions which, in turn, may be more true than anything else has been thus far.

One of the troubles with what are otherwise good theories in the various fields of science is the claim to infallibility that is so often built into their structure. Even those theories which are built upon objective observation or upon firsthand experience make this claim by their failure to admit that what is observed is not revealed but only construed. In fact, the more objectively supported the theory at the time of its inception, the more likely it is to cause trouble after it has served its purpose. A conclusion supported by the facts is likely to be a good one at the time it is drawn. But, because facts themselves are open to reconstruction, such a theory soon becomes a dogmatism that may serve only to blind us to new perceptions of the facts.

Take, for example, the body of theoretical assumptions that Freud propounded out of his experience with psychoanalysis. There was so much truth in what he said—so much new truth. But, like most theories of our times, psychoanalysis, as a theory, was conceived as an absolute truth, and, moreover, it was designed in such a manner that it tended to defy both logical examination and experimental validation. As the years go by, Freudianism, which deserves to be remembered as a brave outpost on the early frontier of psychological thought, is condemned to end its days as a crumbling stockade of proprietary dogmatism. Thus, as with other farseeing claims to absolute truth, history will have a difficult time deciding whether Freudianism did more to accelerate psychological progress during the first half of the twentieth century than it did to impede progress during the last half.

This business of absolutism in modern science and the havoc it creates is a matter that has been given a good deal of thought in recent decades. It has been attacked on several fronts. First of all, modern science has itself attacked older dogmatisms through its widespread use of the method of experimentation. But experimentation, if assumed to be a way of receiving direct revelations from nature, can often be found living quite happily side by side with modern dogmatisms of the lowest order.

There is nothing especially revelational about events that happen in an experimental laboratory—other events that happen elsewhere are just as real and are just as worthy of attention. Even the fact that an event took place in a manner predicted by the experimenter gives it no particular claim to being a special revelation from nature. That an experimenter's predictions come true means only that he has hit upon one of many possible systems for making predictions that come true. He may be no more than a wee bit closer to a genuine understanding of things as they really are. Indeed, the fact that he has hit upon one such way of predicting outcomes may even blind him to alternatives which might have proved far more productive in the long run.

Absolutism is coming under other forms of attack. It has been pointed out, for example, that the subject-predicate form of our Indo-European languages has led us to confound objects with what is said about them. Thus every time we open our mouths to say something we break forth with a dogmatism. Each sentence, instead of sounding like a proposal of an idea to be examined in the light of personal experience, echoes through the room like the disembodied rumblings of an oracle. Even as we try to describe a theory of personal constructions of events, one that stands in contrast to theories that claim to spring from events directly, we are caught up in the assumptions and structure of the very language upon which we depend for communication. In view of this fact, we can think of no better way of disclaiming the assumptions of our language than by introducing this paper with the paradoxical statement that we are proposing half-truths only.

Motivation Questioned. A second feature of this paper is its outright repudiation of the notion of motivation. Since the topic of the conference series, in which we have been so graciously invited to participate, is "The Assessment of Human Motives," such a repudiation may appear to be in bad taste. It seems a little like being honored with an invitation to preach a sermon in church, and then taking advantage of the solemn occasion in order to present the case for atheism. Yet the present volume on the assessment of human motives may not lose flavor from this kind of seasoning. Perhaps one chapter of heresy may even strengthen the reader's convictions about human motives, just as an occasional rousing speech on atheism might do more than a monotony of sermons to bring a church congregation face to face with its own convictions—or lack of them.

Certainly the repudiation of "motives" as a construct is a major undertaking, not to be ventured into without some thought being given to its consequences. For a period roughly corresponding to the Christian era, metaphysics, including psychology, has conceptualized its spiritual realm in terms of a trichotomy, just as Christianity has envisioned itself in terms of a trinity. The classic trichotomy is variously called by such terms as cognition, conation, and affection; or intellect, will, and emotion; or even, in somewhat more modern terms, thought, action, and feeling. Psychologists keep coming back to this trichotomous division, perhaps because they have never been able to venture beyond it. That we now say we propose to abandon motives will seem to many listeners a kind of unforgivable sin, something like the unforgivable sin of rejecting the Holy Ghost.

In the classic psychological trichotomy, cognition, on the one hand, has been viewed as a realm governed by verbalized rationality, while affection, on the other, has been viewed as a very chaotic, though often pleasant, place where inarticulate irrationality is in command. Conation, the middle category which deals with behavior or determination to act, has been caught between the other two, sometimes believed to be swayed by the rationality of the cognitive mind but at other times suspected of having a secret allegiance to the whimsical irrationality of feeling and emotion.

REPUDIATION OF MOTIVATION AS A CONSTRUCT

Reconciling Rationality and Irrationality. Because the topic of motivation falls into this disputed area where modern man has had such a difficult time reconciling rationality with irrationality, we propose to start our serious discussion at this particular point. We should like to deal with those matters which are called rational—and therefore by quirk of our language structure assumed actually to be rational—together with those matters which are called irrational—for the same reason—both in the very same psychological terms. In doing so we shall, if our previous experiences repeat themselves, be perceived by some persons to be capitulating to the classic rationalism of Thomas Aquinas and by others as giving hostages to the supposed intuitive irrationality of Freud, Rogers, or Sullivan. Not that we really mind being bracketed with any of these great names; but rather the burden of our comments, it seems to us, rests on other grounds.

This is the risk we take. Why? Why will some see this as conforming to classic rationality and others see it as lapsing into irrationality? We have already mentioned the tendency to confound objects with what is said about them. Some philosophers, Bertrand Russell being possibly the first and foremost, have seen this tendency to confound words and facts as being embedded in the subject-predicate structure of our language. But it involves also the highly questionable *law of the excluded middle*, a law accepted as a basic principle of logic for the past twenty-four hundred years, though now under sporadic attack.

Law of the excluded middle: What this law proposes is that for any proposition there is only one alternative. I call an object a spade. There is only one alternative to calling it a spade—to call it not a spade! I can't say, "to heck with it," or "who cares," or "who brought that up," or that the object cannot be sensibly called either a spade or not a spade; I have to stick with one or the other. Once the object is accused of being a spade it has to plead innocent or guilty, or I have to plead its innocence or guilt in its behalf.

Subject-predicate fallacy: Now, if we combine this dictum with the subject-predicate mode of thought we put ourselves in a stringent position with respect to our world. We call an object a spade. Not only do we therefore imply that it is a spade because we cannot say that it is not a spade, but we put the onus of choosing between the two alternatives on the object itself. We disclaim responsibility for our propositions and try to make the objects we talk about hang themselves on the horns of the dilemmas we invent for dealing with them. If a woman is accused of being a witch, she has to be either a witch or not a witch—it is up to her. The speaker disclaims all responsibility for the dilemma he has imposed upon her.

For centuries Western man has roamed his world impaling every object he has met on the horns of the dilemmas he chose to fashion out of his language. In fact, an individual, if he was very bright and had a vocabulary well stocked with psychological terms, could do a pretty substantial job of impaling himself. Recently so many people have learned to do it in so many ingenious ways that apparently half the world will have to be trained in psychotherapy in order to keep the other half off its own hooks. Yet, even so, it may be that what most of the psychotherapists are doing is lifting people off one set of hooks and hanging them on other more comfortable, more socially acceptable, hooks.

Let us see if we can make this point a little clearer. For example, on occasion I may say of myself—in fact, on occasion I *do* say of myself—"I am an introvert." "I," the subject, "am an introvert," the predicate. The language form of the statement clearly places the onus of being an introvert on the subject—on me. What I actually am, the words say, is an introvert.

The listener, being the more or less credulous person to whom I make the statement, says to himself, "So George Kelly is an introvert—I always suspected he was." Or he may say, "Him an introvert? He's no introvert," a response which implies scarcely less credulity on the part of my listener. Yet the proper interpretation of my statement is that I *construe* myself to be an introvert, or, if I am merely being coy or devious, I am inveigling *my listener into construing* me in terms of introversion. The point that gets lost in the shuffle of words is the psychological fact that I have identified myself in terms of a personal construct —"introversion." If my listener is uncritical enough to be taken in by this quirk of language, he may waste a lot of time either in believing that he must construe me as an introvert or in disputing the point.

In clinical interviewing, and particularly in psychotherapeutic interviewing, when the clinician is unable to deal with such a statement as a personal construction, rather than as fact or fallacy, the hour is likely to come to a close with both parties annoyed with each other and both dreading their next appointment. But more than this, if I say of myself that I am an introvert, I am likely to be caught in my own subject-predicate trap. Even the inner self—my self—becomes burdened with the onus of actually being an introvert or of finding some way to be rid of the introversion that has climbed on my back. What has happened is that I named myself with a name and, having done so, too quickly forgot who invented the name and what he had on his mind at the time. From now on I try frantically to cope with what I have called myself. Moreover, my family and friends are often quite willing to join in the struggle.

A third possibility—relevance: Now, back specifically to the law of the excluded middle. Here, too, we find a failure to take into account a psychological fact, the fact that human thought is essentially constructive in nature and that even the thinking of logicians and mathematicians is no exception. I say that I am an introvert—whatever that is. If I now go ahead and apply the law of the excluded middle I come up with the dilemma that I must continue to claim either to be an introvert or not an introvert—one or the other. But is this necessarily so? May not introversion turn out to be a construct which is altogether irrelevant? If it is not relevant is it any more meaningful to say that I am not an introvert than to say that I am? Yet classical logic fails to make any distinctions between its negatives and its irrelevancies, while modern psychology ought to make it increasingly clear to each of us that no proposition has more than a limited range of relevance, beyond which it makes no sense either to affirm or deny. So we now ought to visualize propositions which are not universal in their range of application but useful only within a restricted range of convenience. For each proposition, then, we see three alternatives, not two: It can be affirmed, it can be denied, or it can be declared irrelevant in the context to which it is applied. Thus we argue, not for the inclusion of the long excluded middle—something between the "Yes" and the "No"—but for a third possibility that is beyond the meaningful range of yes and no.

Apply this more psychological way of thinking to the proposition, "I am an introvert." Instead of lying awake trying to decide whether I am or am not an introvert, or taking frantic steps, as so many do, to prove that I am not, I simply go off to sleep with the thought that, until the construct of introversion is demonstrated to be of some practical usefulness in my case, there is no point of trying to decide whether I am or not, or what to do about it if I am. Thus we treat the subject-predicate problem and the excluded middle problem in pretty much the same way—we insist on demonstrating relevance before we lose any sleep over a proposition.

Summary: Let us try to summarize our criticisms of the two features of Western thought which went unchallenged for more than two thousand years. First of all, there is the dogmatism of subject-predicate language structure that is often presented under the guise of objectivity. According to this dogmatism, when I say that Professor Lindzey's left shoe is an "introvert," everyone looks at his shoe as if this were something his shoe was responsible for. Or if I say that Professor Cattell's head is "discursive," everyone looks over at him, as if the proposition had popped out of his head instead of out of mine. Don't look at his head! Don't look at that shoe! Look at me; I'm the one who is responsible for the statement. After you figure out what I mean you can look over there to see if you make any sense out of shoes and heads by construing them the way I do. It will not be easy to do this, for it means abandoning one of the most ancient ways of thinking and talking to ourselves.

As far as the law of the excluded middle in this particular context is concerned, whether or not a person has ever heard of this law, or whether he has ever sat down to puzzle out a similar notion on his own, the law is an everyday feature of nearly every educated man's more intellectualized thought processes. The law says, assuming that the term "introvert" ever has meaning, that that shoe, at which we looked a moment ago, has to be construed either as an introvert or as not an introvert; it has simply got to be seen as one or the other. There is no middle ground.

Some people argue against the law of the excluded middle by claiming that the shoe could be a little introvertish, but not completely introvert, or that it could be a little nonintrovertish, though not wholly nonintrovert. This is the notion of shades of gray that can be perceived between black and white. But this notion of reifying the excluded middle by talking about grays is not what we are proposing. In fact, we see this gray thinking as a form of concretism that merely equivocates and fails to get off the ground into the atmosphere of abstraction.

What we are saying, instead, is that "introversion" may well enough be a term that has meaning in some contexts, but that it does not go well with shoes. Since it does not apply to shoes, it makes no more sense to say that Professor Lindzey's left shoe is not an introvert than to say that it is. Thus we see three possibilities, not two, as the law would insist: The shoe is an introvert; the shoe is not an introvert; and the shoe does not fall within the context of the construct of introversion vs. nonintroversion. The third possibility is not a middle proposition in any intermediate sense but rather a kind of outside—beyond-the-pale —kind of proposition.

So much for a summary of this section of our discourse. In spite of our criticisms, let us not say that the inadequacies we have pointed out prevented our language and thought from leading us along a path of progress. Remember that we believe that half-truths serve to pave the way toward better truths. Time spent with a half-truth is not necessarily wasted; it may have been exceedingly profitable. In order to appreciate a half-truth one has to examine two things; what it replaced and what it led up to. Let us see what the kind of thing we have been criticizing actually replaced. Let us compare it with more primitive modes of language and thought.

From Magic to Fallacy in Two Thousand Years. Western thinking, which has pretty much overrun the world recently, takes the very practical view that a word is beholden to the object it is used to describe. The object determines it. This is a moderate improvement over the so-called magical way of thinking which has it that the object is beholden to the word. The improvement has been the basis of scientific thinking, particularly the experimentalism that has psychologists and others bubbling with so much excitement these days.

Let us see how the improvement works. Say the word and the object will jump out at you—that is magical thinking—very bad! Prod the object and the word will jump out at you—that is objective thinking; very good! Worth publishing! Say "Genie, come genie" and hope that a genie will pop out of the bottle—that is magical; no good! Kick the bottle until either a genie pops out or does not pop out—now that is *science!*

But there is something a person can do besides shouting, "Genie, come genie," or kicking the bottle through a series of statistically controlled experiments. He can ask himself, and the other people who have worked themselves up over the genie business, just what they are trying to get at. This is what the skilled psychotherapist does in dealing with the thoughts of man. His approach is based on the notion that "genie" is a construct someone erected in order to find his way through a maze of events. It is not a substitute for experimentation but a useful prelude to it. It is a proper substitute, however, for random measurement of verbalizations.

Meaning and the Man. This is the way we see the matter: Magical thinking has it that the object is beholden to the word—when the word is spoken, the object must produce itself. So-called objective thinking, under which it has been possible to make great scientific progress, says that the word is beholden to the object—kick the bottle to validate the word. If, however, we build our sciences on a recognition of the psychological nature of thought we take a third position—the word is beholden to the person who utters it, or, more properly speaking, to the *construction* system, that complex of personal constructs of which it is a part.

This concern with personal meaning should prove no less valuable to the scientist than it has to the psychotherapist. It stems from the notion that, when a person uses a word, he is expressing, in part, his own construction of events. One comes to understand the communication, therefore, not by assuming the magical existence of the word's counterpart in reality and then invoking that counterpart by incantation; nor does he understand it by scrounging through a pile of accumulated facts to see if one of them will own up to the word; rather, he understands the communication by examining the personal construction system within which the word arose and within which it came to have intimate meaning for the individual who attempted to communicate.

Now What Happens to Motivation? How does this apply to motives? We have already said that we do not even use the term as a part of our own construction system, yet it enters our system, perforce, as a matter to be construed. If a person catches his friends in the act of using such a term as "motives," how does he act? Does he put his fingers in his ears? Does he start kicking the bottle of reality to see if it produces the phenomenon? If it fails, shall he accuse his friends of irrationality? We think not.

Again, if we so much as start to inquire into motivation as a construct, do we not thereby reify it? Or if we deal with a realm which so many believe is essentially irrational in nature, are we not capitulating ourselves to irrationality? And if we attempt to think rationally about the behavior of an individual who is acting irrationally, are we not closing

our eyes to an irrationality that actually exists? Are we not hiding behind a safe intellectualism? All of these questions rise out of the long-
accepted assumptions of a subject-predicate mode of thought that tries
to make reality responsible for the words that are used to construe it.
Because of the currency of this kind of interpretation we run the risk
we mentioned a few moments ago—the risk of being bracketed with
either the classic rationalists or the modern intuitionists.

Actually we are neither. Our position is that of a psychology of personal constructs (Kelly, 1955), a psychologist's system for construing
persons who themselves construe in all kinds of other ways. Thus I,
Person A, employ Construct A', a component construct within my own
construction system, to understand Construct B', a component construct
with Person B's construction system. His B' is not a truth revealed to
him by nature. Nor is my A' revealed to me by his human nature. Construct A' is my responsibility, just as B' is his. In each instance the
validity of the construct rests, among other things, upon its prophetic
effectiveness, not upon any claim to external origin, either divine or
natural.

Now let us hope we are in a safe position to deal with the assessment
of human motives without appearing either to reify them or to talk
nonsense. Our discussion might as well start where our thinking started.

REPUDIATION OF THE MOTIVATION
CONSTRUCT FOR DIAGNOSIS

Some twenty years or more ago a group of us were attempting to provide a traveling psychological clinic service to the schools in the State
of Kansas. One of the principal sources of referrals was, of course,
teachers. A teacher complained about a pupil. This word-bound complaint was taken as prima-facie grounds for kicking the bottle—I mean,
examining the pupil. If we kicked the pupil around long enough and
hard enough we could usually find some grounds to justify any teacher's
complaint. This procedure was called in those days, just as it is still
called, "diagnosis." It was in this manner that we conformed to the
widely accepted requirements of the scientific method—we matched
hypothesis with evidence and thus arrived at objective truth. In due

course of time we became quite proficient in making something out of teachers' complaints, and we got so we could adduce some mighty subtle evidence. In short, we began to fancy ourselves as pretty sensitive clinicians.

Now, as every scientist and every clinician knows and is fond of repeating, treatment depends upon diagnosis. First you find out what is wrong—really wrong. Then you treat it. In treatment you have several alternatives; you can cut it out of the person, or you can remove the object toward which the child behaves improperly, or you can remove the child from the object, or you can alter the mechanism he employs to deal with the object, or you can compensate for the child's behavior by taking up a hobby in the basement, or teach the child to compensate for it, or, if nothing better turns up, you can sympathize with everybody who has to put up with the youngster. But first, always first, you must kick the bottle to make it either confirm or reject your diagnostic hunches. So in Kansas we diagnosed pupils, and having impaled ourselves and our clients with our diagnoses, we cast about more or less frantically for ways of escape.

After perseverating in this classical stupidity—the treatment-depends-on-objective-diagnosis stupidity—for more years than we like to count, we began to suspect that we were being trapped in some pretty fallacious reasoning. We should have liked to blame the teachers for getting us off on the wrong track. But we had verified their complaints, hadn't we? We had even made "differential diagnoses," a way of choosing up sides in the name-calling games commonly played in clinical staff meetings.

Two things became apparent. The first was that the teacher's complaint was not necessarily something to be verified or disproved by the facts in the case, but was, rather, a construction of events in a way that, within the limits and assumptions of her personal construction system, made the most sense to her at the moment. The second was the realization that, in assuming diagnosis to be the independent variable and treatment the dependent variable, we had got the cart before the horse. It would have been better if we had made our diagnoses in the light of changes that do occur in children or that can be made to occur, rather than trying to shape those changes to independent but irrelevant psychometric measurements or biographical descriptions.

"Laziness." What we should like to make clear is that both these difficulties have the same root—the traditional rationale of science that leads us to look for the locus of meaning of words in their objects of reference rather than in their subjects of origin. We hear a word and look to what is talked about rather than listen to the person who utters it. A teacher often complained that a child was "lazy." We turned to the child to determine whether or not she was right. If we found clear evidence that would support a hypothesis of laziness, then laziness was what it was—nothing else—and diagnosis was complete. Diagnosis having been accomplished, treatment was supposed to ensue. What does one do to cure laziness? While, of course, it was not quite as simple as this, the paradigm is essentially the one we followed.

Later we began to put "laziness" in quotes. We found that a careful appraisal of the teacher's construction system gave us a much better understanding of the meaning of the complaint. This, together with some further inquiry into the child's outlook, often enabled us to arrive at a vantage point from which we could deal with the problem in various ways. It occurred to us that we might, for example, help the teacher reconstrue the child in terms other than "laziness"—terms which gave her more latitude for exercising her own particular creative talents in dealing with him. Again, we might help the child deal with the teacher and in this way alleviate her discomfort. And, of course, there was sometimes the possibility that a broader reorientation of the child toward himself and school matters in general would prove helpful.

We have chosen the complaint of "laziness" as our example for a more special reason. "Laziness" happens to be a popular motivational concept that has widespread currency among adults who try to get others to make something out of themselves. Moreover, our disillusionment with motivational conceptualization in general started with this particular term and arose out of the specific context of school psychological services.

Our present position regarding human motives was approached by stages. First we realized that even when a hypothesis of laziness was confirmed there was little that could be said or done in consequence of such a finding. While this belief originally appeared to be less true of other motivational constructs, such as appetite or affection, in each instance the key to treatment, or even to differential prediction of outcomes, appeared to reside within the framework of other types of constructs.

Another observation along the way was that the teachers who used the construct of "laziness" were usually those who had widespread difficulties in their classrooms. Soon we reached the point in our practice where we routinely used the complaint of "laziness" as a point of departure for reorienting the teacher. It usually happened that there was more to be done with her than there was to be done with the child. So it was, also, with other complaints cast in motivational terms. In general, then, we found that the most practical approach to so-called motivational problems was to try to reorient the people who thought in such terms. Complaints about motivation told us much more about the complainants than it did about their pupils.

This generalization seems to get more and more support from our clinical experience. When we find a person who is more interested in manipulating people for his own purposes, we usually find him making complaints about their motives. When we find a person who is concerned about motives, he usually turns out to be one who is threatened by his fellow men and wants to put them in their place. There is no doubt that the construct of motives is widely used, but it usually turns out to be a part of the language of complaint about the behavior of other people. When it appears in the language of the client himself, as it does occasionally, it always—literally always—appears in the context of a kind of rationalization apparently designed to appease the therapist, not in the spontaneous utterances of the client who is in good rapport with his therapist.

One technique we came to use was to ask the teacher what the child would do if she did not try to motivate him. Often the teacher would insist that the child would do nothing—absolutely nothing—just sit! Then we would suggest that she try a nonmotivational approach and let him "just sit." We would ask her to observe how he went about "just sitting." Invariably the teacher would be able to report some extremely interesting goings on. An analysis of what the "lazy" child did while he was being lazy often furnished her with her first glimpse into the child's world and provided her with her first solid grounds for communication with him. Some teachers found that their laziest pupils were those who could produce the most novel ideas; others, that the term "laziness" had been applied to activities that they had simply been unable to understand or appreciate.

Construed Alternatives. It was some time later that we sat down and tried to formulate the general principles that undergirded our clinical experiences with teachers and their pupils. The more we thought about it, the more it seemed that our problems had always resolved themselves into questions of what the child would do if left to his own devices rather than questions about the amount of his motivation. These questions of what the child would do seemed to hinge primarily on what alternatives his personal construction of the situation allowed him to sense. While his construed alternatives were not necessarily couched in language symbols, nor could the child always clearly represent his alternatives, even to himself, they nonetheless set the outside limits on his day-to-day behavior. In brief, whenever we got embroiled in questions of motivation we bogged down, the teachers bogged down, and the children continued to aggravate everybody within earshot. When we forgot about motives and set about understanding the practical alternatives which children felt they were confronted by, the aggravations began to resolve themselves.

What we have said about our experiences with children also turned up in our psychotherapeutic experiences with adults. After months or, in some cases, years of psychotherapy with the same client, it did often prove to be possible to predict his behavior in terms of motives. This, of course, was gratifying; but predictive efficiency is not the only criterion of a good construction, for one's understanding of a client should also point the way to resolving his difficulties. It was precisely at this point that motivational constructs failed to be of practical service, just as they had failed to be of service in helping children and teachers get along with each other. Always the psychotherapeutic solution turned out to be a reconstruing process, not a mere labeling of the client's motives. To be sure, there were clients who never reduced their reconstructions to precise verbal terms, yet still were able to extricate themselves from vexing circumstances. And there were clients who got along best under conditions of support and reassurance with a minimum of verbal structuring on the part of the therapist. But even in these cases, the solutions were not worked out in terms of anything that could properly be called motives, and the evidence always pointed to some kind

of reconstruing process that enabled the client to make his choice between new sets of alternatives not previously open to him in a psychological sense.

APPROACH TO A NEW PSYCHOLOGICAL THEORY

Now, perhaps, it is time to launch into the third phase of our discussion.
We started by making some remarks of a philosophical nature and from
there we dropped back to recall some of the practical experiences that
first led us to question the construct of motivation. Let us turn now
to the formulation of psychological theory and to the part that motivation plays in it.

A half century ago William McDougall published his little volume,
Physiological Psychology (1905). In the opening pages he called his
contemporary psychologists' attention to the fact that the concept of
energy had been invented by physicists in order to account for movement of objects, and that some psychologists had blandly assumed that
they too would have to find a place for it in their systems. While Mc-
Dougall was to go on in his lifetime to formulate a theoretical system
based on instinctual drives and thus, it seems to us, failed to heed his
own warning, what he said about the construct of energy still provides us
with a springboard for expounding a quite different theoretical position.

The physical world presented itself to preclassical man as a world of
solid objects. He saw matter as an essentially inert substance, rather
than as a complex of related motion. His axes of reference were spatial
dimensions—length, breadth, depth—rather than temporal dimensions.
The flow of time was something he could do very little about, and he
was inclined to take a passive attitude toward it. Even mass, a dimen-
sion which lent itself to more dynamic interpretations, was likely to be
construed in terms of size equivalents.

Classical man, as he emerged upon the scene, gradually became aware
of motion as something that had eluded his predecessors. But for him
motion was still superimposed upon nature's rocks and hills. Inert matter was still the phenomenon, motion was only the epiphenomenon.
Action, vitality, and energy were the breath of life that had to be
breathed into the inertness of nature's realities. In Classical Greece this

thought was magnificently expressed in new forms of architecture and sculpture that made the marble quarried from the Greek islands reach for the open sky, or ripple like a soft garment in the warm Aegean breeze. But motion, though an intrinsic feature of the Greek idiom, was always something superimposed, something added. It belonged to the world of the ideal and not to the hard world of reality.

The Construct of Motivation Implies That Man Is Essentially Inert. Today our modern psychology approaches its study of man from the same vantage point. He is viewed as something static in his natural state, hence something upon which motion, life, and action have to be superimposed. In substance he is still perceived as like the marble out of which the Greeks carved their statues of flowing motion and ethereal grace. He comes alive, according to most of the psychology of our day, only through the application of special enlivening forces. We call these forces by such names as "motives," "incentives," "needs," and "drives." Thus, just as the physicists had to erect the construct of energy to fill the gap left by their premature assumption of a basically static universe, so psychology has had to burden itself with a construct made necessary by its inadequate assumption about the basic nature of man.

We now arrive at the same point in our theoretical reasoning at which we arrived some years earlier in appraising our clinical experience. In each instance we find that efforts to assess human motives run into practical difficulty because they assume inherently static properties in human nature. It seems appropriate, therefore, at this juncture to re-examine our implied assumptions about human nature. If we then decide to base our thinking upon new assumptions we can next turn to the array of new constructs that may be erected for the proper elaboration of the fresh theoretical position.

In This Theory the Construct of Motivation Is Redundant in Explaining Man's Activity. There are several ways in which we can approach our problem. We could, for example, suggest to ourselves, as we once suggested to certain unperceptive classroom teachers, that we examine what a person does when he is not being motivated. Does he turn into some kind of inert substance? If not—and he won't—should we not follow up our observation with a basic assumption that any person is motivated, motivated for no other reason than that he is alive? Life itself could be defined as a form of process or movement. Thus, in designating man as our object of psychological inquiry, we should be taking it for granted that movement is an essential property of his being, not something that has to be accounted for separately. We should be talking about a form of movement—man—not something that has to be motivated.

Pursuant to this line of reasoning, motivation ceases to be a special topic of psychology. Nor, on the other hand, can it be said that motivation constitutes the whole of psychological substance, although from the standpoint of another theoretical system it might be proper to characterize our position so. *Within our system,* however, the term "motivation" can appear only as a redundancy.

How can we further characterize this stand with respect to motivation? Perhaps this will help: Motivational theories can be divided into two types, push theories and pull theories. Under push theories we find such terms as drive, motive, or even stimulus. Pull theories use such constructs as purpose, value, or need. In terms of a well-known metaphor, these are the pitchfork theories on the one hand and the carrot theories on the other. But our theory is neither of these. Since we prefer to look to the nature of the animal himself, ours is probably best called a jackass theory.

Thus far our reasoning has led us to a point of view from which the construct of "human motives" appears redundant—redundant, that is, as far as accounting for human action is concerned. But traditional motivational theory is not quite so easily dismissed. There is another issue that now comes to the fore. It is the question of what directions human actions can be expected to take.

The Construct of Motivation Is Not Needed to Explain Directionality of Movement. We must recognize that the construct of "motive" has been traditionally used for two purposes; to account for the fact that the person is active rather than inert, and also for the fact that he chooses to move in some directions rather than in others. It is not surprising that, in the past, a single construct has been used to cover both issues; for if we take the view that the human organism is set in motion only by the impact of special forces, it is reasonable to assume also that those forces must give it direction as well as impetus. But now, if we accept the view that the organism is already in motion simply by virtue of its being alive, then we have to ask ourselves if we do not still require the services of "motives" to explain the directionality of the movement. Our answer to this question is "No." Let us see why.

Here, as before, we turn first to our experiences as a clinician to find the earliest inklings of a new theoretical position. Specifically, we turn to experiences in psychotherapy.

Clinical experience: When a psychologist undertakes psychotherapy with a client he can approach his task from any one of a number of viewpoints. He can, as many do, devote most of his attention to a kind of running criticism of the mistakes the client makes, his fallacies, his irrationalities, his misperceptions, his resistances, his primitive mechanisms. Or, as others do, he can keep measuring his client; so much progress today, so much loss yesterday, gains in this respect, relapses in that. If he prefers, he can keep his attention upon his own role, or the relation between himself and his client, with the thought that it is not actually given to him ever to know how the client's mind works, nor is it his responsibility to make sure that it works correctly, but only that he should provide the kind of warm and responsive human setting in which the client can best solve his own problems.

Any one of these approaches may prove helpful to the client. But there is still another approach that, from our personal experience, can prove most helpful to the client and to the psychotherapist. Instead of assuming, on the one hand, that the therapist is obliged to bring the client's thinking into line, or, on the other, that the client will mysteriously bring his own thinking into line once he has been given the proper setting, we can take the stand that client and therapist are conjoining in an exploratory venture. The therapist assumes neither the position of judge nor that of the sympathetic bystander. He is sincere about this; he is willing to learn along with his client. He is the client's fellow researcher who seeks first to understand, then to examine, and finally to assist the client in subjecting alternatives to experimental test and revision.

The psychologist who goes at psychotherapy this way says to himself, "I am about to have the rare opportunity of examining the inner workings of that most intricate creation in all of nature, a human personality. While many scholars have written about the complexity of this human personality, I am now about to see for myself how one particular personality functions. Moreover, I am about to have an experienced colleague join me in this venture, the very person whose personality is to be examined. He will help me as best he can, but there will be times when he cannot help, when he will be as puzzled and confused as I am."

When psychotherapy is carried out in this vein the therapist, instead of asking himself continually whether his client is right or not, or whether he himself is behaving properly, peers intently into the intimate psychological processes which the unusual relation permits him to see. He inquires rather than condemns. He explores rather than rejects or approves. How does this creature, man, actually think? How does he make choices that seem to be outside the conventionalized modes of thought? What is the nature of his logic—quite apart from how logicians define logic? How does he solve his problems? What ideas does he express for which he has no words?

Conventional psychological concepts: Out of this kind of experience with psychotherapy we found ourselves becoming increasingly impatient with certain standard psychotherapeutic concepts. "Insight" was one of the first to have a hollow sound. It soon became apparent that, in any single case, there was any number of different possible insights that could be used to structure the same facts, all of them more or less true. As one acquires a variety of psychotherapeutic experience he begins to be amazed by how sick or deviant some clients can be and still surmount their difficulties, and how well or insightful others can be and yet fall apart at every turn. Certainly the therapist who approaches his task primarily as a scientist is soon compelled to concede that unconventional insights often work as well or better than the standardized insights prescribed by some current psychological theory.

Another popular psychotherapeutic concept that made less and less sense was "resistance." To most therapists resistance is a kind of perverse stubbornness in the client. Most therapists are annoyed by it. Some accuse the client of resisting whenever their therapeutic efforts begin to bog down. But our own experiences with resistance were a good deal like our experiences with laziness—they bespoke more of the therapist's perplexity than of the client's rebellion. If we had been dependent entirely on psychotherapeutic experiences with our own clients we might have missed this point; it would have been too easy for us, like the others, to blame our difficulties on the motives of the client. But we

were fortunate enough to have opportunities also for supervising therapists, and here, because we were not ourselves quite so intimately involved, it was possible to see resistance in terms of the therapist's
naiveté.

When the so-called resistance was finally broken through—to use a
psychotherapist's idiom—it seemed proper, instead of congratulating
ourselves on our victory over a stubborn client, to ask ourselves and our
client just what had happened. There were, of course, the usual kinds of
reply, "I just couldn't say that to you then," or "I knew I was being
evasive, but I just didn't know what to do about it," etc.

But was this stubbornness? Some clients went further and expressed
it this way, "To have said then what I have said today would not have
meant the same thing." This may seem like a peculiar remark, but from
the standpoint of personal construct theory it makes perfectly good
sense. A client can express himself only within the framework of his
construct system. Words alone do not convey meaning. What this
client appears to be saying is this: When he has the constructs for
expressing himself, the words that he uses ally themselves with those
constructs and they make sense when he utters them. To force him to
utter words which do not parallel his constructs, or to mention events
which are precariously construed, is to plunge him into a chaos of
personal nonsense, however much it may clarify matters for the therapist. In short, our experience with psychotherapy led us to believe that
it was not orneriness that made the client hold out so-called important
therapeutic material, but a genuine inability to express himself in terms
that would not appear, from his point of view, to be utterly miscon-
strued.

Perhaps these brief recollections of therapeutic experiences will suffice
to show how we began to be as skeptical of motives as direction-finding
devices as we were skeptical of them as action-producing forces. Over
and over again, it appeared that our clients were making their choices,
not in terms of the alternatives we saw open to them, but in terms of
the alternatives they saw open to them. It was their network of constructions that made up the daily mazes that they ran, not the pure realities
that appeared to us to surround them. To try to explain a temper tantrum or an acute schizophrenic episode in terms of motives only was
to miss the whole point of the client's system of personal dilemmas.

The child's temper tantrum is, for him, one of the few remaining choices left to him. So for the psychotic; with his pathways structured the way they are in his mind, he has simply chosen from a particular limited set of alternatives. How else can he behave? His other alternatives are even less acceptable.

We have not yet fully answered the question of explaining directionality. We have described only the extent to which our therapeutic experiences led us to question the value of motives. But, after all, we have not yet found, from our experience, that clients do what they do because there is nothing else they can do. We have observed only that they do what they do because their choice systems are definitely limited. But, even by this line of reasoning, they do have choices, often bad ones, to be sure, but still choices. So our question of directionality of behavior is narrowed down by the realization that a person's behavior must take place within the limited dimensions of his personal construct system. Yet, as long as his system does have dimensions, it must provide him with some sets of alternatives. And so long as he has some alternatives of his own making we must seek to explain why he chooses some of them in preference to others.

"Neurotic paradox":   Before we leave off talking about clinical experience and take up the next and most difficult phase of our discussion, it will do no harm to digress for a few moments and talk about the so-called neurotic paradox. O. H. Mowrer has described this as "the paradox of behavior which is at one and the same time self-perpetuating and self-defeating" (1950, p. 486). We can state the paradox in the form of a question, "Why does a person sometimes persist in unrewarding behavior?" Reinforcement theory finds this an embarrassing question, while contiguity theory, to which some psychologists have turned in their embarrassment, finds the converse question equally embarrassing, "Why does a person sometimes *not* persist in unrewarding behavior?"

From the standpoint of the psychology of personal constructs, however, there is no neurotic paradox. Or, to be more correct, the paradox is the jam which certain learning theorists get themselves into rather than the jam their clients get themselves into. Not that clients stay out of jams, But they have their own ingenious ways of getting into them and they need no assistance from us psychologists. To say it another way, the behavior of a so-called neurotic client does not seem paradoxical to him until he tries to rationalize it in terms his therapist can understand. It is when he tries to use his therapist's construction system that the paradox appears. Within the client's own limited construction system he may be faced with a dilemma but not with a paradox.

Perhaps this little digression into the neurotic paradox will help prepare the ground for the next phase of our discussion. Certainly it will help if it makes clear that the criteria by which a person chooses between the alternatives, in terms of which he has structured his world, are themselves cast in terms of constructions. Not only do men construe their alternatives, but they construe also criteria for choosing between them. For us psychologists who try to understand what is going on in the minds of our clients it is not as simple as saying that the client will persist in rewarding behavior, or even that he will vacillate between immediate and remote rewards. We have to know what this person construes to be a reward, or, still better, we can bypass such motivational terms as "reward," which ought to be redefined for each new client and on each new occasion, and abstract from human behavior some psychological principle that will transcend the tedious varieties of personalized motives.

If we succeed in this achievement we may be able to escape that common pitfall of so-called objective thinking, the tendency to reify our constructs and treat them as if they were not constructs at all, but actually all the things that they were originally only intended to construe. Such a formulation may even make it safer for us to write operational definitions for purposes of research, without becoming lost in the subject-predicate fallacy. In clinical language it may enable us to avoid concretistic thinking—the so-called brain-injured type of thinking —which is what we call operationalism when we happen to find it in a client who is frantically holding on to his mental faculties.

Now we have been procrastinating long enough. Let us get on to the most difficult part of our discussion. We have talked about experiences with clients who, because they hoped we might be of help to them, honored us with invitations to the rare intimacies of their personal lives and ventured to show us the shadowy processes by which their worlds were ordered. We turned aside briefly in our discussion to talk about the neurotic paradox, hoping that what we could point to there would help the listener anticipate what needed to come next. Now we turn again to a more theoretical form of discourse.

Man Links the Past with the Future—Anticipation. If man, as the psychologist is to see him, exists primarily in the dimensions of time, and only secondarily in the dimensions of space, then the terms which we erect for understanding him ought to take primary account of this view. If we want to know why man does what he does, then the terms of our whys should extend themselves in time rather than in space; they should be events rather than things; they should be mileposts rather than destinations. Clearly, man lives in the present. He stands firmly astride the chasm that separates the past from the future. He is the only connecting link between these two universes. He, and he only, can bring them into harmony with each other. To be sure, there are other forms of existence that have belonged to the past and, presumably, will also belong to the future. A rock that has rested firm for ages may well exist in the future also, but it does not link the past with the future. In its mute way it links only past with past. It does not anticipate; it does not reach out both ways to snatch handfuls from each of the two worlds in order to bring them together and subject them to the same stern laws. Only man does that.

If this is the picture of man, as the psychologist envisions him—man, a form of movement; man, always quick enough, as long as he is alive, to stay astride the darting present—then we cannot expect to explain him either entirely in terms of the past or entirely in terms of the future. We can explain him, psychologically, only as a link between the two. Let us, therefore, formulate our basic postulate for a psychological theory in the light of this conjunctive vision of man. We can say it this way: *A person's processes are psychologically channelized by the ways in which he anticipates events.*

The Nature of Personal Constructs. Taking this proposition as a point of departure, we can quickly begin to sketch a theoretical structure for psychology that will, undoubtedly, turn out to be novel in many unexpected ways. We can say next that man develops his way of anticipating events by construing, by scratching out his channels of thought. Thus he builds his own maze. His runways are the constructs he forms, each a two-way street, each essentially a pair of alternatives between which he can choose.

Another person, attempting to enter this labyrinth, soon gets lost. Even a therapist has to be led patiently back and forth through the system, sometimes for months on end, before he can find his way without the client's help, or tell to what overt behavior each passageway will lead. Many of the runways are conveniently posted with word signs, but most of them are dark, cryptically labeled, or without any word signs at all. Some are rarely traveled. Some the client is reluctant to disclose to his guest. Often therapists lose patience and prematurely start trying to blast shortcuts in which both they and their clients soon become trapped. But worst of all, there are therapists who refuse to believe that they are in the strangely structured world of man; they insist only that the meanderings in which they are led are merely the play of whimsical motives upon their blind and helpless client.

Our figure of speech should not be taken too literally. The labyrinth is conceived as a network of constructs, each of which is essentially an abstraction and, as such, can be picked up and laid down over many different events in order to bring them into focus and clothe them with personal meaning. Moreover, the constructs are subject to continual revision, although the complex interdependent relation between constructs in the system often makes it precarious for the person to revise one construct without taking into account the disruptive affect upon major segments of the system.

In our efforts to communicate the notion of a personal construct system we repeatedly run into difficulty because listeners identify personal constructs with the classic view of a concept. Concepts have long been known as units of logic and are treated as if they existed independently of any particular person's psychological processes. But when we use the notion of "construct" we have nothing of this sort in mind; we are talking about a psychological process in a living person. Such a construct has, for us, no existence independent of the person whose thinking it characterizes. The question of whether it is logical or not has no bearing on its existence, for it is wholly a psychological rather than a logical affair. Furthermore, since it is a psychological affair, it has no necessary allegiance to the verbal forms in which classical concepts have been traditionally cast. The personal construct we talk about bears no essential relation to grammatical structure, syntax, words, language, or even communication; nor does it imply consciousness. It is simply a psychologically construed unit for understanding human processes.

We must confess that we often run into another kind of difficulty. In an effort to understand what we are talking about, a listener often asks if the personal construct is an intellectual affair. We find that, willy-nilly, we invite this kind of question because of our use of such terms as thought and thinking. Moreover, we are speaking in the terms of a language system whose words stand for traditional divisions of mental life, such as "intellectual."

Let us answer this way. A construct owes no special allegiance to the intellect, as against the will or the emotions. In fact, we do not find it either necessary or desirable to make that classic trichotomous division of mental life. After all, there is so much that is "emotional" in those behaviors commonly called "intellectual," and there is so much "intellectualized" contamination in typical "emotional" upheavals that the distinction becomes merely a burdensome nuisance. For some time now we have been quite happy to chuck all these notions of intellect, will, and emotion; so far, we cannot say we have experienced any serious loss.

Now we are at the point in our discourse where we hope our listeners are ready to assume, either from conviction or for the sake of argument, that man, from a psychological viewpoint, makes of himself a bridge between past and future in a manner that is unique among creatures, that, again from a psychological viewpoint, his processes are channelized by the personal constructs he erects in order to perform this function, and, finally, that he organizes his constructs into a personal system that is no more conscious than it is unconscious and no more intellectual than it is emotional. This personal construct system provides him with both freedom of decision and limitation of action—freedom, because it permits him to deal with the meanings of events rather than forces him to be helplessly pushed about by them, and limitation, because he can never make choices outside the world of alternatives he has erected for himself.

The Choice Corollary. We have left to the last the question of what determines man's behavioral choices between his self-construed alternatives. Each choice that he makes has implications for his future.

Each turn of the road he chooses to travel brings him to a fresh vantage point from which he can judge the validity of his past choices and elaborate his present pattern of alternatives for choices yet to be made. Always the future beckons him and always he reaches out in tremulous anticipation to touch it. He lives in anticipation; we mean this literally; *he lives in anticipation!* His behavior is governed, not simply by *what* he anticipates—whether good or bad, pleasant or unpleasant, self-vindicating or self-confounding—but by *where* he believes his choices will place him in respect to the remaining turns in the road. If he chooses this fork in the road, will it lead to a better vantage point from which to see the road beyond or will it be the one that abruptly brings him face-to-face with a blank wall?

What we are saying about the criteria of man's choices is *not* a second theoretical assumption, added to our basic postulate to take the place of the traditional beliefs in separate motives, but is a natural outgrowth of that postulate—a corollary to it. Let us state it so. *A person chooses for himself that alternative in a dichotomized construct through which he anticipates the greater possibility for extension and definition of his system.*

Such a corollary appears to us to be implicit in our postulate that a person's processes are psychologically channelized by the ways in which he anticipates events. For the sake of simplification we have skipped over the formal statement of some of the intervening corollaries of personal construct theory: the corollary that deals with construing, the corollary that deals with the construct system, and the corollary that deals with the dichotomous nature of constructs. But we have probably covered these intervening ideas well enough in the course of our exposition.

What we are saying in this crucial *Choice Corollary* gives us the final ground for dismissing motivation as a necessary psychological construct. It is that if a person's processes are channelized by the ways in which he anticipates events he will make his choices in such a way that he apparently defines or extends his system of channels, for this must necessarily be his comprehensive way of anticipating events.

At the risk of being tedious, let us recapitulate again. We shall be brief. Perhaps we can condense the argument into three sentences. First we saw no need for a closet full of motives to explain the fact that man was active rather than inert; there was no sense in assuming that he was inert in the first place. And now we see no need to invoke a concept of motives to explain the directions that his actions take; the fact that he lives in anticipation automatically takes care of that. Result: no catalogue of motives to clutter up our system and, we hope, a much more coherent psychological theory about living man.

Footnotes. At this point our discourse substantially concludes itself. What we have left to offer are essentially footnotes that are intended to be either defensive or provocative, perhaps both. Questions naturally arise the moment one begins to pursue the implications of this kind of theorizing. One can scarcely take more than a few steps before one begins to stumble over a lot of ancient landmarks that remain to serve no purpose except to get in the way. Perhaps it is only fair that we spotlight some of these relics in the hope of sparing our listeners some barked intellectual shins.

Is this a dynamic theory? This is the kind of question our clinical colleagues are likely to ask. We are tempted to give a flat "No" to that question. No, this is not what is ordinarily called a dynamic theory; it intentionally parts company with psychoanalysis, for example—respectfully, but nonetheless intentionally. However, if what is meant by a "dynamic theory" is a theory that envisions man as active rather than inert, then this is an all-out dynamic theory. It is so dynamic that it does not need any special system of dynamics to keep it running! What must be made clear, or our whole discourse falls flat on its face, is that we do not envision the behavior of man in terms of the external forces bearing upon him; that is a view we are quite ready to leave to the dialectic materialists and to some of their unwitting allies who keep chattering about scientific determinism and other subject-predicate forms of nonsense.

Is this rationalism revisited? We anticipated this question at the beginning of our discussion. We are tempted to answer now by claiming that it is one of the few genuine departures from rationalism, perhaps the first in the field of psychology. But here is a tricky question, because it is not often clear whether one is referring to extrapsychological rationalism or to an essential-psychological rationalism that is often imperfect when judged by classical standards and often branded as "irrationality," or whether the question refers simply to any verbalized structure applied to the behavior of man in an effort to understand him.

Certainly ours is not an extrapsychological rationalism. Instead, it frankly attempts to deal with the essential rationalism that is actually demonstrated in the thinking of man. In doing so it deals with what is sometimes called the world of the irrational and nonrational.

But, in another sense, our interpretation, in its own right and quite apart from its subject matter, is a psychologist's rationale designed to help him understand how man comes to believe and act the way he does. Such a rationale approaches its task the way it does, not because it believes that logic has to be as it is because there is no other way for it to be, not because it believes that man behaves the way he does because there is no other way for him to react to external determining forces, nor even because the rationale's own construction of man provides him with no alternatives, but, rather, because we have the hunch that the way to understand all things, even the ramblings of a regressed schizophrenic client, is to construe them so that they will be made predictable. To some persons this approach spells rationalism, pure and simple, probably because they are firmly convinced that the nether world of man's motives is so hopelessly irrational that anyone who tries to understand that world sensibly must surely be avoiding contact with man as he really is.

Finally, there is the most important question of all; how does the system work? That is a topic to be postponed to another time and occasion. Of course, we think it does work. We use it in psychotherapy and in psychodiagnostic planning for psychotherapy. We also find a place for it in dealing with many of the affairs of everyday life. But there is no place here for the recitation of such details. We hope only that, so far as we have gone, we have been reasonably clear, and a mite provocative, for only by being both clear and provocative can we give our listeners something they can set their teeth into.

ADDENDUM

The invitation to prepare this paper was accompanied by a list of nine issues upon which, it was presumed, would hinge the major differences to be found among any group of motivational theorists. On the face of it such a list seems altogether fair. But one can scarcely pose even one such question, much less nine of them, without exacting hostages to his own theoretical loyalties. And if a correspondent answers in the terminology of the questions posed, he in turn immediately bases his discourse on the assumptions of an alien theory. Once he has done that he will, sooner or later, have to talk as if the differences he seeks to emphasize are merely semantical.

Yet the nine questions need to be met, if not head on, at least candidly enough to be disposed of.

How Important Are Conscious as Opposed to Unconscious Motives in Understanding Human Behavior? We do not use the conscious-unconscious dichotomy, but we do recognize that some of the personal constructs a person seeks to subsume within his system prove to be fleeting or elusive. Sometimes this is because they are loose rather than tight, as in the first phase of the creative cycle. Sometimes it is because they are not bound by the symbolisms of words or other acts. But of this we are sure, if they are important in a person's life, it is a mistake to say they are unconscious or that he is unaware of them. Every day he experiences them, often all too poignantly; the point is that he cannot put his finger on them or tell for sure whether they are at the spot the therapist has probed for them.

When does a person fall back upon such loosened thinking? Or when does he depend upon constructs that are not easily subsumed? Ordinarily when one is confronted with confusion (anxiety) the first tendency is to tighten up; but beyond some breaking point there is a tendency to discard tight constructions and fall back upon constructs that are loose or which have no convenient symbolizations. It is in the human crises that it becomes most important to understand the nature of a person's secondary lines of defense.

What Is the Relative Importance of Direct as Opposed to Indirect Techniques for Assessing Human Motives? Let us change the word "motives" to "constructs." They are not equivalent, of course, but "motives" play no part in our system, whereas "constructs" do. If we ask a person to express his constructs in words, and we take his words literally, then we may say, perhaps, that we are assessing his constructs "directly." If we assume that his words and acts have less patent mean-

ings and that we must construe him in terms of a background understanding of his construct system, shall we say that we have used a more
"indirect" technique? But is anything more direct than this? Perhaps
the method that takes literal meanings for granted is actually more indirect, for it lets the dictionary intervene between the client and the
psychologist. If time permits, we vote for seeking to understand the
person in the light of his personal construct system.

**Is It Essential in Assessing Motives to Provide Some Appraisal of the
Ego Processes, Directive Mechanisms, or Cognitive Controls That Intervene between the Motive and Its Expression?** "Ego" is a psychoanalytic
term; we still don't know what it means. "Cognitive" is a classical term
that implies a natural cleavage between psychological processes, a
cleavage that confuses everything and clarifies nothing; let's forget it.
The notion of a "motive," on the one hand, and "its expression," on
the other, commits one to the view that what is expressed is not the
person but the motivational gremlins that have possessed him. Finally,
if the term "directive mechanisms" is taken in a generic sense, then we
can say that we see these as in the form of constructs formulated by the
person himself and in terms of which he casts his alternatives. What
we need to assess are these personal constructs, if we wish to understand
what a person is up to.

**In Assessing Human Motives How Important Is It to Specify the Situ-
ational Context within Which the Motives Operate?** Each of a client's
constructs has a limited range of convenience in helping him deal with
his circumstances. Beyond that range the construct is irrelevant as far
as he is concerned. This is the point that was so long obscured by the
law of the excluded middle. Knowledge, therefore, of the range of convenience of any personal construct formulated by a client is essential
to an understanding of the behavior he structures by that construct.

**How Necessary Is Knowledge of the Past in the Assessment of Con-
temporary Motivation?** It is not absolutely necessary but it is often convenient. Events of the past may disclose the kind of constructions that
the client has used; presumably he may use them again. Events of the
past, taken in conjunction with the anticipations they confirmed at the
time, may indicate what has been proved to his satisfaction. Again,
events of the past may indicate what the client has had to make sense
out of, and thus enable us to surmise what constructions he may have

had to formulate in order to cope with his circumstances. Finally, since some clients insist on playing the part of martyrs to their biographical destinies, therapy cannot be concluded successfully until their therapists have conducted them on a grand tour of childhood recollections.

At This Time Is the Area of Motivation More in Need of Developing Precise and Highly Objective Measures of Known Motives or Identifying Significant New Motivational Variables? Neither.

In Attempting to Understand Human Motivation Is It Advisable at Present to Focus upon One or a Small Number of Motivational Variables, or Should an Effort be Made to Appraise a Wide Array of Variables? Human impetus should be assumed as a principle rather than treated as a variable or group of variables.

What Is the Relative Importance of Detailed Studies of Individual Cases as Compared to Carefully Controlled Experimental Research and Large-Scale Investigations? All three have their place in the course of developing psychological understanding. The detailed case studies provide excellent grounds for generating constructs. Experimental research, in turn, permits us to test out constructs in artificial isolation. Large-scale investigations help us put constructs into a demographic framework.

Is There a Unique and Important Contribution to the Understanding of Human Motives That Can Be Made at Present through the Medium of Comparative or Lower-Animal Studies That Cannot Be Duplicated by Means of Investigations Utilizing Human Subjects? No.

REFERENCES

Kelly, G. A. *The psychology of personal constructs.* 2 vols. New York: Norton, 1955.
McDougall, W. *Physiological psychology.* London: Dent, 1905.
Mowrer, O. H. *Learning theory and personality dynamics.* New York: Ronald, 1950.

LEON FESTINGER

Stanford University

3 *The motivating effect of*
cognitive dissonance

Since this paper represents a contribution to a conference on the Assessment of Human Motives, I feel a particular responsibility to say something about my conception of psychological motivation—how should motives be defined and conceptualized, how should theories about human motives be stated, how should research on human motives be carried forward? Regrettably, when I started to write this paper, and tried to formulate my ideas about human motivation, it turned out to be an incredibly difficult task. The major source of this difficulty was, I think, that my conceptions of human motivation have all been implicit rather than explicitly and coherently verbalized to myself. Furthermore, I could not, and still cannot see any satisfactory, clear-cut distinctions between concepts concerning human motivations and other psychological concepts with respect to either theory construction or research planning. In the light of this situation, there seemed two courses which I could follow. I could try to infer from my own work and my thinking the nature of my implicit conceptions of motivation, or I could exemplify these implicit notions by presenting here some of the recent theoretical and empirical work I have been doing which concerns a hypothesized human motive. Rather than choose between these alternatives, I decided to do a little of both.

MOTIVATION AS A THEORETICAL CONCEPT

Any specifically defined human motive must, it seems to me, be treated as a hypothetical construct. The specified motive is nothing more than a notion which the psychologist invents in an attempt to explain certain behavior which he observes. For example, we may observe in our own culture that people frequently expend considerable energy to do something well, that is, to do it better than they had done before or to do it better than someone else. In an attempt to explain this kind of behavior one might postulate the existence of an "achievement need." Someone else might try to explain the same phenomena by postulating the existence of an "ego-protection need." Still another person, somewhat more ambitious than the first two, might contend that he can derive the whole thing by postulating a "survival need." All three of these would be hypothetical constructs, and the choice among them would have to be on the basis of which one explains the most data most efficiently. One cannot, and must not, choose on the basis of questions such as, "Are people aware of the existence of such needs or motives?", "Is there a physiological basis for such a need or motive?" or "Does it sound plausible?" These are all irrelevant issues to raise. The only valid issue is whether or not the hypothetical construct is useful, that is, functions better than other constructs in explaining the data.

Before anyone agrees too readily with what I have just said, I want to point out that I have been talking virtual nonsense, because what I have said so far is incomplete. I have stated that the choice among different postulated human needs which attempt to deal with the same behavioral phenomena should be guided by which of them explains the data best. But no single hypothetical construct can explain anything. Before it can do any explaining it must be part of a theory or at least part of a hypothesis. Thus it turns out that one cannot choose among alternative hypothetical human needs apart from the theory in which these constructs are imbedded. And if a postulated human need is not part of a theory or hypothesis, one cannot evaluate it at all. Indeed, if it is not part of a theory it is not performing any explanatory function and, apart from perhaps adding a gratifying technical ring to our language, it is useless. If someone, for example, postulates the existence of an "affiliation need," this means nothing unless he also tells us what this need is supposed to do, that is, how this need, as an independent variable, is related to some dependent variable, or, to state it another way, how this need state motivates behavior. If the person who postulates such an "affiliation need" says, "By giving a questionnaire or a projective test I can measure individual differences with respect to this need, and these measures relate to how much time the person spends with other people," it is still not satisfactory. In essence, one would then be saying only that the stronger the "affiliation need," the greater was the amount of affiliative behavior. Surely this does not constitute a hypothesis with much explanatory power.

What kind of things then does one want to say about human needs and motives? On a general level, the answer to this question is simple. If one is going to postulate some specific need which is part of a theoretical system, one would like to include the following things:

1. Some hypotheses in which the hypothetical need appears as a dependent variable. These hypotheses, in essence, state theories about the variables which affect the magnitude of the need. These variables, let us call them antecedent variables, should ideally be conceptually defined with sufficient clarity to make possible two kinds of empirical operation. One of these is the identification of measurable aspects of the life history of a person which would affect the magnitude of the antecedent variables, thus affecting the magnitude of the need in that person. The other is the identification of immediate situational factors which affect the magnitude of the antecedent variables, thus enabling experimental manipulation.

2. Some hypotheses in which the hypothetical need appears as an independent variable. These hypotheses state theories concerning the consequences for behavior of the existence of the need in different situations.

If one looks at the problem in this way, a number of things become clear. The greater the number of different antecedent conditions which affect the magnitude of the need, and the greater the number of consequent behaviors which are motivated *by* the need, the greater is the usefulness, as an explanatory device, of the postulated need and of the theory concerning it. If there is only one behavioral consequence, then postulating the existence of the need does not help. At this level there would be an unlimited number of possible needs one could postulate which would simply duplicate exactly the chaos of the empirical world.

Another point to be made is that it is essential to define and deal with both antecedent variables and consequent behaviors. It is highly unsatisfactory simply to show that two consequent behaviors relate to one another. If I obtain verbal responses in a given situation and show that this verbal behavior bears a relation to some nonverbal behavior, I have merely shown that both behaviors are dependent in part on the same variables. Calling one of these behaviors a "measure of the need" does not help the situation at all. Both are dependent variables and sooner or later one must show a relation between dependent and independent variables.

I have one last general point to discuss. How can one measure the magnitude of a human need? From the preceding discussion it is clear that one cannot measure it directly. One can measure antecedent conditions which supposedly affect the magnitude of the need, or one can measure behavioral consequences motivated by the need. The situation is precisely similar to the problem of measuring any hypothetical construct. One can measure it only through the variables which affect it or through the effects it has on other variables. To obtain a measure of the magnitude of some hypothetical need one should, then, first demonstrate a relation between the hypothesized antecedent and consequent variables. One can then regard measures of any of these variables as, at least in part, a measure of the magnitude of the need. What one usually tries to do is to select as a measure some consequent behavior which is most closely related to the postulated need in the sense that it is least affected by other variables.

The preceding remarks conclude what I have to say, in general, about human motivation. They represent neither an exhaustive analysis nor a profound discussion of the problem. Rather, they almost border on truisms and platitudes from philosophy of science. Let us, however, keep this discussion in mind for a while.

COGNITIVE DISSONANCE AS A MOTIVATING STATE

I shall now turn to a consideration of one particular hypothetical concept on which I have been working for some years (Festinger, 1957). I hope that this example will illustrate concretely many of the general remarks I have made. First of all, I should like to postulate the existence of *cognitive dissonance* as a motivating state in human beings. Since most of you probably never heard of cognitive dissonance, I assume that so far I have been no more informative than if I had said that I wish to postulate X as a motivating state. I will try, then, to provide a conceptual definition of cognitive dissonance. Let me start by trying to convey, in a loose way, what I have in mind. Afterward we can arrive at a more formal conceptual definition.

Definition of Dissonance. The word "dissonance" was not chosen arbitrarily to denote this motivating state. It was chosen because its ordinary meaning in the English language is close to the technical meaning I want to give it. The synonyms which the dictionary gives for the word "dissonant" are "harsh," "jarring," "grating," "unmelodious," "inharmonious," "inconsistent," "contradictory," "disagreeing," "incongruous," "discrepant." The word, in this ordinary meaning, specifies a relation between two things. In connection with musical tones, where it is usually used, the relation between the tones is such that they sound unpleasant together. In general, one might say that a dissonant relation exists between two things which occur together, if, in some way, they do not belong together or fit together.

Cognitive dissonance refers to this kind of relation between cognitions which exist simultaneously for a person. If a person knows two things, for example, something about himself and something about the world in which he lives, which somehow do not fit together, we will speak of this as cognitive dissonance. Thus, for example, a person might know that he is a very intelligent, highly capable person. At the same time, let us imagine, he knows that he meets repeated failure. These two cognitions would be dissonant—they do not fit together. In general, two cognitions are dissonant with each other if, considering these two cognitions alone, the obverse of one follows from the other. Thus, in the example we have given, it follows from the fact that a person is highly capable that he does not continually meet with failure.

The phrase "follows from" that was used in the previous two sentences needs some explaining. Without going into it in too great detail here, I should like to stress that we are concerned with psychological implication and not necessarily logical implication. The psychological implication which one cognition can have for another cognition can arise from a variety of circumstances. There can be psychological implication because of experience and what one has learned. Thus, if a person is out in the rain with no umbrella or raincoat, it follows from this that he will get wet. There can also be psychological implication because of cultural mores and definition. If one is at a highly formal dinner party, it follows from this that one does not pick up the food with one's fingers. I do not have the time to be thorough or exhaustive in my discussion here, but I hope I have sufficiently explained the concept of dissonance so that we can proceed.

How Cognitive Dissonance Resembles Other Need States. Thus far I have said nothing about the motivating aspects of cognitive dissonance. This is the next step. I wish to hypothesize that the existence of cognitive dissonance is comparable to any other need state. Just as hunger is motivating, cognitive dissonance is motivating. Cognitive dissonance will give rise to activity oriented toward reducing or eliminating the dissonance. Successful reduction of dissonance is rewarding in the same sense that eating when one is hungry is rewarding.

In other words, if two cognitions are dissonant with each other there will be some tendency for the person to attempt to change one of them so that they do fit together, thus reducing or eliminating the dissonance. There are also other ways in which dissonance may be reduced but, not having the time to go into a complete discussion of this, I would rather confine myself to this one manifestation of the motivating character of cognitive dissonance.

Data Needed to Demonstrate the Motivating Character of Cognitive Dissonance. Before proceeding, let us consider for a moment the kinds of data one would like to have in order to document the contention that cognitive dissonance is a motivating state. One would like to have at least the following kinds of data:

1. Determination at Time 1 that a state of cognitive dissonance exists.

This could be done either by measurement or by experimental manipulation.

2. Determination at Time 2 that the dissonance has been eliminated or reduced in magnitude.

3. Data concerning the behavioral process whereby the person has succeeded in changing some cognition, thus reducing the dissonance.

Actually, the above three items are minimal and would probably not be sufficient to demonstrate cogently the validity of the theory concerning cognitive dissonance. Consider the following example. We have determined for a certain person that at one time he believes that tomatoes are poisonous and also knows that his neighbor eats them continually with apparently no ill effect. A dissonance between these two cognitions certainly exists. We then observe that he talks to people about it, shows evidence of being bothered by it, and at a later time, no longer believes that tomatoes are poisonous. The dissonance has been eliminated. But this example would not be very convincing. There are too many alternative ways of understanding this change in the person's belief about tomatoes. He is simply, someone might say, being responsive to the real world.

The kind of data that would be more convincing concerning the motivating aspects of dissonance would be data concerning instances where the dissonance was reduced in the other direction, such as is exemplified in the old joke about the psychiatrist who had a patient who believed he was dead. After getting agreement from the patient that dead men do not bleed, and being certain that the patient understood this, the psychiatrist made a cut on the patient's arm and, as the blood poured out, leaned back in his chair, smiling. Whereupon the patient, with a look of dismay on his face, said, "Well, what do you know, dead men *do* bleed." This kind of thing, if it occurred actually, would be harder to explain in alternative ways.

In other words, one has to demonstrate the effects of dissonance in circumstances where these effects are not easily explainable on the basis of other existing theories. Indeed, if one cannot do this, then one could well ask what the usefulness was of this new notion that explained nothing that was not already understood. Consequently, in order to persuade you of the validity of cognitive dissonance and its motivating characteristics I will give two examples where dissonance reduction produced results somewhat contrary to what one would expect on the basis of the operation of other human motives.

Some Examples of Unusual Manifestations of Dissonance Reduction.

Example 1: One rather intriguing example comes from a pair of studies of rumors following disasters. Prasad (1950) systematically recorded rumors which were widely current immediately following an especially severe earthquake in India, in 1934. The quake itself, a strong and prolonged one, was felt over a wide geographical area. Actual damage, however, was quite localized and, for a period of days, communication with the damaged area was very poor. The rumors were collected in the area which felt the shock of the earthquake but which did not suffer any damage. We are, then, dealing with communication of rumors among people who felt the shock of the earthquake but who did not see any damage or destruction.

While Prasad reports little concerning the emotional reactions of people to the quake, it is probably plausible to assume that these people who knew little about earthquakes had a strong reaction of fear to the violent and prolonged shaking of the ground. We may also assume that such a strong fear reaction does not vanish immediately but probably persists for some time after the actual shock of the quake is over.

Let us speculate about the content of the cognition of these persons. When the earthquake was over they had this strong, persistent fear reaction but they could see nothing different around them, no destruction, no further threatening things. In short, a situation had been produced where dissonance existed between cognition corresponding to the fear they felt and the knowledge of what they saw around them which, one might say, amounted to the cognition that there was nothing to be afraid of.

The vast majority of the rumors which were widely circulated were rumors which, if believed, provided cognition consonant with being afraid. One might even call them "fear-provoking" rumors, although, if our interpretation is correct, they would more properly be called "fear justifying" rumors. The following are a fair sample of the rumors which Prasad collected:

There will be a severe cyclone at Patna between January 18 and January 19. (The earthquake occurred on January 15.)

There will be a severe earthquake on the lunar eclipse day.

A flood was rushing from the Nepal borders to Madhubani.

January 23 will be a fatal day. Unforseeable calamities will arise.

Here, then, is an instance where the reduction of dissonance produced results which looked like fear arousal.

If this explanation is correct in accounting for the prevalence of these "fear-justifying" rumors, there is one clear implication, namely, that if rumors had been collected among persons living *in* the area of destruction, few, if any, of such rumors would have been found. Those persons directly in the area of destruction caused by the earthquake were, undoubtedly, also frightened. Indeed, their fear reaction would very likely have been even stronger than that of the persons who merely felt the shock of the quake. But for the people in the area of destruction, no cognitive dissonance would have been created. The things they could see around them, the destruction, the wounded and killed, would produce cognition which would certainly be consonant with feeling afraid. There would be no impulse or desire to acquire additional cognitions which fit with the fear, and fearful rumors of the type so prevalent outside the area of destruction should have been absent.

Unfortunately, Prasad presents no data on rumors which circulated inside the area of destruction following the earthquake. There is, however, another study reported by Sinha (1952) which bears on this. This study reports a careful collection of rumors following a disaster in Darjeeling, India, a disaster which was fully comparable to the earthquake in terms of destruction and loss of life but which, unfortunately for purposes of comparison, did not arise from an earthquake but from a landslide. Nevertheless, it must have produced considerable fear among the people. Sinha directly compares the two when, in describing the landslide disaster he states:

There was a feeling of instability and uncertainty similar to that which followed the Great Indian Earthquake of 1934. (p. 200)

There is, however, one important difference between the study reported by Prasad and the one reported by Sinha. While the rumors following the earthquake were collected among persons outside of the area of destruction, the rumors which Sinha reports were collected from persons in Darjeeling who actually were in the area and witnessed the destruction. Since for these people there would have been no dissonance —what they saw and knew was quite consonant with being afraid—we would not expect disaster rumors to arise and spread among them.

Actually, in Sinha's report, there is a complete absence of rumors predicting further disasters or of any type of rumor that might be regarded as supplying cognition consonant with being afraid. The contrast between the rumors reported by Sinha and those reported by Prasad is certainly strong.

Example 2: Another intriguing example of the reduction of dissonance in a startling manner comes from a study I did together with Riecken and Schachter (1956) of a group of people who predicted that, on a given date, a catastrophic flood would overwhelm most of the world. This prediction of the catastrophic flood had been given to the people in direct communications from the gods and was an integral part of their religious beliefs. When the predicted date arrived and passed there was considerable dissonance established in these people. They continued to believe in their gods and in the validity of the communications from them, and at the same time they knew that the prediction of the flood had been wrong. We observed the movement as participants for approximately two months preceding and one month after this unequivocal disproof of part of their belief. The point of the study was, of course, to observe how they would react to the dissonance. Let me give a few of the details of the disproof and how they reacted to it.

For some time it had been clear to the people in the group that those who were chosen were to be picked up by flying saucers before the cataclysm occurred. Some of the believers, these mainly college students, were advised to go home and wait individually for the flying saucer that would arrive for each of them. This was reasonable and plausible, since the data of the cataclysm happened to occur during an academic holiday. Most of the group, including the most central and most heavily committed members, gathered together in the home of the woman who received the messages from the gods to wait together for the arrival of the saucer. For these latter, disproof of the prediction, in the form of evidence that the messages were not valid, began to occur four days before the predicted event was to take place. A message informed them that a saucer would land in the back yard of the house at 4:00 P.M. to pick up the members of the group. With coat in hand they waited, but no saucer came. A later message told them there had been a delay—the saucer would arrive at midnight. Midst absolute secrecy (the neighbors and press must not know), they waited outdoors on a cold and snowy night for over an hour, but still no saucer came. Another message told them to continue waiting, but still no saucer came. At about 3:00 A.M. they gave up, interpreting the events of that night as a test, a drill, and a rehearsal for the real pickup which would still soon take place.

Tensely, they waited for the final orders to come through—for the messages which would tell them the time, place, and procedure for the actual pickup. Finally, on the day before the cataclysm was to strike, the messages came. At midnight a man would come to the door of the house and take them to the place where the flying saucer would be parked. More messages came that day, one after another, instructing them in the passwords that would be necessary in order to board the saucer, in preparatory procedures such as removal of metal from clothing, removal of personal identification, maintaining silence at certain times, and the like. The day was spent by the group in preparation and rehearsal of the necessary procedures and, when midnight came, the group sat waiting in readiness. But no knock came at the door, no one came to lead them to the flying saucer.

From midnight to five o'clock in the morning the group sat there struggling to understand what had happened, struggling to find some explanation that would enable them to recover somewhat from the shattering realization that they would not be picked up by a flying saucer and that consequently the flood itself would not occur as predicted. It is doubtful that anyone alone, without the support of the others, could have withstood the impact of this disproof of the prediction. Indeed, those members of the group who had gone to their homes to wait alone, alone in the sense that they did not have other believers with them, did not withstand it. Almost all of them became skeptics afterward. In other words, without easily obtainable social support to begin reducing the dissonance, the dissonance was sufficient to cause the belief to be discarded in spite of the commitment to it. But the members of the group that had gathered together in the home of the woman who received the messages could, and did, provide social support for one another. They kept reassuring one another of the validity of the messages and that some explanation would be found.

At fifteen minutes before five o'clock that morning an explanation was found that was at least temporarily satisfactory. A message arrived from God which, in effect, said that He had saved the world and stayed the flood because of this group and the light and strength this group had spread throughout the world that night.

The behavior of these people from that moment onwards presented a revealing contrast to their previous behavior. These people who had been disinterested in publicity and even avoided it, became avid publicity seekers. For four successive days, finding a new reason each day, they invited the press into the house, gave lengthy interviews, and attempted to attract the public to their ideas. The first day they called all the newspapers and news services, informed them of the fact that the world had been saved and invited them to come and get interviews. The second day, a ban on having photographs taken was lifted, and the newspapers were once more called to inform them of the fact and to invite them to come to the house and take pictures. On the third day they once more called the press to inform them that on the next afternoon they would gather on their front lawn singing and that it was possible a space man would visit them at that time. What is more, the general public was specifically invited to come and watch. And on the fourth day, newspapermen and about two hundred people came to watch the group singing on their front lawn. There were almost no lengths to which these people would not go to attract publicity and potential believers in the validity of the messages. If, indeed, more and more converts could be found, more and more people who believed in the messages and the things the messages said, then the dissonance between their belief and the knowledge that the messages had not been correct could be reduced.

These examples, while they do illustrate attempts to reduce dissonance in rather surprising directions, still leave much to be desired. One would also like to be able to show that such dissonance-reduction phenomena do occur under controlled laboratory conditions and that the magnitude of the effect does depend upon the magnitude of the dissonance which exists. Consequently, I will describe for you a laboratory experiment which we have just completed at Stanford, one in which we investigated the reduction of dissonance following experimental manipulation of the magnitude of dissonance. The obtained results are, in my opinion, not easily interpreted in terms of other existing theories.

An Experimental Investigation. In this experiment, we created dissonance in the subjects by inducing them to say something which was at variance with their private opinion. It is clear that this kind of situation does produce dissonance between what the person believes and what he knows he has said. There are also cognitive consonances for the person. His cognitions concerning the things that induced him to make the public statement are consonant with his knowledge of having done it. The total magnitude of the dissonance between all other relevant cognitions taken together and the knowledge of what he has publicly said will, of course, be a function of the number and importance of the dissonances in relation to the number and importance of the consonances. One could, then, manipulate the total magnitude of dissonance experimentally by holding everything constant and varying the strength of the inducement for the person to state something publicly which was at variance with his private opinion. The *stronger* the inducement to do this, the *less* would be the over-all magnitude of dissonance created.

Let us imagine a concrete situation. Suppose a number of people have had an experience to which they reacted negatively. Each of these persons, then, let us say, is offered a different amount of money to tell someone else that the experience was very pleasant and enjoyable. In each case, let us further imagine, the amount of money offered is at least large enough so that the person accepts the money and engages in the overt behavior required. Certainly, after telling someone that the experience was enjoyable, there is a dissonance between his cognition of what he has said and his own private opinion.

This dissonance could, clearly, be reduced if the person persuades himself that the experience was, indeed, fairly pleasant and enjoyable, that is, if he changes his private opinion so that it corresponds more closely with what he has said. The greater the dissonance, the more frequently should one observe such subsequent attitude change. We would expect then that, after the person had told someone else that the experience was pleasant and enjoyable, he would change his private opinions concerning the experience to some extent. We would further expect that the more money he was given to induce him to make the public statement, the smaller would be the subsequent opinion change, because less dissonance had been created initially.

Now for the details of the experiment. I will describe it as it proceeded for the subject, with occasional explanatory comments. Each subject had signed up for a two hour experiment on "measures of performance." The subjects were all students from the Introductory Psychology course at Stanford where they are required to serve a certain number of hours as subjects in experiments. When the student arrived he was met by the experimenter and, with a minimum of explanation, was given a repetitive motor task to work on. He packed a frame full of little spools, then emptied it, then packed it again, and so on for a half hour. He was then given another task to do in which he turned rows of pegs, each a quarter turn, then turned them all another quarter turn, and so on for another half hour. When he had finished, the experimenter informed him that the experiment was over, thanked him for his participation, and proceeded to explain to him what the experiment was about and what its purpose was.

From our point of view, the purpose of this initial part was to provide for each subject an experience which was rather dull, boring, and somewhat fatiguing. The student, however, believed this to be the whole experiment. The explanation of the experiment given to the student was that the experiment was concerned with the effect of preparatory set on performance. He was told that there were two conditions in the experiment, one of these being the condition he had experienced where the subject was told nothing ahead of time. The other condition, the experimenter explained, was one in which the subject, before working on the tasks, was led to expect that they were very enjoyable, very interesting, and lots of fun. The procedure for subjects in this other condition, the experimenter explained, proceeded in the following manner. A person working for us is introduced to the waiting subject as someone who has just finished the experiment and will tell the prospective subject a little about it. This person who works for us then tells the waiting subject that the experiment is very enjoyable, interesting, and lots of fun. In this way, the subjects in the other condition are given the set we want them to have. This concluded the false explanation of the experiment to the student and, in the control group, nothing more was done at this point.

In the experimental groups, however, the experimenter continued by telling the subject that he had a rather unusual proposal to make. It seems that the next subject is scheduled to be in that condition where he is to be convinced in advance that the experiment is enjoyable and a lot of fun. The person who works for us and usually does this, however, although very reliable, could not do it today. We thought we would take a chance and ask him (the student) to do it for us. We would like, if agreeable to him, to hire him on the same basis that the other person was hired to work for us. We would like to put him on the payroll and pay him a lump sum of money to go tell the waiting subject that the experiment is enjoyable, interesting, and fun; and he was also to be on tap for us in case this kind of emergency arises again.

There were two experimental conditions which we actually conducted. The procedure was absolutely identical in both except for the amount of money that the subjects were paid as "the lump sum." In one condition they were paid one dollar for their immediate and possible future services. In the other condition they were paid twenty dollars. When the student agreed to do this, he was actually given the money and he signed a receipt for it. He was then taken into the room where the next subject was waiting and introduced to her by the experimenter, who said that the student had just been a subject in the experiment and would tell her a bit about it. The experimenter then went out, leaving student and the waiting subject together for two and a half minutes. The waiting subject was actually a girl in our employ. Her instructions were very simple. After the student had told her that the experiment was interesting, enjoyable and lots of fun, she was to say something like, "Oh, a friend of mine who took it yesterday told me it was dull and that if I could I should get out of it." After that she was simply supposed to agree with whatever the student said. If, as almost always happened, the student reaffirmed that the experiment was fun, she was to say that she was glad to hear it. The following is a typical record of this interchange which was recorded on a tape recorder for all subjects.

STUDENT: It's quite a deal.

GIRL: Is it?

STUDENT: Yeah—it's kind of fun. You play with pegs and spools. I don't know what it's supposed to test, but it's a lot of fun.

GIRL: I'm living over at Moore. I have a friend who took the experiment last week and she wouldn't tell me what she did but she said it was very boring.

STUDENT: I don't know—it's kind of fun when you get going at it.

GIRL: Oh, really? Well, I'm relieved to hear you say that in a way. Gosh, I was kind of worried.

STUDENT: It's kind of interesting to play with those things. I can't figure out what they're trying to test but it's kind of fun.

GIRL: You sit there trying to figure out what it is, huh?

STUDENT: (laughs) I guess so. It's kind of fun—fun to work on. It's interesting to do something with your hands. Lots of fun. What class you in—sophomore?

GIRL: No, senior.

STUDENT: Senior? (*laughs*) Quite a difference.

GIRL: Yeah. I wanted to get some Psych in before I graduate. (*few seconds silence*)

STUDENT: Quite a challenge. Yeah. Some of them are fun—some of them don't seem to have much point to them. (*Here the subject talked for a few seconds about other experiments he had taken*).

When the experimenter returned, after two and a half minutes, he sent the girl into the experimental room, telling her he would be there in a few minutes. He then obtained the student's phone number in order to continue the fiction that the student was to be available for future services of like nature. The experimenter then thanked the subject and made a brief speech in which he said that most subjects found the experimental tasks very interesting and enjoyed them, and that, when he thinks about it, he will probably agree. The purpose of this brief speech is to provide some cognitive material which the subject can use to reduce dissonance, assuming that such dissonance exists. The identical speech is, of course, made to the control subjects, too.

The only remaining problem in the experiment was to obtain a measure of what each subject honestly thought privately about the tasks on which he had worked for an hour. It seemed desirable, naturally, to obtain this measure in a situation where the subject would be inclined to be very frank in his statements. It also seemed desirable to obtain these measures quite independently of the actual experiment. This was done in the following manner. It had previously been announced by the instructor in the Introductory Psychology class that, since students were required to participate in experiments, the Psychology Department was going to do a study to assess the value of the experiences they had. The purpose of this, the instructor had explained, was to help improve the selection of experiments in the future. They were told that a sample of them, after serving in experiments, would be interviewed about them. It would be to their advantage, and to the advantage of future students in the course, for them to be very frank and honest in these interviews.

In our experiment, the student was told that someone from Introductory Psychology probably wanted to interview him. The experimenter confessed ignorance about what this impending interview was about but said he had been told that the subject would know about it. Usually at this point the subject nodded his head or otherwise indicated that he did, indeed, know what it was about. The experimenter then took him to an office where the interviewer was waiting, said good-bye to the subject, and left.

The interview itself was rather brief. Four questions were asked, namely, how interesting and enjoyable the experiment was, how much the subject learned from it, how important he thought it was scientifically, and how much he would like to participate in a similar experiment again. The important question, for us, is the first one concerning how interesting and enjoyable the experiment was, since this was the content area in which dissonance was established for the experimental subjects. The subject was encouraged to answer the question in some detail and then was asked to rate, on a scale running from -5 to $+5$, how he felt about it. The other questions were included to make the interview realistic and also to provide a comparison, since there seemed little reason to believe that there would or should be any difference among the three conditions on the questions concerning how much they learned and how important the experiment was. There might, of course, be differences on the question concerning their desire to partici-pate in a similar experiment, the answers to which would undoubtedly reflect, in part, how much they liked this one.

Needless to say, since it is standard practice, after the interview was concluded, the experimenter, the student, and the girl who posed as the waiting subject were brought together, and the truth about the whole experiment was explained in detail to the subject's satisfaction.

Some of you may wonder about the effectiveness of the experimental procedure. Were the subjects really taken in by all of it? Actually, if you have been wondering about this, let me assure you that it is a legitimate thing to wonder about. It took us several months of preliminary work to get the procedure in a form so that subjects did not become suspicious. In its present form, the procedure I have described works well. Of the forty subjects, twenty in each of the two experimental conditions (there were, of course, also twenty control subjects, but here there is no prob-lem) only 5 gave evidence of suspecting that the experiment really dealt with having him talk to the waiting subject. These few subjects, of course, had to be omitted from the data.

Let us look, then, at what the results show. Figure 1 shows the average rating, for each of the three conditions, for the question concerning how interesting and enjoyable the experiment was. A rating of —5 meant extremely dull and boring, +5 meant extremely interesting and enjoy-able, and 0 meant neutral. The subject could, of course, rate his reaction to the experiment anywhere between —5 and +5. The average rating for the control group is represented as a horizontal dotted line across the figure. It is done this way since the data from the control group actually provide a base line. This is how subjects reacted to the experiment after having gone through it and having been told exactly the same things that the experimental subjects were told. They simply were never asked to, and never did, tell the waiting subject that the experiment was inter-esting, enjoyable, and lots of fun. It turns out that, on the average, the control group rates the experiment —.45 for how enjoyable it was, slightly below neutral. In the One Dollar experimental condition there is a definite increase over the control group. Here the average rating is +1.35, definitely on the positive side of the scale and significantly different from the control group at the 1 per cent level of confidence. In other words, in the One Dollar condition the dissonance between their private opinion of the experiment and their knowledge of what they had said to the waiting subject was reduced significantly by changing their private opinion somewhat, to bring it closer to what they had overtly said.

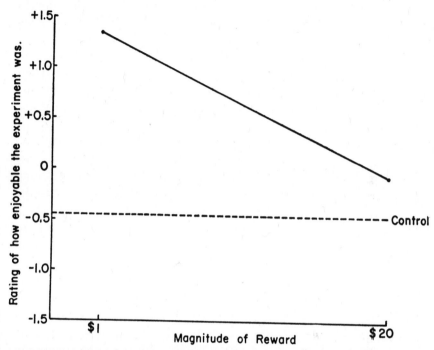

Figure 1. *Relation between magnitude of reward used to elicit compliance and subsequent rating of how enjoyable the experiment was.*

But now let us turn our attention to the Twenty Dollar condition. Here the magnitude of dissonance experimentally created was less than in the One Dollar condition because of the greater importance of the cognition that was consonant with what they knew they had done. It seems undeniable that twenty dollars is a good deal more important than one dollar. There should hence be less pressure to reduce the dissonance, and indeed, the average rating for the Twenty Dollar condition is —.05, only slightly above the Control condition and significantly different from the One Dollar condition at the 2 per cent level of confidence.

While I will not take the time to present the data on the other questions in detail, I will say that there were no significant differences on any of the other questions among the three conditions in the experiment. On the scale concerning how much they feel they learned from the experiment, the three means are virtually identical. On their desire to participate again in a similar experiment and on how scientifically important they think it is, the results are in the same direction as those we have shown, but the differences are smaller and not significant.

There is just one other point I would like to discuss about the data from this experiment. What are the possible alternative interpretations? Clearly, any interpretation which seeks to explain the opinion change in terms of reward or reinforcement is doomed to failure, since the smaller reward led to the larger opinion change. Janis and King (1954; King and Janis, 1956) have published two experiments in which they show that opinion change occurs after a person has made a speech favoring a particular point of view. They offer an explanation of their results mainly in terms of rehearsal of arguments, thinking up new arguments, and in this way convincing themselves. Could this be an explanation of the difference between the One and Twenty Dollar conditions? On the surface it appears implausible, since such an explanation would demand that the subjects in the One Dollar condition would have tried harder to be persuasive when talking to the waiting girl than the subjects in the Twenty Dollar condition. This would seem unlikely since, if anything, having received more money, they should be *more* motivated to do a good job in the Twenty Dollar condition. However, strange things sometimes happen; with this possibility in mind, we obtained recordings of the discussion between the subjects and the waiting girl. These have been rated for persuasiveness, number of different things the subject says, and other conceivably relevant variables. The ratings were, of course, done in ignorance of the experimental condition by two separate raters. The reliability of the independent ratings varies between .6 and .9. The ratings used in the actual analysis of the data were settled on by discussion of disagreements between the two raters. It turns out that there are no large differences between the two experimental conditions in what the subject said or how he said it. As one might expect, the small differences which do exist are in the direction favoring the $20 condition. In the $20 condition the subjects are a bit more emphatic about saying the experiment was interesting and enjoyable. Personally, I have not been able to think of any very satisfactory alternative explanation of the results. It is precisely this difficulty of devising alternative explanations that makes these results strongly supportive of the dissonance interpretation.

SUMMARY AND CONCLUSIONS

I should like to summarize a bit before concluding. I started out, as you will recall, by making a number of rather general remarks about human motivation. In these general remarks I did not discuss the nature of human motives but rather the circumstances under which hypothesizing the existence of a specific motive was fruitful and useful. I then proceeded to propose to you that the existence of cognitive dissonance was a motivating state and I attempted to illustrate the validity and usefulness of his concept. The evidence for the validity and usefulness of conceiving cognitive dissonance as motivating is as follows:

1. Evidence that the existence of cognitive dissonance sometimes leads to behavior that appears very strange indeed when viewed only from the standpoint of commonly accepted motives. Here I have had time only to give two examples illustrating this phenomenon.

2. Evidence that the amount of reduction of dissonance is a direct function of the magnitude of dissonance which exists. I illustrated this by describing a laboratory experiment where, under controlled conditions, the magnitude of dissonance was experimentally manipulated.

There is at least one further point that I would have liked to have made, and would have if I had supporting data. If cognitive dissonance is indeed a motivating state, one would like to be able to show that, assuming that individual differences exist, which they almost certainly do, that those persons for whom it is more highly motivating react more strongly. In order to do this one would first have to have some way of measuring the degree to which cognitive dissonance is painful or uncomfortable for the individual. This I do not as yet have. It is, though, one of the clearly important goals of the future.

I stress this lack, not so much to emphasize that a measure of individual differences is missing, but rather to re-emphasize what I consider an important procedural point. I do not think it will be maximally fruitful in the long run to begin by developing tests to give measures of the strength of some hypothesized human need, and then to attempt to discover how this need operates. I believe strongly that it is better to proceed in the reverse order. After one has demonstrated the validity and usefulness of some hypothesized need is the time to start measuring individual variation. One then knows much more clearly what one is trying to measure, why one is trying to measure it, and to what the individual measure should relate.

REFERENCES

Festinger, Leon. A *theory of cognitive dissonance*. Evanston, Ill.: Row-Peterson, 1957.

———, Riecken, H. W., and Schachter, S. *When prophecy fails*. Minneapolis: University of Minnesota Press, 1956.

Janis, I. L., and King, B. T. The influence of role-playing on opinion change. *J. abnorm. soc. Psychol.*, 1954, 49, 211-218.

King, B. T., and Janis, I. L. Comparison of the effectiveness of improvised versus non-improvised role-playing in producing opinion changes. *Human Relations*, 1956, 9, 177-186.

Prasad, J. A comparative study of rumors and reports in earthquakes. *Brit. J. Psychol.*, 1950, 41, 129-144.

Sinha, D. Behavior in a catastrophic situation: a psychological study of reports and rumors. *Brit. J. Psychol.*, 1952, 43, 200-209.

GEORGE S. KLEIN

New York University

4 *Cognitive control and motivation*[1]

Some years ago my co-workers and I proposed a concept of cognitive control that would center attention upon a person's typical strategies of perceiving, remembering, and thinking (Klein and Schlesinger, 1949; Klein, 1950; Holzman and Klein, 1954; Klein, 1954). We suggested that such inveterate regulative tendencies—*cognitive attitudes,* we came to call them—might account for some of the differences among people that always appear in perceptual and cognitive studies. More recently it became clear to us that a variety of cognitive attitudes contributes to self-consistency in a person's behavior, and we have tried to take note of such a structural arrangement of cognitive attitudes by referring to it as *cognitive style.* In proposing these concepts of cognitive attitude and style, there was at the back of our minds a feeling that while motivation-in-perception studies were rectifying older sins of omission, they were also assuming that if only a drive is intense enough it can bend any and all cognitive structures to its aim. While no one committed himself

[1] I owe much to the stimulating and helpful comments of friends and colleagues who read this paper many drafts ago. Robert R. Holt, Gardner Murphy, Irving Paul, and David Rapaport especially earn my gratitude, and they are to be absolved from the inadequacies of formulation and clarity that remain.

blatantly to such an overstatement, the drift of empirical work seemed to be moving steadily toward it. Some way had to be found in theory of providing for effective perceiving without renouncing the possible pervasiveness of motivational influence upon thought.

The behavior patterns in which we sought evidences of cognitive attitudes seemed clearly to reflect direction in thought, but as we learned more about them it also became clear that they lacked the characteristics ordinarily ascribed to drives. For instance, a rather common notion of drive speaks of it as goal-directed behavior which involves, in Tolman's words, a "readiness to get to and manipulate in consummatory fashion (or to get from) certain types of objects" (1951, p. 288). Yet the behavior patterns of cognitive attitudes seemed by no means committed to a search for particular objects, nor were they linked in any clear-cut way to particular forms of satisfaction. Cognitive attitudes seemed to be purposive without having the character of a drive and thus demanding satisfaction. They had much in common with what Gordon Allport (1935) has called "instrumental attitudes," since they involved not so much *what* a person was typically trying to get at (drive satisfaction) as the *how*, his ways and means of getting there. In fact, they were able to account in some measure for individual differences even in innocuous, sexless, contentless, aggression-free tasks of the glamourless psychophysical experiment.

It dawned on us that our most reliable estimates of such individual controls actually occurred in settings that ensured optimal performance, relatively uncomplicated by anxiety and by conflictual connotations of the stimuli. That is, when subjects felt involved without being threatened their patterns seemed to stand out. It seemed best, then, to consider the purposiveness in cognitive attitudes in terms best suited to their most obvious accomplishment in behavior, rather than as an expression of drive satisfaction: as ways of contacting reality, whereby one's intentions are coordinated with the properties, relations, and limitations of events and objects.

Thus conceived, cognitive attitudes seemed to resemble what psychoanalysts have called "character defenses." However, to regard them as "defenses" could be misleading, because they were not obviously tied to specific demands or conflicts, as the precise meaning of "defense" should imply. If in particular experimental conditions they seemed to have an instrumental function in helping to bring about reduction of a drive (say if we were to see evidence of a cognitive attitude in the way a hungry person typically goes about getting his food), or if they brought about an outcome in behavior that could be thought of as defensive, these did not really describe the essential behavior pattern of the cognitive attitude; they referred to its possible consequences, its secondary outcomes. Furthermore, to view them in such specific terms of drive reduction or defense leaves unexplained (1) that they seem to reflect highly generalized forms of control, as likely to appear in a person's perceptual behavior as in his manner of recall and recollection; and (2) that activation of one rather than another cognitive attitude in a person's repertoire depends not so much on the drive tension of the moment as upon the requirements posed by the adaptive *task* with which he had to cope.

Working from the psychoanalytic assumption that thought originates in the enforced postponement of drive satisfaction (Freud, 1900, 1911), I found it useful to consider cognitive attitudes as contributing to drive activity in a secondary way, by modulating, facilitating, or inhibiting the effects of a temporarily active drive upon behavior (Klein, 1954). They seemed to ensure that drive-organized behavior would also be realistic behavior, for they represented strategies of reality contact which were probably the outcomes of a person's long and repeated efforts to deal adequately and with "least action" with classes of situations typically encountered en route to drive satisfaction. If the problem of motivation were merely how to get the organism into action, cognitive attitudes would be irrelevant to drive. But motivation involves direction in behavior, the production of certain results—some perceivable change which meets subjective standards of adequacy, standards of a workable fit with the nature of things. If a given result is to be achieved, behavior must be provided not only with a motor but with a steering wheel and a map—which cognitive attitudes supply.

A study reported three years ago seemed to encourage this thesis (Klein, 1954). The main purpose of this investigation was to see how reactions to thirst would differ when different cognitive attitudes are brought to bear upon a task. The thirsty and sated groups were made up of people who in an earlier testing situation responded in contrasting ways to interfering, task-irrelevant stimulus meanings. The experimental tasks had in common a single essential feature: the stimulus *contents,* either thirst-related or neutral themes, were of no help to the subject as he went about the task; in fact, they could be only distracting, a hindrance to accurate performance. For instance, in a size estimation task pictures were pasted on the surfaces of the disks which subjects were to judge for over-all size. It was expected that *all* thirsty subjects would cope with the tasks in characteristic ways different from sated subjects, especially when confronting thirst-related themes in the stimuli. The results, however, were not so simple. Thirst *generally* did produce deviations in cognitive behavior, but in different ways in the two thirsty groups. These differences were consistent with the subjects' performance on the earlier selection task, which had posed somewhat similar adaptive hurdles. Thus the effects of drive seemed better understandable when we knew the requirements of a task and the cognitive attitudes relevant to it. If drives bend cognitive behavior, there are evidently limits to this plasticity, limits imposed in part by options presented by the situation, in part by the objects with which a person has to deal, and in part by the cognitive attitudes called into play by the adaptive problems confronting him. The experiment seemed to tell us that drive, with its associated situation sets, goal sets, and incentives, is the piper that calls most of the tunes, but not the tempo or the style with which they are played.

There seemed, then, good reason to postulate two bases of regulation in behavior: control structures having what we may term an *accommodative* function in behavior—that of coordinating intentions and the structural matrix of objects and events; and drive structures, which give behavior segments either an instrumental or a consummatory significance in terms of goal sets. This distinction proved to have its troubles, however. The main one was how to describe the "force" of drive independently of its partners in interaction. Try as we would, it was impossible to define the pushing or impelling quality of thirst apart from the cognitive tools of perceiving and cognition which it presumably pushes. Further reflection on the nature of thirst in our experiment created doubts about the wisdom of conceiving drives simply as a pushing agent which produces behavior. Thirst, like the so-called "higher needs," is evidently very much a cognitive event linked in some way to somatic deficit, though not necessarily requiring such deficit for arousal, but always implicating intentions and conceptualizations as well as a range of consummatory objects. The processes "pushed" somehow determine the "push" itself. Clearly, a more adequate conception of drive should house both the delaying principles *and* the specific object aims, sets, intentions, and incentives implied by the concept of drive.

The study gave us a useful perspective to the issue of directedness in behavior. It emphasized for us that behavior reflects direction and control, but in a fashion that does not render it exclusively at the mercy of the demand aspect of drives, or helplessly prey to environmental forces. There needs to be provision for a scheme of regulation that produces structural guarantees of autonomy in a person's behavior; guarantees that ensure that thinking and behavior are products of internal demands, on the one hand, which recruit only certain environmental structures and motor activities for their own requirements; and, on the other, of accommodative processes which are simultaneously responsive to adaptive intentions and to the inherent structural arrangements of things and events. "Instinctual danger," remarked Anna Freud, "makes a man wise." By being responsive to drive aims and to reality alike, thought and behavior achieve paradoxically a certain freedom from both masters (Hartmann, 1951; Rapaport, 1958).

CONTROL STRUCTURES IN DRIVE

In the pages that follow I will try to place these component motivations of thought in a somewhat more workable relation to each other within a general conception of drive. Admittedly, the proposals are speculative and tentative. But there is no escaping the necessity of keeping step, however halting, with empirical developments of the last decade which have made more glaring the insufficiencies of older conceptions of drive. Of course it is hazardous to hope that any theory or concept can provide a sacrosanct shelter in these times of rapid empirical change. But such change calls for an accelerating of theory building, not for a retreat from it. As Hebb remarked, theorizing today is like skating on thin ice; keep moving or drown.

Older notions of "interaction" are not very helpful in relating drives to structures of cognitive control. The conception of drive as an independent entity designed to provide for internally coerced, selective behavior came about at a time when purpose and intention had to be grafted on to an unwilling host. However, it brought into psychology a fundamentally unspecifiable force, conceptions of which often retreat to the metaphors of an energy language. Other defects seem obvious now. For one thing, it is impossible to define the drive presumed to interact with cognition without implicating in the definition the very structure supposedly pushed. Hebb (1949) and Jacob (1954) have argued, and our results certainly bear them out, that even a so-called somatic drive like thirst cannot be defined solely in terms of a tissue lack. The dehydrated condition of the body would not itself create a call for water were it not for some kind of relating (cognitive) activity associated with the somatic tension. Also, it is difficult to bring a conception of an independent pushing agent into line with the fact that behavior can be differently organized in people even while showing the integrative pull of the same goal set or incentive. Neither is it easy to hold such a conception and still provide for the fact that, although behavior is selective, it responds quite efficiently to existing environmental arrangements.

It seems more parsimonious to follow Woodworth's (1918), Woodworth and Schlosberg's (1954), and Hebb's (1949) lead and think of drive as a construct which refers, on the one hand, to the "relating" processes—the meanings—around which selective behavior and memories are organized; and in terms of which goal sets, anticipations, and expectations develop, and, on the other hand, to those processes which accommodate this relational activity to reality. In this way drive is defined solely in terms of behavior and thought products. Emphasis is thereby placed where it belongs; in Hebb's words, upon the directedness, patterning, and the timing of behavior, since these are after all the essential problems which provoked motivation concepts in the first place.

The first characteristic of drive is that it involves a goal set, a requirement for object qualities appropriate to it. Drives bring the organism into readiness for certain things, certain meanings. The relational core of a drive is, therefore, conceptual activity. Conceptual activity may be said to have a *recruiting* or *priming* effect upon behavior, whereby the activated concepts and memories reinforce certain sensory stimuli and not others, predisposing thought and behavior toward or away from particular objects and events through associated motor facilitations, and providing a framework for bringing order to registered sensory events. In speaking of "drive activity" we imply that there exists a requirement for appropriate stimulations of a certain range and class. In short, drive is a construct (not an observed datum) that is useful in expressing, first of all, not so much the urge toward something as a demand *for* something. This demand we could call the *recruitment* and *priming* aspect of drive structure.

In the sense that drive activity may be said to recruit objective facts, making them part of the organism's fund of experience, we can also speak of stimuli as signals and mediators of objective facts. Since any object is actually a complex arrangement, only certain impingements become stimuli (signals) and only certain properties of an object are experienced as such. Drive activity is in part defined by this selection. Perception is indispensable to this selective adjustment to things; percepts reflect the relevance of objects to drives.

A drive, however, is said to be adaptive only when its manifestations respect, so to speak, the inherent organization of distal events and objects, and this limitation brings us to the second aspect of drive structure. In most contexts (at least in our usually pragmatic waking life), we bring the attractions and repulsions provoked by drive activity to some realistic relation to what things are—to environmental probabilities, and to the opportunities that situations present. Behavior accommodates itself to the sense-conveyed logic of things. A crucial component of this accommodative process, to which Troland (1932) first called attention in his conception of "retroflex," involves a sort of back action of the environment on the cortex; *changes of behavior* provoked by contact with segments of reality are themselves perceived, and the consequences of the contact can be reported back to the cortex in terms of benefit or injury, leading to reinforcement, facilitation, or inhibition of the behavior change.

Cognitive structures are indispensable to this general accommodative effort involving action and an informational return from objects, and the reason must be that they are provided with means of imposing an order upon receptor events which will accord with the relatively constant attributes of objects and events. Perceptual experience amply testifies to this fact. Regardless of the recruitment fostered by active drive aims, perception seems assured a certain essential independence by certain structuring processes which are directly responsive to objects and relations; e.g., *pregnanz* tendencies in experiencing forms, one-sidedness of contour, etc. Indeed, all the tendencies which Gestaltists called attention to in their principles of perceptual grouping and form illustrate this autonomy of perceptual processes.

Particularly impressive evidence of the intimate coordination of perceptual experience with the actual properties of objects themselves appears in Ivo Kohler's studies (1951, 1952). In experiments modeled after the classic studies by Stratton (1897), Kohler observed the effects of wearing inverting prisms for months at a time. Eventually, subjects showed great improvement in visual motor coordinations. But the most striking findings were the clear-cut indications, following the long period of motor rehabituation, that the visual field righted itself *perceptually*. While learning obviously occurred here, it was learning that involved *perceptual* accommodation to *actual* properties of the external spatial framework.

That such coordination with reality structures occurs in every purposive commerce with objects seems to be, then, an inescapable fact. That is, the activity of drive consists not simply of arousal or even of readying the organism for particular goals. It includes specific ways of dealing with the environment; it involves accommodative structures. Since cognitive attitudes describe a person's typical accommodative patterns in confronting reality, they are thus best conceived as integral aspects of his drive structures; they are initiated by any intention (not necessarily conscious) which calls for realistic appraisal and assessment. Behavior, then, embodies both recruiting and accommodative functions. To put the matter somewhat differently: drive aim, drive consummation, and mode of cognitive control are simply different vantage points for viewing the *same* behavior.

Considering behavior in terms of its development, the present conception also implies that modifications of drive aims and of accommodative structures go hand in hand. This is essentially Piaget's (1952) view. For him, psychological reality is a product of action and feedback out of which schemata of reality form and then change. He shows how "abstract intelligence," in the form of ideas, derives from "sensory-motor intelligence," which is rooted in inborn reflexes, among which are the sucking reflexes. The ideas that develop around the activity of the sucking reflex illustrate this process. In the early stages an object does not exist "in its own right"; it exists only as something to suck, and there are no psychological distinctions among objects in this respect. However, in recruiting objects—giving them "meaning" as sucking objects—the active sucking schema changes and refines itself, and the sucking movement becomes different with different objects. Much of our learning comes down to such accommodative differentiation.

THE BEHAVIOR SEGMENT IN ACCOMMODATIVE ACTIVITY

The accommodative side of drive activity—the "reality principle" in operation—deserves closer scrutiny, since it is here that cognitive attitudes and styles are to be observed. I should like to offer at this point a definition of the natural boundaries of an adaptive behavior segment. It may be said to consist of sensory, cognitive, and motor events linked both serially and in parallel coupling to one another and to an initiating intention or task set (not necessarily in this particular sequence) in a propagation of influence, terminating in a particular change which is experienced as "adequate" to the initiating intention (Troland, 1932).

Even when drive recruitment is clearly present, it cannot account for all selection and choice in behavior; selection has another source in adaptive intentions. An intention which requires us to deal with things and relations as they are, narrows responses to certain properties of objects and events and to the restraints these pose to action upon them. A thirsty person still considers differences between the *picture* of an ice-cream soda and the real thing; in an experiment, he is generally capable of judging size without giving way to the desire to drink. Intention initiates the back-action process referred to earlier; it endows certain behavior changes with potential influence, these in turn enhancing or inhibiting behaviors which favor or bar the intention, as the case may be. Specific intentions may, of course, undergo modification in the feedback or back action of environmental objects and events, even while all processes in this interplay serve a single recruitment aim. In any one adaptive segment, an intention and its associated goal set start the process. As behavior encounters objects, modified intentions propagate

new changes. But the revised intentions remain commensurate with the
initiating goal set and adaptive intention. If my intention is to navigate
a motorboat to the opposite shore, I must "intend" to press the starter,
guide my progress to avoid other boats, etc., although the main objective
remains unwavering.

One may slice behavior for purposes of analysis into any segment,
gross or minute, of long or of short duration, which shows the boundaries of an intention on the one side and a behavioral change *experienced* as attaining the intention on the other. Selecting the smallest
possible yet apt segment for analysis, say, for describing a cognitive attitude in behavior, is not an easy matter and is always more or less an
arbitrary abstraction from a more comprehensive adaptive effort. Relevance to the particular control involved is crucial. On this basis one
may choose a unit taking minutes or one spanning years. In any event
the unit chosen will have the same initiating and terminal characteristics
described above.

I should like to emphasize one feature of this conception: it stresses
an *experienced* attainment as the natural terminus of an adaptive behavior segment. This characteristic calls attention to the fact that simply
the attainment of an objective is not enough to define the terminus of a
behavior unit. A behavioral change may be entirely adequate to an adaptive intention; i.e., it may actually attain an intended objective, but it
may not be experienced as such, and behavior will continue. Examiners
are familiar with the response pattern on the Block Design test of the
Wechsler-Bellevue, where a subject unwittingly arranges the blocks in
the "right" solution, fails to perceive its correctness, and upsets it. There
are also familiar instances where confirmation is experienced too im-
petuously. In still another variation, one's standards of adequacy may be
too high; one will simply never accept *any* perceived change as "adequate." Obviously, such standards will be reflected in the entire course
of events and behavior *leading up* to the terminal change, and this relation provides a crucial observation focus for defining different cognitive attitudes. There is real advantage, then, in distinguishing *experienced* confirmations of attainment from the fact of behavioral change
alone. The distinction gives us a basis for expecting cognitive styles to
be different where standards of "adequacy" or of an acceptable "fit" are

different.[2] An incidental implication of this is that the *experienced* attainment may be crucial in learning, i.e., in the "reinforcement" of behavior, on the theory, as Woodworth (1947) has developed it, that adequate *results* of activity are more likely to make sense to the learner than will simply a motor response or a perception. Now, if cognitive style contributes to such experiences of confirmation, it may also be expected to affect the course of learning.

Operational definition of such a frankly "subjective" experience of attainment presents, of course, easily recognized difficulties. What is an acceptable criterion of such awareness of "adequate" change? The experience may consist of some indication by the subject that a choice, a movement, a perception, or a judgment he makes is "OK," "good enough," "big enough," etc. Whether the experience of attainment should be a *perceived* change, or some indication of the subject's *reflection* or *judgment* upon the adequacy of a behavior change is a difficult matter and must be decided within the framework of actual investigation. But difficult as it may be to decide upon such operational criteria, I do not think we can bypass the problem. The main issue is not that of preferring a "subjective" indicator where a behavioral one might do, but of recognizing that *it makes a difference for the next steps taken by a person on a task whether or not he is aware of the significance of a change.*

Figure 1 summarizes the supposed behavioral unit which emanates from an active, recruiting matrix of concepts and from an accommodative intention (I), and which terminates in a behavioral change experienced as confirmatory. The adaptive behavioral unit is pictured as an extended series of events *outward*; arrows are also shown pointing in the *reverse* direction to indicate the recruiting force of the initiating goal set and its associated accommodative intention. The symbols "I.1. . . . . I.n" refer to modifications in adaptive intention resulting from successive environmental encounters and from the altered situation continually revealed by perception. Terminating the sequence is a behavior change experienced (e.g., via perception, thought, or imagery) as attainment.

---

[2] Note, for instance, Gardner's evidence (1953) of generalized dispositions for broad or narrow equivalence ranges in discriminative behavior.

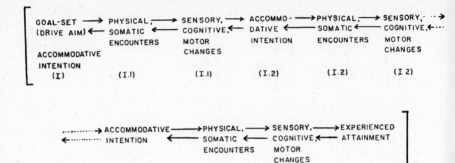

Figure 1. *Adaptive behavior segment.*

Note that action and thought are not conceived in any rigidly fixed sequential relation. In this conception of action upon, and back action from, objects the main thing is *not* that stimuli produce motor activity but that they induce a *change* of activity of the organism terminating in an *experienced* result—a change in behavior which stimulates the receptors and which may be perceived or otherwise experienced. At the same time, the terminus of an adaptive behavior unit is not simply a response—motor or otherwise—as conventional S-R conceptions would have it but the experienced attainment of aim.

In an adaptive behavior segment, perceptions and actions are united solely by the requirements of an intention, not by an unalterable relation in terms of sequence alone; both contribute to the intention, and hence both are interpretable on the same terms. Motor response does not necessarily *follow* perception. Neither is it necessarily the executor of perception, although it is an indispensable component of a more comprehensive adaptive effort. Motor activity can have different functions within the over-all strategy employed en route to the terminating change. In the object assembly test of the Wechsler-Bellevue Test, trial-and-error movements may provide opportunities for *perceptual* restructuring; we may move a block and *then* see the crucial relation. Ivo Kohler's studies (1951, 1952) offer vivid testimony to the possibility that motor rehabituation may actually be an important *antecedent* condition for restructuring the perceptual experience itself. The role of perception and motor activity in reflecting the course of behavioral change initiated by an adjustive requirement is lost when we rigidly adhere to the older model of stimulus, followed by perception, followed by motor response.

We are by now so habituated to defining our units of analyses of cognition in terms of different qualitative varieties of experience, such as *perception, memory, imagery, judgment,* etc., that we overlook their embeddedness in the total sensorimotor exchange. We are accustomed to take as a dependent variable perception or some motor activity rather than the integrated adaptive unit itself. It is not fruitful to restrict descriptions of a cognitive attitude to the confines of motor behavior or to the perceptual components of the more inclusive behavior sequence. The level of analysis of cognitive attitude must be the total accommodative sequence implementing a goal set, not simply that segment of it which is "perceptual" or "memory" or "motor."

To review the main considerations to this point: the behavior unit appropriate to the study of cognitive attitudes is the sequence of stimuli and responses necessary to produce an experienced significant result. The child creeping to get a toy exemplifies such a complex, yet integrated unit of responses, with back actions from objects en route provoking new stimulations, inhibiting some, facilitating others, and finally producing a terminal experienced attainment. The integrating factor in an adaptive behavior unit is the goal set—the objective or aim, e.g., to judge size in an experiment, or to look for food when one is hungry. Within this orientation determined by goal sets, the cognitive attitude unfolds *in* the reaction. Cognitive attitude refers to the organizing principles that guide this interplay of action and transaction and determine what will be considered an *adequate* perceived result.

The idea of drive as a *meaning-inducing* field of activity implemented by *accommodative structures* makes it easier to use the concept of drive to account for behavior. (a) It avoids the dilemma of an unanalyzable push "interacting" with processes having no basic relation to them; (b) it makes simpler a consideration of control structures as themselves outcomes of drive activity, and of drive aims as becoming transformed through the accommodating effects of these structures; (c) it accords well with the notion that cognition, involving concepts and categories, is always motivated, and at the same time warns us that motivated cognition is not always—in fact, most of the time need not be— "distorting" and "autistic." (d) Any behavior segment may be looked at from the standpoint of the developmental level of drive aims and the level of accommodative strategy reflected in it. Accommodative strategies—cognitive attitudes and styles—are presumed to undergo developments that parallel changes in drive structure (i.e., goal sets and associated conceptual structures); they include those accommodative modes associated with early drive organizations as well as highly differentiated later modes. (e) Finally, it helps us to conceive of *regression* as well as development in cognitive behavior. At any single developmental level, behavior segments express the ratio of recruitive to accommodative activity reflected in them. In circumstances where behavior reflects maximal recruitment and minimal accommodation, it is not likely to be adaptive. Examples of such a mode of response would be hallucinated drive objects, symbolized representations, condensations, and other forms of what Freud has called primary-process modes of thought. In accordance with psychoanalytic conceptions, regression would involve drive aims and control structures lower down in a developmental hierarchy, these moving thought and behavior in accordance with cognitive attitudes and styles typical of earlier, less differentiated stages of drive organization.

This conception of control structures assumes that the organisms's behavior moves toward achieving freedom from the selective tyranny of drive aims; and toward acquiring controlling structures that reduce the coerciveness of stimulations at sensory surfaces, a thesis elaborated by Rapaport (1958). The paradox pointed out earlier of an effectively oriented organism which is yet pervasively motivated is resolved in the present conception of drive. Our view of drive structure as combining accommodative and recruitive functions tells us that autonomy from drive aims and from stimulation can be only *relative*, since the recruiting activity of drives provides insurance against capricious steering of behavior by environmental stimulation. On the other hand, drive aims always implicate instrumental and accommodative structures of thought. Complete autonomy from environmental stimulation implies a wholly recruitive responsiveness to drives, and accommodative activity prevents such a possibility. In short, delay and postponement are intimately involved in the workings of drive: every cognitive process has *potentially* implications for drive organization; every drive implicates cognitive controlling structures.

ACCURACY AND EFFECTIVENESS IN
MOTIVATED PERCEIVING

I should now like to consider the issue of accuracy in perceiving so that it will be possible to see how cognitive attitudes and styles may guide perception and cognition in various ways, yet each in its own way adaptive and motivated. Discussions of motivated perception have been confused by the assumption that if perception is accurate it cannot be drive-determined; that accurate perception is somehow less "subjective" and therefore less relevant to personality theory, which should deal with the idiosyncratic and thus autistic determinants of experience. Presumably, according to this assumption, only in "wrong" or "distorted" perceptions can we find the influence of drives and personality dispositions.

First of all, let us be clear that demonstrations of effective perceiving do *not* indicate absence of motivation. Perception is always part of a larger *adaptive* act which brings some but not all qualities of objects into our experience. We are not randomly and helplessly responsive to stimuli; drive structures are fundamental guarantors of this selectivity.

Even the typical psychophysical experiment in which maximal accuracy is intended is not free of motivated selection. Rather, the experimental setting creates what we may call a "motivational reduction screen" which hopefully cajoles a subject into maintaining a particular intention as a basis for reporting what he sees. Sometimes the screen isn't effective, and other motives peek through. Certainly the subject's report is conditioned by this fact. In a tachistoscopic experiment, Morris Eagle was testing subjects for their recognition limens with gradually increased exposures of a simple line drawing—a triangle. As exposures lengthened, one subject kept repeating that he saw "nothing." He gave this report so far beyond the usual liminal limits that the experimenter became suspicious. He himself looked into the tachistoscope, and the triangle appeared clear as day. He again showed the triangle and asked the subject what he saw, and this time came the response, "Nothing, only the same old triangle." Had he been seeing this for some time? "Yes," the subject replied. Well, why didn't he say so? The subject replied, "Well, it didn't seem reasonable to me that you would have built such a complex, huge apparatus just to show a little old triangle."

The example illustrates the active process of sifting and choosing among alternatives, which always narrows a subject's report of his perception. It is also possible to show that sets and interests are involved in the perception itself, even while the perception shows fidelity to constant features of a physical stimulus. Zangwill (1937) has shown how different preparatory sets produce different perceptions of the same contoured surfaces, and that later inability to recognize these stimuli is traceable to the differences in the earlier perceptual context. One of the stimuli had a double hump. In one condition where the subject was prepared to see animals, the contours were typically represented in perceived animal forms (e.g., camel); in another condition a set to see "mountains" produced a corresponding translation of the same form. Motivation, this experiment tells us, does not simply create perceptions out of whole cloth, nor does it simply distort; its influence consists in the coordination of receptor information with the interest of the moment and with the concepts appropriate to this interest. Perception is directed and organized in terms of goal sets, even when it yields experiences that correspond pretty closely to the structure of something really "out there."

The Zangwill study tells us also that perception is very much a *conceptual* process, even while closely coordinated with the structural logic of things and with environmental probabilities. Professor Boring tells of a biologist friend who showed him drawings of the same microscopic specimen before and after the discovery of chromosomes. None of the drawings showed chromosomes before; there were plenty to be seen afterward! (Boring, 1953) Essentially the same point was made experimentally by Wallach (1956) with respect to the operation of texture gradients which Gibson has shown are so crucial to the perception of slant (1950). Wallach demonstrated that either set or recognition is needed to make texture an effective stimulus for perceived slant. As Wallach (1956) puts it: "This is not to say that texture gradients have nothing to do with perceived slant. Rather it is that memory and set serve to make the texture gradient effective. . . . Such a memory is brought into play either through recognition of familiar objects that are usually seen at a slant or by a set. A set may be due to experimental instructions as in Gibson's research or to preceding exposures as in our own experiments. Once a texture gradient has become effective, its steepness can then influence the angle of the perceived slant." An experiment reported by Pieron (1955) also neatly illustrates this allegiance of perception to schema. Put a plumb line in front of your eye while you are wearing Ivo Kohler's prisms which invert the visual field, and the string, which first appeared to climb miraculously, will seem to return after a while, and the weight to lower—to come back toward the bottom. The experiment seems to show that, given gravity as a frame of reference, we experience our vision as "wrong"; then perception corrects itself. Here, even though perception is clearly accommodative, it is also very much a conceptual activity.

A basic confusion in speaking of accurate perception in an absolutistic way is to mistake a finite number of characteristics of an object or an event (perceivable by the experimenter) as the totality of what is *potentially* perceivable. The apparent singularity of an "object" is deceptive. An object is no one thing; it comprises complex relations, some experienced, some not, depending on availability of the concepts basic to the perception. Our concepts being more circumscribed than the actual number of properties of things, we see at best only part of the world in every so-called "accurate" perception. "For when you come to think of it," muses Thomas Mann's Felix Krull, "which is the real shape of the glowworm, the insignificant little creature crawling about on the palm of your hand, or the poetic spark that swims through the summer night?" Accuracy can refer only to the degree of correspondence of a percept to a *single* attribute of an object—and only a measurable one at that; it has nothing to do with seeing the "whole" object.

The history of art and science gives fair warning that we ought not to be betrayed by the directness of our perceptual experience into thinking that our concepts, and therefore our percepts, of any "single" thing can ever be complete. Today's "conventional," workable reality is tomorrow's barrier to exploring different aspects of the same things. That is why the artist's activity in his unceasing efforts to tease out new forms from nature is also basically destructive; he must destroy well-traveled conventions about reality in order to "create" (i.e., to "see") a new form. It is no accident that artists test low in object constancy. The artist continually tries to penetrate to formal properties of things. His perception isn't necessarily more accurate than conventional experience;

he simply penetrates to properties that may be currently irrelevant to ordinary effective perception.

This fact perhaps partially explains why many relations that are brought to our consciousness by an artist may be experienced by us as repugnant, because of what they contradict and undo of conventional, effective, well-practiced indisputables in our perceptual life.[3] The price we pay for efficient perception is partial blindness. The artist, like the scientist, supplies the categories and concepts which will become to-morrow's conventional perceptual realities.

Therefore the concept of accurate perception can be especially mis-chievous if it leads us to assume that there is a finality to perceptual development, a plateau in what *can* be seen. Perception pursues mean-ings, not exhaustive accuracy or totality. The course of perceptual de-velopment is not so much that of achieving the limits of discriminability or of exhausting the perceivable qualities of objects but one of develop-ing a succession of working models of objects and events. The fact that most of our perceptions represent coordinations with physical stimuli, as psychophysical studies repeatedly show us, must not keep us from recognizing that "literal" perceptions are still *selected* perceptions.

It is also necessary to keep in mind that effectiveness is a develop-mental matter. Perception is *differently effective* at different stages of de-velopment; it is not necessarily *less "accurate"* at earlier stages than later on. As drive aims change with development, perception will reflect differ-ent adaptive purposes and different conceptual structures; standards of effectiveness will change. The perceptions that "satisfy" the child, that coordinate his behavior to the relations within and among things will differ from the adult's. For the *child's* developmental stage, and in the tasks that he sets for himself, *his* perceptions need be no less effective (and in that sense no less accurate) than those of the adult just because they are different. The child who sees the physiognomies of a form rather than its details of texture and shape is not less responsive to what is actually *in* the stimulus object. His perceptions are inaccurate to an adult world which judges him against a conventional standard. If "accuracy" is to have any sensible usage in perceptual theory it can refer

[3] Such feelings of "repugnance" are certainly not wholly explained by the experi-ence of contradiction. Possibly they reflect a reaction to unconscious drive structures activated by the artist's focus, as Ehrenzweig (1953) suggested. Meanings on several levels, each in a different drive matrix, may be apprehended.

only to effective coordination between the properties of things and our concepts and perceptions of them; *stage* of development partly defines criteria of *"adequacy"* or *"effectiveness."*

This understanding gives us a sounder basis for conceiving of "regression" in perception. We cannot be certain that altered perceptions in unusual states of consciousness (e.g., mescalinization) are hallucinatory; they may represent a fresh slant on things, i.e., coordinations with physical properties that our adult pragmatic concern for *effective*, adaptive perceiving usually excludes. A "regression" may reactivate an older conceptual matrix of psychophysical coordination—a different rule of organizing experience. Seeing things in a novel way under such conditions is not necessarily seeing them in a wrong way—in any absolute sense. Behavioral regression involves the adaptive *aims* associated with earlier goal sets and concepts, but with these it invokes earlier adaptive *means*. Therefore not all instances of regression must be taken to represent a helpless capitulation to drive satisfaction at the cost of adaptiveness.

These considerations of effective perception illuminate the adaptive character of cognitive attitudes and styles. To say that they are adaptive means, not so much that they provide, in different degrees, an accurate translation of reality, but that they provide in each instance a *workable fit*. The concept of cognitive attitude alerts us to the individually varying standards of such a working fit in the "feedback" strategies that guide perceptual, cognitive, and motor activity. It provides for the fact that individuals differ in how "accurate" perception has to be in order to be *effective* for the purpose at hand. In order to meet a subjective standard of "big enough" or "small enough," cognition musters complex processes that make possible perceptual contact with the sizes, slant, and colors of things, and it incorporates these processes into a larger "feedback" strategy that includes appropriate conceptual and motor activity. The significance of "feedback" activity is that it coordinates the phases of perceptual-cognitive-motor action and reaction with drive aims, on the one hand, and with environmental structures and probabilities, on the other. Different phases of the total cognitive event would, then, be expected to reflect the larger adaptive strategy. We should not be surprised to find the rate at which figure-ground differentiation occurs or the extent to which small differences are elided or heightened in awareness will vary from person to person, and yet that each tendency will have specific adaptive importance; such variations could simply represent the consequences of differing strategies in one of the phases of the total adaptive cognitive act, each appropriate to the particular task.

A psychophysical study at the University of Stockholm by Johansson, Dureman, and Sälde (1955) illustrates the point. To most observers, the perceived motion of a single object moving in a visual field increases considerably when a second object moving with the same speed in the opposite direction is introduced. However, individuals differed. Scores made by subjects of one extreme indicated that the static frame of reference was dominant in perceived movement; the scores made by the remaining subjects indicated that the influence of the second moving object was completely predominant. The suggestion that these opposing trends reflected more comprehensive adaptive strategies came from the fact that individual differences in this simple task were also related to social attitudes of withdrawal and isolation. The experiment demonstrates a stylistic influence upon a basically stable psychophysical function. It also points up the possibility, too often ignored in personality studies, that cognitive style may be profitably explored in investigations on psychophysical relations of physical stimulation to behavior, and not only in vague or reduced conditions of stimulation which are usually presumed to be the only basis for defining regulatory constants in behavior.

Effective perception does not mean uniform perception among people; conversely, individual differences in perception do not necessarily imply "distorting" mechanisms. *Scanning, leveling, field independence* (Schlesinger, 1954; Holzman, 1954; Witkin *et al.*, 1954), while distinctive reality orientations, may still for the subjects involved reflect "adequate" modes of making sense of reality, of dealing with it in ways that are appropriate to adaptive intentions.

STRUCTURE OF COGNITIVE ATTITUDES AND STYLES

I turn now to a closer look at cognitive attitudes and their arrangements in cognitive styles. A detailed summary of empirical studies of specific cognitive attitudes and styles is now being prepared (Gardner *et al.*). Here I will limit myself to a few general characteristics of these control structures, to some of the principles we followed in detecting them in behavior, and to a few of the research possibilities generated by the concept of cognitive style.

A cognitive attitude describes a way of organizing a transmitted array of information. The organization may take place in the course of peripheral transmission, though the evidence for this is still scanty; the loci of cognitive attitudes are probably more to be sought beyond the sensory projection areas (Bruner, 1957b; Osgood, 1957). They have the status of intervening variables and define rules by which perception, memory, and other basic qualitative forms of experience are shaped. However, the empirical limits of the assumed generality of cognitive attitudes and styles are at present by no mean clear (Klein, 1950).

A cognitive attitude is triggered by a *situation*, a requirement to adapt, not simply by a physical stimulus. In order, then, to detect the control components—the cognitive attitudes—in behavior, one must know a person's explicit intentions and the circumstances he has to adapt to, particularly the *options* offered by the situation he is coping with. Intention implies, for one thing, that certain qualities of *experience*, and not others, will be implicated in the adaptive effort—one can be set to discriminate *perceptually*, or to *remember*, or to *image*. Intention also restricts the range of behavior possibilities that a person will consider relevant. For many intentions, simply noting the presence or absence of something will be adequate; other circumstances and different intentions may require a deeper probe. Intentions establish the premises of coordinations with environmental events. A Rorschach card shown in the usual way ("What might this be?") poses a problem for which any number of solution strategies are apt. One can range from responses closely anchored to *perceptions* to frank inferences and judgments of vague possibility. Were the same stimulus card presented in the form: "Find all the animals on this card," it is by no means certain that the cognitive attitudes called forth in both conditions would be the same. From the standpoint of measurement the intentional matrix of a task is all important. Obviously, when response options and intentions are limited, the range of possible cognitive strategies is narrowed also. It would be foolish, except in pathological instances, to expect to see the cognitive attitude of leveling in the action of switching on the room light. Of course, many situations are of this nature, a single intention coinciding with a single option.

Clearly, a person can take up different cognitive attitudes which vary in appropriateness to different circumstances of task and intention. The particular cognitive attitude exhibited most typically by a person is not necessarily the one which is most apt for a particular situation or adaptive intention. Indeed, pathology in cognitive control is perhaps seen in just such failures of coordination between cognitive attitude and adaptational requirements. In an apparent motion situation, a schizophrenic subject kept seeing the movement of two squares of light as "a penis darting back and forth." Now the physiognomic propensity illustrated in this response may relate to a distinctive cognitive attitude, as other studies have indeed suggested (Klein, 1950), but in this instance it was inappropriate to the task defined by instructions. Different cognitive attitudes can, however, be equally effective, and lead to *varying*, equally "veridical" experiences.

Some Process Components of Cognitive Attitudes. Cognitive attitudes may be studied from the vantage point of processes that seem to be fundamentally implicated in adaptive commerce with environmental structures. I will limit myself to two such processes: *attention deployment* and *anticipation*.

1. *Attention deployment*: In speaking of attention cathexes I am using Freud's conception of an amount of cathexis which a proximal stimulus must attract if it is to become conscious (Freud, 1900, 1911). Availability and deployment of attention cathexis are presumably vital matters in the development and maintenance of cognitive structures Rapaport *et al.*, 1945; Rapaport, 1951, 1957).

Consider the consequences of high or low availability of the fixed amount of attention cathexis. One could argue that hysterics have to maintain so high a level of *counter*cathexis (to maintain repression) that there is not sufficient attention cathexis available for new concepts to form. Attention cathexis insures the proper "feedback" between psychological structure and object until such time as the object has acquired representation, and attention cathexis can be released to other adaptive efforts. In this way it is analogous to the wooden scaffolding and molds that hold poured cement. If you keep them on a sufficient time, it becomes possible to remove the scaffolding, and the cement will hold. Where there is insufficient attention cathexis, the gradients of dissipation are great. A hint of this possibly crucial role of attention cathexis in the building of stable concepts appears in David Elkind's unpublished finding that the complexity of concepts of quantity in children is highly correlated with their digit span.

A cognitive attitude which we now call *"scanning"* (Schlesinger, 1954) shows a distinctive quality of attention deployment. In the scanning attitude, attention is broadly and intensively deployed. The scanner is aware of a broad array of background qualities of a stimulus field. His investment is intensely incorporative, characterized by a constant, close look. The consequences of this deployment of attention cathexis in cognitive behavior are many, and lead to successful predictions of degrees of object constancy (they take on easily a retinal attitude), and to the degree of facility in extracting embedded figures (the Witkin-embedded figures task [1950]). It is interesting, by the way, that practically all the myopic subjects in one of our samples were strongly characterized by the scanning attitude. Paradoxically, these myopics were hyperaware of small stimulus differences (Gardner *et al.*).

Other studies disclose that the scanning attitude involves not only intense concentration on the central task but an indiscriminate peripheral sensitivity that renders many aspects of the field available to conscious recall. A study of incidental recognition by Holzman (1957), involving the Müller-Lyer illusion, found that scanners could quite accurately reproduce the areas bounded by the arrowheads in the stimulus despite the fact that they had not been "set" beforehand to acquire this information.

Other cognitive attitudes my co-workers and I have studied also involve distinctive patterns of attention deployment. Holzman (1954) found it to be characteristic of the *leveling* attitude that successive stimuli tended to lose their identity. Also, on a task requiring subjects to ignore the word context of colors and to read only the colors alone, the levelers' performance became progressively slowed over a period of time. On a time-error task they showed a steep gradient of dissipation with respect to incoming stimuli; hence, compared to sharpeners, they were more affected by an interpolated stimulus on their successive judgments of weights.

2. *Anticipation:* Accommodative structures include structuralized patterns that guide the selection of concepts and steer action. These we call *anticipations* or *sets.* They define the range of alternatives for which a person is perceptually or cognitively "ready." Anticipations are crucial to coordinations of concepts with objects and therefore to the development of control strategies. Restrictions on the patterning of anticipations seem to be reflected in the various cognitive attitudes.

Levelers and sharpeners differ with respect to flexibility in the requirement to shift from one set to another. The capacity to alter anticipations in accordance with slight gradients of stimulation contributes to the sensitivity of sharpeners in their responses to a series of squares gradually changing in size (Holzman, 1954). Smith and Klein (1953) presented subjects with a succession of Gottschaldt designs in which one of two test figures was embedded. When a design containing the *second* figure was shown, levelers perceptibly slowed up at this change; they did not easily give equal weight to both alternatives after the run of designs which contained only the first figure.

Another cognitive attitude we have studied, *constricted control,* also reflects a distinctive anticipatory pattern, which showed up in conditions where subjects have to cope with perceived incongruencies (Klein, 1954). Trying to resolve an experience of ambiguity, some subjects tended to lean heavily upon certain easily apprehended physical features of the situation; when instructions allowed them to choose among different conflicting cues to steer judgment, they tended to favor the more directly confirmable cues. In the apparent motion situation alluded to earlier, their motion thresholds were determined in large measure by the authoritatively given explanation of "reality" in the situation (that the objects were not really moving); their motion thresholds were relatively high (Gardner *et al.*). The anticipatory pattern of the more flexibly controlled subjects under conditions of perceived incongruity tended to be one of poised, uncommitted readiness.

Secondary Consequences of Cognitive Attitudes—Cognitive Style. I have referred to *cognitive style* as an arrangement of cognitive attitudes of perhaps another structural order. One reason for this assumption is that we have found cognitive attitudes to be associated with behavior tendencies that are not easily encompassed by the strategic principles defining the specific attitudes. Possibly such behavioral correlates reflect a superordinate level of control within the personality system. One basis for conceiving of this possibility is to think of certain types of behavior as a *secondary adaptation* to a cognitive attitude, after continual and repeated reliance upon the attitude. For instance, the leveling attitude produces an oversimplified world. The leveler adjusts to this world, and his means of doing so become attributes of his cognitive style. Cognitive style may describe the balance that is struck between what is left askew as a result of the attitudinal elisions and the person's capacity to handle them. The blurring of temporally extended stimuli characteristic of levelers could lead to a relatively impoverished conceptual structure. Applying a fundamentally limited set of categories which "work" for him, the leveler could conceivably feel no further need for "close listening." The associated qualities of ingenuousness and naiveté and the experiences of surprise that we find quite frequently in levelers are conceivably secondary consequences of the attitude.

When we turn to those people for whom the *scanning* attitude is typical, it is clear that here a too close attentional investment—the hard, close look—could have secondary consequences of another kind. For one thing, as Bruner (1957a) has pointed out, the price of the constant close look is a slowdown in the identifying and categorizing of relevant details; a crucial loss can occur in the small interval available for adjusting. Possibly anticipation would also be impaired because the close inspection prevents speedy appraisal of alternatives. It is not perhaps surprising that doubt, uncertainty, and mistrust are prominent accompaniments of the scanning attitude.

These and other correlates of cognitive attitudes stood out when we investigated different "person-clusters," each containing a heavy representation of scanners (Gardner *et al.*). In one of these clusters, scanning appeared in the context of *sharpening, narrow equivalence range in categorizing,* and *constricted response to ambiguity.* A distinctive cognitive style characterized the scanning subjects in this attitudinal context. The dominant impression this group gave was one of intense control and inhibition, with very pronounced intellectualizing tendencies, pervasive experiences of ambivalence, mistrust, expectations of being hurt. They regarded the world as a source of malevolence and danger, and had a generally pessimistic outlook on the present and the future. They seemed preoccupied with issues of mastery, and they were intensely self-absorbed (e.g., they made an unusually large number of references to body parts on the Rorschach). They felt guilty, dissatisfied with their achievements, and their contacts with objects and people were darkened by aggression. At the same time they were intensely absorbed in the rejecting and threatening world of people and things.

Some Investigative Applications: 1. Style of commerce with environmental structures and its stability may be an important safeguard against regressive behavior. An interesting step has been taken by Holt (1957) toward extending predictions from cognitive style to evidences of "regressive" thinking. The departure points of his work are the assumptions derived from psychoanalytic theory, that the course of drive development is toward progressively more differentiated levels, and that there exists the potentiality that thought will revert to earlier modes of drive-organized thinking ("primary-process" modes of thought, in Freud's terms). Holt says that perhaps the dispositions to primary-process forms of thought and the varieties of such reversions will be dictated by the conditions and possibilities afforded by cognitive style. He has developed a set of indices concerning the amount, type, and manner of control of primary-process thinking in Rorschach responses. Preliminary findings indicate that subjects with definably contrasting cognitive styles are distinguishable on the indices. Comparing constricted and flexible control subjects, he found a distinct trend:

Flexible Ss gave slightly higher percentages of drive-directed content and an average of twice as many formal manifestations of the primary process. Constricted Ss tended to give drive content, or responses involving condensation, for example, either with signs of disturbance or else flatly and, as it were, unconsciously or naively. By contrast, the sexual or aggressive content in the flexible Ss' Rorschachs were typically couched in a way more acceptable as social communication. (Holt, 1957).

Possibly, then, cognitive style has an important role either in limiting or providing opportunities for thinking to revert to primary-process modes. This suggestion holds out the possibility that cognitive style may be helpful in understanding individual variations in the "regressed" behavior influenced by mescaline and lysergic acid.

2. Structures, once formed, seem to require a guaranteed supply of

their appropriate level of stimulation—a particular frequency of contact with particular realms of objects and properties of objects (Hebb, 1955a; Piaget, 1952; Rapaport, 1958). Drastic alterations in the level of environmental stimulation—too low or too high—can cause adaptive structures to lose their effectiveness. This is suggested strikingly by the McGill studies on the effects of isolation (Bexton *et al.*, 1954; Hebb, 1955a, b) and in Lifton's (1956) descriptions of the "thought reform" procedures in Communist China. Depriving accommodative structures of their required optimal level of stimulation perhaps makes it possible for behavior to be dominated more easily by the recruitment aspect of drives, and for behavior to regress to developmentally earlier cognitive styles.

Presumably drastic changes in stimulation would wreak havoc with cognitive attitudes and styles, but in different ways. If the requirements for adequate or optimal stimulation vary in different cognitive styles, we should expect that stimulus deprivation in the manner of the McGill studies will produce predictably different effects. There is evidence that levelers organize stimulus sequences according to low common denominators of object structures (Holzman, 1954; Gardner *et al.*). We also find that leveling Ss tend to show little curiosity. The optimal stimulus requirement set by this adaptive strategy may be different from that for the scanning attitude where absorption in detailed perceptual contact with object and things seems to pervade adaptive efforts. Scanning imposes greater demands for more varied and frequent stimulation, and it seems quite possible that wholesale and prolonged elisions of stimulation may quickly devastate thought and produce a distinctive regressive pattern. Leo Goldberger's (1958) studies of individual differences in the effects of sensory deprivation will perhaps illuminate the role of cognitive attitude and style when opportunities for adaptive "feedback" are thwarted by restrictions of stimulation. Studies of the effects either of extreme reduction or of oversupply of stimulation provide an opportunity to explore the possibility that cognitive attitude and styles provide a measure of restraint against domination of thought by the recruitment aspect of drives, and that cognitive style will in part determine the regressive consequences of radical deprivations or overloading of stimulation.

3. Controls involve the monitoring, sifting, and reduction of sense-

conveyed stimuli. We used to take it for granted that such "gating," as Bruner (1957a) calls it, occurs at the higher centers alone. Reception itself was supposed to be indiscriminate, limited only by the inherent structural limitations of the receptor surfaces. Hebb (1957) tells us that a good deal of such sorting out may occur prior to cortical "encoding" and "decoding." The extraordinary sensitivity of the sensory apparatus makes it reasonable to look for such a screening process prior to transmission to the cortex; otherwise, cortical channels to the higher centers would be hopelessly jammed. Freud (1920) envisioned a "sensory barrier" which accomplishes the first filtering of stimuli, and this was in fact the basis for his postulation of "pre-ego defenses." An experiment by Hernandez-Péon, Scherrer, and Jouvet (1956) demonstrates the possibility of a filtering process at the receptor surfaces. They were able to show in cats that spike potentials in the cochlear nucleus, elicited by audible clicks, disappear when a distracting object (e.g., a mouse or a fish odor) suddenly captures the cat's attention, as if the auditory stimuli were selectively "blocked" at the cochlear nucleus itself rather than at the higher centers.

Some of the tests in our studies of cognitive attitude suggest that the selective action of some cognitive attitudes may reach back in part to the level of proximal stimulation and the receptor surfaces themselves. The indiscriminate hypersensitivity to stimulus details in the scanning attitude indirectly suggests this possibility.

Evidence of cognitive controls in sensory-gating processes comes from another quarter. A number of studies (Klein, Spence, et al., 1955; Smith, Spence and Klein, 1957; Bach and Klein, 1957) have employed the technique of producing a subliminal stimulus by exposing two stimuli briefly and in rapid succession so that only the second of the pair can definitely be seen. It was found that the consciously seen form—the second of the pair—takes on a different appearance in certain respects, an effect evidently induced by the subliminal, temporally adjacent stimulus. However, this influence was found to vary with more general reaction tendencies of the subjects. Though the relation between these response dispositions and what we have here called cognitive attitudes and style are not yet worked out, the possibility exists that adaptive controls of this kind may effect the intake itself as well as the organizational fate of receptor excitations.

I have tried to review some issues of control structures that participate in behavior, and their relation to drives. I have tried to point up their basis in the unceasing accommodative exchanges that spring from motivations.

We are only at the beginnings of an adequate conception of control structures, their relation to one another, and their composition. How structure itself is to be conceived is an overriding issue. The efforts of Floyd Allport (1955), Piaget (1952), and Hebb (1949) are perhaps the most powerful wedges yet driven into this problem. Then there is the question of the nature of the system in which structures develop, a matter at the very heart of theories of personality integration. We are moving toward an eventual model of a hierarchy of subsystems, each a governor of those below, yet each, like perception, preserving a certain autonomy from those above. A crude analogy would be the relation of a bay to the larger ocean body of which it is an integral subsystem, its *relative* independence vouchsafed by its land outlines which give its water currents distinctive qualities, but nonetheless capable of overrule by insistent events of the more embracing ocean system. This seems to be the fascinating theme of personality itself, at once its paradox and achievement: its allegiance both to drive aims and to environmental structures and probabilities, and its relative autonomy from both.

REFERENCES

Allport, F. H. *Theories of perception and the concept of structure.* New York: Wiley, 1955.

Allport, G. W. Attitudes. In C. Murchison (ed.), *A handbook of social psychology.* Chap. 17. Worcester: Clark University Press, 1935. Pp. 798-844.

Bach, S., and Klein, G. S. The effects of prolonged subliminal exposures of words. *Amer. Psychologist,* 1957, 12, 397-398.

Bexton, W. H., Heron, W., and Scott, T. H. Effects of decreased variation in sensory environment. *Canad. J. Psychol.,* 1954, 8, 70-76.

Boring, E. G. The role of theory in experimental psychology. *Amer. J. Psychol.,* 1953, 66, 169-184.

Bruner, J. S. On perceptual readiness. *Psychol. Rev.,* 1957a, 64, 123-152.

———. Going beyond the information given. In J. S. Bruner *et al., Contemporary approaches to cognition.* Cambridge, Mass.: Harvard University Press, 1957b. Pp. 41-69.

Eagle, M. The effects of subliminal stimuli of aggressive content upon conscious cognition. Ph.D. dissertation, on file New York University Library. 1958.

Ehrenzweig, A. *The psychoanalysis of artistic vision and hearing.* New York: Julian Press, 1953.

Freud, Anna. *The ego and the mechanisms of defense.* (Trans. by C. Baines.) New York: Int. Univ. Press, 1946.

Freud, S. *The Interpretation of Dreams.* Vol. V. Chap. 7. The Standard Edition of the Complete Psychological Works of Sigmund Freud. (Transl. by J. Strachey.) London: Hogarth Press, 1953. (Originally published in 1900.)

———. Formulations regarding the two principles of mental functioning. In S. Freud, *Collected papers.* Vol. IV. London: Hogarth Press, 1946. Pp. 13-21. (Originally published in 1911.)

———. The unconscious. In *Collected Papers.* Vol. IV. London: Hogarth, 1946. Pp. 98-136. (Originally published in 1915.)

———. *Beyond the pleasure principle.* Vol. XVIII. The Standard Edition of the Complete Psychological Works of Sigmund Freud. (Trans. by J. Strachey.) London: Hogarth Press, 1955. (Originally published in 1920.)

Gardner, R. W. Cognitive styles in categorizing behavior. *J. Pers.,* 1953, 22, 214-233.

———, Holzman, P. S., Linton, Harriet B., Spence, D. P., and Klein, G. S. *Exploratory studies of cognitive consistencies.* (To be published.)

Gibson, J. J. The perception of visual surfaces. *Amer. J. Psychol.,* 1950, 63, 367-384.

Goldberger, L. Individual differences in the effects of perceptual isolation as related to Rorschach manifestations of the primary process. Ph.D. dissertation, on file New York University Library. 1958.

Hartmann, H. Ich-Psychologie und Anpassungsproblem. *Int. Z. Psychoanal.,* 1939, 24, 62-135. [Translation, Ego psychology and the problems of adaptation (abridged). In D. Rapaport (ed.), *Organization and pathology of thought.* New York: Columbia University Press, 1951. Pp. 362-396.]

———, Kris, E., and Lowenstein, R. Comments on the formation of psychic structure. In *The psychoanalytic study of the child.* Vol. II. New York: Int. Univ. Press, 1946. Pp. 11-38.

Hebb, D. O. *The organization of behavior.* New York: Wiley, 1949.

———. The mammal and his environment. *Amer. J. Psychiat.,* 1955a, 111, 826-831.

———. Drives and the C.N.S. (Conceptual Nervous System). *Psychol. Rev.,* 1955b, 62, 243-254.

———. Perception and perceptual learning. Address given at Eastern Psychological Association, New York, 1957.

Heider, F. Thing and medium. Trans. by F. Heider and G. Heider from Ding und Medium. *Symposion (Verlag der Philosophischen Akademie),* Erlangen I, 1927. Pp. 109-157.

Hernandez-Péon, R., Scherrer, R. H., and Jouvet, M. Modification of electric activity in the cochlear nucleus during "attention" in unanesthetized cats. *Sci.*, 1956, *123*, 331-332.

Heron, W., Bexton, W. H., and Hebb, D. O. Cognitive effects of a decreased variation to the sensory environment. *Amer. Psychologist*, 1953, 8, 366.

Holt, R. R. Cognitive style and primary process. Paper given at 30th Anniversary Celebration, Harvard Psychological Clinic, June, 1957.

Holzman, P. S. The relation of assimilation tendencies in visual, auditory, and kinesthetic time-error to cognitive attitudes of leveling and sharpening. *J. Pers.*, 1954, *22*, 375-394.

————. Focussing: a style of reality contact. *Amer. Psychologist*, 1957, *12*, 388.

————, and Klein, G. S. Cognitive system-principles of leveling and sharpening: individual differences in assimilation effects in visual time-error. *J. Psychol.*, 1954, *37*, 105-122.

Jacob, P. *The behavior cycle.* Ann Arbor: Edwards, 1954.

Johansson, G., Dureman, I., and Sälde, H. Motion perception and personality. I. *Acta Psychol.*, 1955, *11*, 289-296.

Klein, G. S. The personal world through perception. In R. R. Blake and G. V. Ramsey (eds.), *Perception: an approach to personality.* New York: Ronald, 1950. Pp. 328-355.

————. Need and regulation. In M. R. Jones (ed.), *Nebraska symposium on motivation.* Lincoln: University of Nebraska Press, 1954. Pp. 224-274.

————. Perception, motives and personality. In J. S. McCary (ed.), *Psychology of personality: six modern approaches.* New York: Logos, 1956.

————, and Schlesinger, H. J. Where is the perceiver in perceptual theory? *J. Pers.*, 1949, *18*, 32-47.

————, Spence, D. P., Holt, R. R., and Gourevitch, Susannah. Cognition without awareness: subliminal influences upon conscious thought. *Amer. Psychologist*, 1955, *10*, 380. (To be published, *J. abnorm. soc. Psychol.*)

Kohler, I. *Uber Aufbau und Wardlungen der Wahrnehmungswelt.* Vienna: Rohrer, 1951.

————. Rehabituation in perception. Trans. by H. Gleitman from I. Kohler, Ungerwohnung in Wahrnehmungsbereich. *Die Pyramide*, 1952, Vols. 5, 6, 7.

Lifton, R. J. "Thought reform" of Western civilians in Chinese Communist prisons. *Psychiatry*, 1956, *19*, 173-195.

Murphy, G. Affect and perceptual learning. *Psychol. Rev.*, 1956, *63*, 1-15.

Murray, H. A. Facts which support the concept of need or drive. *J. Psychol.*, 1936, *3*, 27-42.

Osgood, C. E. A behavioristic analysis of perception and language as cognitive phenomena. In J. S. Bruner *et al., Contemporary approaches to cognition.* Cambridge, Mass.: Harvard University Press, 1957. Pp. 75-118.

Piaget, J. *The origins of intelligence in children.* (Trans. by Margaret Cook.) New York: Int. Univ. Press, 1952.

Pieron, H. In A. Michotte *et al., La perception.* Symposium de l'Association de psychologie scientifique de langue française. Bibliothèque Scientifique Internationale, 1955. Pp. 7-15.

Rapaport, D. *The organization and pathology of thought.* New York: Columbia University Press, 1951.

————. Cognitive structures. In J. S. Bruner *et al., Contemporary approaches to cognition.* Cambridge, Mass.: Harvard University Press, 1957. Pp. 157-200.

————. The theory of ego autonomy; a generalization. *Bull. Menninger Clin.,* 1958, 22, 13-35.

————, Schafer, R., and Gill, M. *Diagnostic psychological testing.* Vols. I and II. Chicago: Yearbook Publishers, 1945-1946.

Schlesinger, H. J. Cognitive attitudes in relation to susceptibility to interference. *J. Pers.,* 1954, 22, 354-374.

Smith, G. J. W., and Klein, G. S. Cognitive controls in serial behavior patterns. *J. Pers.,* 1953, 22, 188-213.

————, Spence, D. P., and Klein, G. S. Subliminal effects of verbal stimuli. *Amer. Psychologist,* 1957, 12, 394. (*J. abnorm. soc. Psychol.,* in press.)

Stratton, G. M. Vision without inversion of the retinal image. *Psychol. Rev.,* 1897, 4, 341-360, 463-481.

Tolman, E. G. A psychological model. In T. Parsons and E. A. Shires (eds.), *Toward a general theory of action.* Cambridge, Mass.: Harvard University Press, 1951. Pp. 285-302.

Troland, L. *The principles of psychophysiology.* Vol. III. *Cerebration and Action.* New York: Van Nostrand, 1932.

Wallach, H. Memory effects in perception. Presented at International Congress of Psychology, Montreal, Canada, 1956.

Witkin, H. A. Individual differences in ease of perception of embedded figures. *J. Pers.,* 1950, 19, 1-15.

————, Lewis, H. B., Hertzman, M., Machover, K., Meissner, P., and Wapner, S. *Personality through perception.* New York: Harper, 1954.

Woodworth, R. S. *Dynamic psychology.* New York: Columbia University Press, 1918.

————. Situation- and goal-set. *Amer. J. Psychol.,* 1937, 50, 130-140.

————. Reinforcement in perception. *Amer. J. Psychol.,* 1947, 60, 119-124.

————, and Schlosberg, H. *Experimental psychology.* New York: Holt, 1954.

Zangwill, O. L. A study of the significance of attitude in recognition. *Brit. J. Psychol.,* 1937, 28, 12-17.

ROY SCHAFER

Yale University School of Medicine

5 *Regression in the service of the ego:*
The relevance of a psychoanalytic concept for
personality assessment

The psychoanalytic concept *regression* is by now well known in clinical psychology and personality theory. Freud (1900) initially introduced and elaborated it to help account for dream phenomena but later extended and revised its application to help account for neurotic and psychotic psychopathology and the disruption of infantile and adolescent development. By and large this usage of the concept has remained dominant. For this reason the mental-mechanism *regression* almost inevitably carries conflictful or ominous implications in our minds. The same is true for the other mental mechanisms, such as projection, denial, and intellectualization. In recent decades, however, as the psychoanalytic theory of the ego has developed, more attention has been paid to how mental mechanisms also may serve adaptive ends. Even regression has begun to be viewed in this light; the result has been the introduction by Ernst Kris (1952) of the concept *regression in the service of the ego.* It is on this specific development in psychoanalytic thought that I will concentrate in this discussion. I will explore the value of this concept in personality-assessment research, or what has been called "the assessment of human motives."

It must be recognized first that the assessment of human motives requires simultaneous assessment of the psychic structures which form, channel, and obstruct motives. Some of these structures, such as well-established defenses, are themselves motives if considered from a certain point of view, while others, such as well-established abstract concepts and patterns of motor coordination, have less motivational character. In either situation, however, a structure may be said to be characterized by the following five features: (1) a slow rate of change; (2) relative autonomy of a primary or secondary nature from instinctual drives;[1] (3) a high degree of automatization as one manifestation of this relative autonomy—that is, structures take on a tool or means character and are not primarily determined in their course by current conflict or adaptive demands on the organism; rather, current internal and external pressures ordinarily merely trigger off the action of these structures; (4) being created not entirely by the individual but being acquired by him in part through learning from and identifying with the family and larger community; these experiences steadily transmit to and sustain in the developing individual traditional structures of experience and action with adaptive (survival) value; (5) being steadily and preferentially available and not being created anew on each occasion of stimulation. Psychic structures are therefore economical as regards energy expenditure in functioning. Concepts and skills, too, are structures in all the aspects defined above, and there can be no question of their economic

---

[1] In recent years psychoanalytic writers have emphasized that the ego must not be thought of as developing out of the id in the course of development; rather, id and ego develop simultaneously out of an originally undifferentiated matrix and they mutually influence and define each other (Kris, Hartmann, and Lowenstein, 1946). Rudiments of ego function and structure, such as learning ability, exist from the beginning, if only as potentialities; the sensory apparatus and sensory and discharge thresholds are also given ego rudiments. Ego functions are not necessarily outgrowths of conflict. In other words, some ego processes have primary autonomy, in contrast to structures which are derived from conflict, which have more or less secondary autonomy. The latter have attained relative independence from conflict during development and become institutions in their own right, and function without being specifically attached to particular drives or conflicts. Many character traits, values, and sublimations are examples of personality characteristics with relative secondary autonomy.

value in behavioral functioning. For assessment purposes, as for therapeutic purposes, we must therefore understand how psychic structures develop and what the rules of their operation are. The same motive operating under different structural conditions is experienced differently by the subject and has different manifestations and different consequences. The concept *regression in the service of the ego* therefore merits discussion in this connection because it clarifies the rules by which psychic structures operate.

One might come to the relevance of *regression in the service of the ego* to personality assessment in a second way. The assessment of human motives requires that we bring to bear the considerations concerning biological and social adaptation first formulated comprehensively within the framework of psychoanalytic theory by Hartmann (1939) and presented in somewhat different terms by Erikson (1950). These formulations emphasize in one respect the study of how motives fit in with, are modified by, and modify organism-environment relations. We cannot understand motives simply from the point of view of instinctual drives, intrapsychic conflict, and maturation. In fact, we cannot fully understand drives, conflict, and maturation without a simultaneous consideration of the adaptive problems and supports of the organism in its environment, and the mechanisms available to it in meeting these problems. Here again *regression in the service of the ego* enters, now as an important adaptive process. In the psychoanalytic literature, *regression in the service of the ego* has been applied in more or less detail to develop our understanding of wit and humor, artistic creativity and the audience's response to it, productive fantasy and imaginative processes, problem solving, sleeping and dreaming, capacity for orgastic experience, ego-building identifications, motherliness, empathy, intimacy, and love, and the therapeutic process, including the hypnotic process and hypnotic state. A concept of such wide and central applicability to human adaptation merits the fullest possible consideration in a discussion devoted to problems of assessment.

A third way of introducing the relevance of this concept—a more immediate and circumscribed way—is to recognize that assessment of motives usually includes the use of projective techniques, and that in understanding the processes whereby these techniques are projective, that is, self-revealing in depth, *regression in the service of the ego* appears to occupy an important place. This place has previously been discussed by Holt (1954), Bellak (1954), and me (1954).

In what follows I plan, first, to offer a general definition of this concept, with illustrations; second, with special reference to art and the comic, to describe the reversal of this regressive process and its culmination in progressive phases in which the products of the regressive movement are elaborated and synthesized; third, to outline conditions that foster and hamper this process; fourth, to consider problems of individual variation; fifth, to sketch, with the help of illustrative test material, the application of this concept to the understanding of responses to several widely used psychological tests and to the understanding of the process of interpreting these responses; and sixth, to mention some implications of the entire discussion for personality-assessment research. In all, this presentation will amount to no more than a preliminary synthesis and illustration of concepts.[2] Such a synthesis is the only basis of formulating the new and more penetrating hypotheses which we need to integrate personality research with psychoanalytic theory. My formulations, above and below, draw heavily on the work of Kris (1952), Hartmann (1939, 1950), Rapaport (1950, 1951a, 1951b, 1951c, 1953a, 1953b, 1957), and Erikson (1950, 1953, 1956), and, of course, Freud (1900, 1905, 1908, 1915, 1921, 1923).

REGRESSION IN THE SERVICE OF THE EGO: DEFINITIONS

Regression in the service of the ego is a partial, temporary, controlled lowering of the level of psychic functioning to promote adaptation. It promotes adaptation by maintaining, restoring, or improving inner balance and organization, interpersonal relations, and work. It is a process which increases the individual's access to preconscious and unconscious contents, without a thoroughgoing sexualization or aggressivization of major ego functions, and therefore without disruptive

---

[2] I will not attempt here a systematic metapsychological presentation of the concept, that is, one which defines its dynamic, economic, and structural referents (and also, following an unpublished discussion of metapsychological analysis by Gill and Rapaport, its genetic and adaptive referents). These three- or five-metapsychological points of view are, however, represented in many details of my discussion.

anxiety and guilt. In other words, the primary and secondary (rela-tive) autonomy of higher ego functions is not impaired; the en-croachment of id tendencies is circumscribed. The process implies central controlling functions in the ego which may suspend some other functions, such as defensive functions and logical functions, and may emphasize genetically primitive mechanisms, such as projection and in-trojection.

A second definition is immediately called for, that of *level of psychic functioning*. For this definition we must consider the distinction in-troduced by Freud between the primary process and the secondary process. The primary process, which is genetically and formally the more primitive, operates with unneutralized drive energies, and its regulative principle is tension reduction (the pleasure principle); it strives toward immediate discharge of energy accumulations by a direct route and through the mechanisms of displacement, condensation, substitute formation, and symbolization. The secondary process oper-ates by the principle of least effort; its energies are relatively neutralized, i.e., relatively bound in motives and structures of a highly socialized nature, and freely available for whichever ego activities of the moment may require energic support; it is oriented toward objective reality; it follows the safest course toward the sought-for object in reality, using delays of impulse, detours, and experimental action in thought, until the suitable object and modes of action have been found.

The contrast between primary process and secondary process may be detailed further. *Thinking*, under the domination of the primary process, tends to be unreflective, timeless, and concrete; under the domination of the secondary process, thinking is reflective, shows time perspective, and uses abstract concepts corresponding to reality relations. Concern-ing *memory* in particular, domination by the primary process means that memories available are organized around the imperative drive or drives, while other memories, not relevant to immediate drive pressures, are unavailable; the contrast to this is conceptual and reality-oriented organization of memories and their free availability, depending on the needs of the real—external as well as internal—situation. Concerning *perception*, the contrast is one of drive selectivity and organization, disregard of total external context, and diffuse, physiognomic, and animistic formal characteristics on the primary side, and, on the secondary side, adaptive selectivity and organization, boundness by objective context, and articulated, stable formal characteristics. From the standpoint of *affects*, primary process involves diffuse, unmodulated affects and affect storms limited in their variability, while secondary process involves articulated, varied, and subtly blended affects. From the standpoint of *motility*, primary-process domination implies rapid spilling over into action and participation, and often grossness of action (as in convulsive laughter), while secondary-process domination implies restrained and modulated motility (as in the smile or the free laugh). Looked at from the standpoint of the *self*, primary-process functioning tends to eliminate the boundaries and inner coherence of the self so that what is thought and what is real are confused, the wish is equivalent to the deed, fantasies are events, and past ego states are present contradictory selves; secondary-process functioning maintains the boundaries and coherence of the self in these respects. From the standpoint of *defense*, the contrast is one of weakness (consciousness overwhelmed by normally unconscious impulses, affects, and fantasies) versus strength. From the standpoint of the *ego ideal*, the contrast is one of megalomanic, unattainable, infantile conceptions versus conceptions relatively more regulated by reality testing or realistic considerations of the possible rather than the exalted. From the standpoint of the superego, the contrast is one of archaic severity versus closeness to the ego. From the standpoint of the *ego as a whole*, the contrast is one of passivity versus activity, respectively, discharge of impulse occurring relatively independently of the ego, or the ego being unable to modify the damming up of impulses by its countercathectic energy distributions versus impulses being discharged by means of the ego's controlling and executive apparatuses or being merely postponed in their discharge by controlling and defensive ego functions (Rapaport, 1953b).

In psychoanalytic discussions the contrasts listed above have often been presented in terms of id versus ego or the system Unconscious versus the systems Preconscious and Conscious. They have been stressed in the study of such phenomena as dreams; extreme fatigue; states of emotional excitement; schizophrenia; altered states of consciousness such as fugues, amnesias, intoxications, and deliria; preliterate cultures; and the behavior of the infant and young child. Werner (1948) has discussed many of these contrasts from a related point of view, and

Piaget's (1928, 1929, 1930, 1932) studies are particularly relevant. Obviously, the contrasts drawn represent ideal polar positions. Any specific behavior must be assessed in terms of its relative position with respect to these poles or in terms of the particular admixture of primary and secondary processes in it. There are all degrees of transition.

To return to *regression in the service of the ego*, it refers, then, to the ego's permitting relatively free play to the primary process in order to accomplish its adaptive tasks. The ego detours through regression toward adaptation. It is warranted to speak here of *regression* insofar as primary process or its close derivatives, normally warded off, are allowed a place in conscious experience; and it is warranted to speak of the process being *in the service of the ego* insofar as the regression serves ego interests (such as being creative or empathic), is relatively easily reversible, and is amenable to productive working over by the ego in terms of its adaptive pursuits.

CREATION OF ART AND THE COMIC

Taking as his starting points comments by Freud on daydreams and creative writing (1908), and on wit in its relation to the unconscious (1905), Kris has discussed at some length the operation of regression in the service of the ego in artistic creativity and in wit and humor. In the so-called inspirational phase of creativity, the artist is more or less immersed in relatively archaic content and archaic, less stable modes of experience. That is to say, ego structures concerned with organized speech, perception, and movement which operate relatively automatically in higher stages of organization may lose their automatized quality and decompose, as it were, into simpler, cruder, and by now strange or startling elements. In the process of de-automatization the raw components of sensory, verbal, and motoric experience may be partially rediscovered. The wit or joke maker may undergo similar changes in moving regressively toward nonsense in word, metaphor, or gesture.[3]

With regard to art and the comic, however, observation makes it

---

[3] In some instances, as in orgastic discharge, the controlled regression involves yielding to biological automatisms; these are not to be confused with psychic automatizations within the ego.

obvious that a subsequent or alternating progressive or elaborational phase is crucial to an adequate end result, which is to say that the regressive process is reversed and the yield of the regressive process is subjected to critical scrutiny, selection, and synthesis. In the end, the regressive yield is shaped into a conceptually and affectively ordered statement or communication that effectively integrates both the experience and intent of the artist or wit and the stringencies of the current reality to which he offers his product. The artist who has first withdrawn into working with introjects, fantasy, and immature modes of experience, returns now to a real and mature relation with others, his audience. In his work he reprojects these introjects with a new and enhanced reality. The successful work of art and the joke are adapted to current situations and to tradition from both of which they derive many of their forms and materials. In part, the contrast between the phase of inspiration and elaboration is that between individualized self-searching and self-expression on the one hand, and craft and tradition on the other. With regard to the joke, a similar process is evident in the necessity of introducing sense into nonsense, as Freud long ago pointed out, thereby eliciting an approving response from others, and appeasing the ego's demand for rationality and the superego's demand for moral restraint.

PSYCHOLOGICAL DETERMINANTS OF REGRESSION IN THE SERVICE OF THE EGO

What are some of the major conditions favoring and hampering artistic and comic *regression in the service of the ego?* The factors to be mentioned are not sharply distinguished from one another. To a great extent they represent somewhat different points of view applied to the same observations. It will be advantageous, however, to mention these factors separately because of their individual connections to a variety of psychoanalytic concepts.

The hampering conditions appear to center chiefly around the unconscious significances of this regressive process. Psychoanalytic study, according to Kris' summary, shows the process to have such prominent unconscious meanings as passivity, sinful and defiant transgression, and magically potent destructiveness toward authority and whatever persons and things are involved, be they external or internalized, real or fantasied. Kris' extensive discussions of society's image of the artist through history, of the artist's image of himself as artist, and of the meanings of schizophrenic art, develop these unconscious meanings clearly. The artist in one form or another has been traditionally linked to the divine on the one hand (e.g., Plato's "divine madness") and on the other to the devil and to rebellion against the divine. These links were literal and explicit in ancient times and are implicit in the bohemian and crackpot stereotype of the artist in current times. These divine and devilish fantasies the artist shares with his audience and in so doing often provides behavioral support for them.

Image magic and word magic, historically and genetically related to ritual and effigy, are also involved in unconscious fantasy about creating. In image and word magic, such as we observe in children's play and fantasy, the intent is to transform the world and not to create an internal experience in the mind of a specific sort. Thus not only does the artist engage in forbidden investigation and exhibitions in his work; he omnipotently controls, manipulates, and destroys by rendition, simplification, distortion, or transformation—by taking over the object, making it his own, and attaining independence from it. The experience of inspiration itself appears to be fantasied as one of passive, feminine receptiveness, both with respect to the father (divine inspiration of old) and the nursing mother (in the blissful feelings of tension reduction, of being filled with supplies from without). Bergler (1944, 1945) has emphasized the attempt to establish psychic autarchy in this process; unconsciously, carrying out the process within oneself means rejecting and destroying the hated mother. Levey (1939, 1940) and Sharpe (1935) have stressed the reparative aspects of the process—its protecting or restoring the mother and the infantile union with her. The artist's reprojection of the object with enhanced reality in his artistic product serves the reparative function.

In addition, creative fantasy derives not only from childhood play but in large measure from early masturbatory fantasy, with its closeness to action and discharge. In its more neutralized aspects fantasy includes the interposing of organizing and delaying factors in the mental experience. These organizing and delaying factors, together with the representation of relatively socialized tendencies in the motivational hierarchy, are aspects of neutralization (delibidinization and deaggres-sivization) of the energies involved in creative fantasy as opposed to asocial daydreaming or too starkly self-revealing "creative" outpourings. Thus, if relatively unneutralized, creative fantasy may also revive or express conflict over masturbation.

Therefore, even though in the service of the ego, that is, fulfilling an adaptive task, the regressive process in creativity may be heavily bur-dened by conflict insofar as anxiety and guilt attach to passivity, femininity, masturbation, destructiveness, maternal rejection, and other tabooed impulses and acts. In fact, the artist, like the wit, has been shown to be dependent on the favorable response of his audience to alleviate his guilt, even if that audience is not the public at large but one or two selected figures in reality or fantasy. The artist's very empha-sis on inspiration appears to alleviate anxiety and guilt by externalizing responsibility for the process and its results: there is an outside source who is responsible—the divine, the devil, the muse, opium, alcohol, nature, etc.

On its part, the audience derives gratification through similar regres-sive and progressive processes within itself. To a significant extent, the audience relies on the artist or joke maker as an external source of responsibility for its pleasure while unconsciously identifying with him. As in the artist, there occurs an intermingling of active and passive ego function.

In brief, it may be said that the variety of dangers involved emanate from the very motives and fantasies that empower creative work. The dangers are reductions of the ego's relative autonomy from the id, dis-turbances of the complex balance between active and passive ego function, and the ego's greater vulnerability to superego condemnation. The preceding discussion has focused on the creative process in the artist and wit; a similar treatment of the phenomena of empathy, intimacy, love, therapeutic involvement, etc., is, of course, necessary and appears to be feasible.

Conditions favoring *regression in the service of the ego* are numerous. Six *overlapping* factors will be mentioned. These factors obviously re-late to existing definitions of ego strength (Fenichel, 1938) and neu-tralization of libidinal or aggressive energies (Erikson, 1956; Hartmann,

1939, 1950; Kris, 1952; Rapaport, 1951b, 1957), and to discussions of factors fostering healthy personality development and maturity (Erikson, 1950, 1953; Olden, 1953; Sullivan, 1947).

First there is required the presence of *a well-developed set of affect signals*. The individual must be relatively secure in his sense of being in touch with his feelings. Here the schizophrenic and the rigid obsessive are hampered. Freud (1926) has described how the ego depends on anxiety signals in order to regulate its defensive and adaptive expenditures of its energy. Actually, we depend on a variety of affect signals all the time. As for *regression in the service of the ego*, when the regressive process threatens to get out of hand, that is, when it comes too close to drives, affects, and fantasies not assimilable in consciousness, appropriate signals will trigger the search for defensive disguise of content or reversal of the entire process. Confidence in these signals makes it safe to regress.

A second condition is *a secure sense of self*, and, more broadly, a well-established ego identity. The considerations of Erikson (1956) and Federn (1952) are particularly relevant here. Moving closer to primary-process domination of functioning means not only that the boundary between id and ego suffers. In orgastic experience and in freedom to sleep and dream, this phenomenon—or capacity—is particularly evident. Anxiety over potential loss of self is central to what is often termed instinctual threat or superego threat. Where there is a secure sense of self and a stable identity, one may tolerate momentary blurring or loss of their boundaries and coherence. Where this security is weak or absent, one must rigidly maintain self-boundaries and organization and a self-definition of a particular sort for fear of having nothing otherwise. The schizophrenic's fear of intimacy conspicuously involves a fear of disintegrating, exploding, being totally engulfed or otherwise losing an already tenuous and fluid self-boundary and inner organization.

A third factor facilitating controlled creative regression is a *relative mastery of early traumata*. With this mastery, the individual may feel free to have subjective experiences which imply in certain respects how it was once to have been a child and to have felt feminine, receptive, helpless, omnipotent, and generally fluid in internal state and object relations. In fact, relative mastery of early traumata implies that the crises and crucial experiences of early development have not been sealed off from the development of the total personality but have been given a place in it and have undergone progressive transformations and working through. This is the sense of Sullivan's (1947) discussion of healthy development, as it is of Erikson's (1953). Olden's (1953) discussion of factors hindering and facilitating adult empathy with children stresses the same point.

A fourth factor is relative *moderateness* rather than archaic severity *of superego pressures* and, in close correlation with this, relative flexibility rather than rigidity or fluidity of defenses and controls. Under favorable conditions of this sort, one may "let go," increase inner awareness and *play* intrapsychically without severe anxiety and guilt and with some degree of pleasure. The limiting and distorting effects of guilt on self-awareness and self-experimentation may reach extreme lengths, of course.

A fifth factor is a *history of adequate trust and mutuality in interpersonal relations,* particularly in the early mother-child relation. Erikson's, Sullivan's, and Olden's discussions, among others, are again relevant. The yield of the regressive process may ultimately be communicated in some form and used in the service of promoting a relation to others (audience, intimates, children, therapist, patients); at the same time it will be internally scrutinized and judged by the ego and superego, on both of which the mother has left a basic imprint. In both respects, a background of adequate trust will support the feeling that what is produced will be empathically and tolerantly acknowledged rather than responded to with panic, withdrawal, or arbitrary punishment. And this feeling will make it safe and pleasurable to regress temporarily.

The sixth and last factor to be mentioned here is the meaningfulness to the larger community of this process that culminates in *self-awareness and personal and effective communication to others.* The need for such cultural meaningfulness has been noted by Kris in his discussion of art and much emphasized by Erikson in his discussion of the ego-identity crisis in adolescence. That is to say, following Erikson, what one has been, is, and aspires to be must be valued by at least a segment of the larger community so that one may become a certain somebody with a sense of wholeness and may preserve this wholeness to advance one's social adaptation and impact. The alternatives are dissociation, ego restriction, or negative identity (becoming all that one is not supposed to be or is most feared by the family and larger community). These alternatives represent various forms of passive ego function predominating over active ego function.

The reader will see that if the preceding propositions concerning favorable conditions were to be put in negative form they would constitute a list of hampering conditions (e.g., poorly developed affect signals, weak sense of self, or weak ego identity, etc.). This list may be added to, though it overlaps, the earlier discussed factors potentially hampering controlled ego regression (e.g., magical meanings, masturbatory activity, shameful passivity and femininity, etc.)

The evidence does not clearly support the idea that creative artists or scientists operate under mostly facilitating conditions. It may well be that some regressive adaptations, such as those involved in direct interpersonal relations (empathy, intimacy, orgasm, therapeutic understanding, and communication), are more dependent on the facilitating conditions discussed than are others, such as artistic, scientific, and comic creativity. And this may be why the list of facilitating conditions is so much more closely tied to conceptions of healthy development and mature personality than they are to observations of gifted artists, comics, and scientists. The key question would here be, "Regression for what?" The further investigation of these suggested differences would be a valuable study in ego psychology, and it would bear on the aptness of applying the concept *regression in the service of the ego* to creative processes in general.

INDIVIDUAL VARIATION

Individual variation has not been ignored in the discussions referred to. Concerning *regression in the service of the ego* in artists, Kris (1952) emphasizes that in actuality we encounter all degrees of transition between ego strength and weakness in this process. The continuum from normal to schizophrenic creative efforts is steadily recognized. Affect signals vary in strength and controllability; anxiety and guilt may get out of hand; the sense of self may be dangerously impaired; early unassimilated traumata may be revived; severe superego and defensive countermeasures may be imposed; and severe disruption of the sense of mutuality and communication with more immediate and more remote members of the community may result. Also varying is the effectiveness of the phase of elaboration in achieving synthesis and communication. Further, we observe variability in the directness of drive representation in awareness, in specific dynamic areas being more accessible than others, in preference for acting out instead of remembering, or for regressing ideationally more in formal respects than in content respects. In this last connection, we seem to encounter formal primitivization without obvious drive representation in certain experiences of problem solving in the sciences and mathematics. Finally, individuals appear to vary in their typical level of psychic functioning: some, like borderline schizophrenics, steadily operate closer to the primary process or at least tend to fluctuate with great amplitude between the primary and secondary poles; others, like compulsives, cling rigidly and ego-restrictively to rationality and full control at all times.

We may add that variation in the typical level of psychic functioning appears to depend significantly on the ego identity of the individual and what it and its community will support. For example, being an artist, a therapist, or a comic supports more controlled ego regression in certain respects than do other identities. Even within one identity the capacity for controlled ego regression varies from one time to another. We may also add that the degree to which the regressive process is voluntary and controlled varies. A regression originally precariously in the service of the ego may go too far and culminate in pathological regression. On the other hand, often the initial process seems more one of pathological regression, and only subsequently may the ego show resiliency and impress the regressive experience into its service. There is even reason to believe that art and wit are often used to recover from or stave off pathological regressive experiences involving large segments of the personality, and that organizational stringencies in work and in the particular medium involved help restore internal organization.

IMPLICATIONS FOR TEST ANALYSIS

Thus far we have defined *regression in the service of the ego*, especially with reference to the primary and secondary processes, we have sketched its place in the creation of art and the comic, and noted the importance of subsequent or alternating elaborative phases, and we have considered psychological conditions that foster and hamper controlled ego regression as well as aspects of individual variation in controlled and uncontrolled regressive experience. What now is the pertinence of these psychoanalytic observations and inferences for the use of tests in personality assessment? First, in using psychological tests we should assess the range and security of *regression in the service of the ego* in each individual. To do this we need a battery of tests, tests varying in their degree of structure and demands for secondary-process functioning. Projective tests like the Thematic Apperception Test and especially the Rorschach Test, being relatively unstructured and personalized, appear to require more regression in the service of the ego, more access to and use of the primary process, than a test like an intelligence test. In these projective tests we require the subject to create something—an image or a fantasy. We give him materials or a medium in which to work, but he is in many respects put in the position of the creative artist and must find within himself forms of experience and contents to elaborate a response. To have free access to a wide range of forms and contents, *regression in the service of the ego* is required; specifically, an enlargement of awareness, a degree of blurring of the distinction between inner and outer, a relaxation of defense, an entrusting of ideas to preconscious and unconscious elaboration, and other processes described above. Otherwise responses will be limited to description, or, what is not far from description, banalities. In the latter case we observe severe restriction of the ego and little capacity to regress for adaptive purposes. The test instructions and stimuli appear to afford the subject a considerable relief from anxiety and guilt by giving him an opportunity to externalize responsibility for many aspects of his responses. Remember that the artist and joke maker need audience response, tradition, and inspirational experience to help them with the same problem.

We observe, moreover, that in the development of responses to projective tests, progressive, elaborational phases are steadily evident. The end result—the response or story—is not normally dreamlike but more or less attuned to the reality of the stimulus and testing situation. We hear from the subject a comprehensible and revelant communication about a creation that "fits in," stimuluswise and situationwise. We find in the subject's verbalization and affective tone established self-awareness and self-boundaries, distance from participation, and curious, interested, playful, and humorous expression. When the regression goes too far and escapes the ego's service, we find fluid, overexpansive, insufficiently worked-out, archaic material, and overparticipation. When the subject does not reestablish the boundary between inner and outer, he may become agitated, hostile, elated, depressed, or severely withdrawn. He lives out his responses. These phenomena we frequently observe in psychotics and some borderline psychotics.

Actually, subjects vary over a continuum in their capacity for creative regression during testing, and they vary in the typical level of functioning from which they must regress to create responses. Also, they vary regarding the areas in which they are free to regress and in their capacity to regain distance and to elaborate and synthesize reality-attuned responses. Defensive requirements, as Bergler (1944, 1945) has pointed out with regard to the artist, may determine which forms and contents of experience are accessible, because revealing one area of depth may be possible only if it helps conceal a more disturbing area. Thus sexual contents may cover hostility or vice versa, passive receptive forms of experience may cover phallic-intrusive forms or vice versa, etc. To illustrate some of the above considerations, I will first present and discuss some illustrative test responses which show regression to image magic and other forms of functioning dominated by the primary process, that is, responses in which regression is not primarily in the service of higher ego functions.

Let us consider first the case of Mr. F.— nineteen years old, single, Jewish, with a history of violent paranoid schizophrenic manifestations for the past year and of at least transient schizophrenic manifestations for more than three years. On Card II of the Rorschach Test (administered by a young woman) he responds as follows: "This looks like a, two little rabbits. These are rabbits, these black spots here, they could be bears, yeah. The red stuff shouldn't be here! It shouldn't be here!

It should be out of it!" Patient is agitated. He puts his head down on the desk. Examiner asks if there is anything else. "Nothing else." He mutters something about bleeding but does not look at card. In the inquiry he is first asked what makes them look like bears; he responds: "They are black and they are shaped like it. You know, cubs. Did you ever see cubs? I saw cubs in the Smoky Mountains National Park. I fed them. It was a lot of fun!" Patient's manner is now pleased and animated. He is then asked what he had in mind about the "red stuff": "It could be blood but I don't want it there!" Patient is again agitated. He is asked if he thought of the blood in relation to the bears or separately: "Where else could it be from but the bears! Here is the front, the face, the ears, the tails, and the paws. It looks as if they had cut their feet and it's bleeding (lower red area). But that stuff up here (upper red): I don't know what that is from. What could that be? I don't know. They must have cut their feet and have a nose bleed. Are you engaged?" There is in this response sequence abundant and obvious evidence of regression to archaic modes of reasoning, image magic, participation, and loss of self-boundary (the distinction between inner and outer or between thought and percept). In addition, the disorder of verbalization evident in his redundancy indicates perceptual and/or conceptual fluidity. His reasoning about the nosebleed is based on the upper red area having a position near—though above—the nose; he follows here a primitive, concrete mode of reasoning rather than a conceptual one. He deals with the picture that he visualizes as if it were a reality situation with ominous implications, and he pronounces a verdict: the red should not be there. His intent is to transform reality and he is not having or communicating an internal experience of the mind. His earlier animation in talking about the cubs had already suggested proneness to lose distance, concreteness, and readiness for participation; while more moderate and more pleasant, that elaboration still had pathological regressive implications. His putting his head down on the desk and his later forwardness with a female tester are further indications of impaired capacity for delay: affects rapidly spill over into acting.

On the fourth Rorschach Card one of his responses develops as follows: "This thing here (lower middle): you want to know what this is? A person's windpipe." Asked in inquiry what made it look like that, he says: "Well, I remember seeing something like that before. You know, a chicken, a chicken's neck. I watched them murder—er—kill chickens once. They wrang the neck and chopped it off. I was sick that day, not from that, though; that didn't bother me." Again asked what made it look like a windpipe specifically: "Well, I have seen a picture of a windpipe. So, if it is real, it is a chicken's neck, but if it is a picture, which this is, it is a windpipe." Of particular significance here is his incomplete separation of what is real and what is imagined. By the end of the inquiry he has to play it both ways: there is a contamination between a concrete association and a current perception.

On Card 6 BM of the TAT, the card showing an elderly woman with her back turned to a young man, he gives this story: "Here is this guy; here is his mother. Are you ready? It is too bad you didn't know shorthand. He's just got fired again and his mother, he told his mother that and she is feeling kind of—she doesn't know what to do. He is a nice looking guy though. He just can't hold on to a job. He is a nice guy though. He had a pretty tough break. You know what happens after that? (The patient stands and looks out window.) He doesn't let things worry him! He says, The hell with them! He doesn't care what people think! Maybe he will find himself some day! (Returns to desk at request of tester but stands at her side.) He gets away from his mother (covers his mouth with his hands) and then he will be okay. Why should I care about that guy in the picture! I have enough of my own problems! (Patient is very angry. Tester asks patient to be seated.) Am I making you nervous? Come on, you don't have to do so much writing!" And on Card 7BM, the card showing the heads of an elderly man and a young man, he gives this story: "(Nervous laugh.) Holy cow! Look at this character! (Nervous laugh.) Holy cow! (Nervous laugh.) I have seen this before too. Here we have a father and son, a father-son relationship here, and the son feels rather gloomy and discouraged. The old man—he has been through the mill and he is supposed to be helping the son out. He tells him not to worry but the son will have to learn for himself. He is much of a character, this guy. (Who is?) The son. This guy looks sad. Most people when they are gloomy don't look like that. He is a jerk! (Patient is angry.) This guy doesn't get anywhere! It is tough luck but he doesn't get anywhere! Two stupid characters if I ever saw them! Taking life too seriously! They should be like me:

Not a worry in the world! (etc.)" The primary process characteristics described in connection with his Rorschach responses clearly reappear here, though now in forms determined by the nature of the TAT situation. Again, the patient is not having an internal experience in the mind but is living out a real event and pronouncing verdicts, struggling after the fact to achieve distance but failing, and falling back on obviously unconvincing and inappropriate denials. Note particularly his defunct reality testing in reasoning that the young man in the second story is a jerk because he does not look the way the patient projectively decided he felt, that is, gloomy.

Consider now excerpts from the Rorschach record of a fifty-five-year-old man, married, with several children, in acute turmoil over an infatuation with a young woman, and diagnostically in a hypomanic and paranoid state. He instantaneously responds to the first Rorschach card: "That is a pelvis. That is a pelvis to me. So you can see I am sexy oriented (laughs) or am I?" His first reaction to Card II: "Well, my instant reaction is that this is another pelvis but they played around with this one and this has something new. Here is the female vulva, here (lower red). These red things here are kidneys (upper red). The open area has no meaning to me other than to make this ridiculous remark: Why the hell did they take the uterus out and left a hole right through her body? Now I see something else. There seem to be a couple of, I am going to call them Teddy bears. You cut off the body below the shoulders. The forepaws, like this, hanging down (demonstrates). The two red spots have no meaning at all in this connection. They have unusually long snouts to kiss with. This is fun! I am beginning to see something myself already (that is, significance in his responses)." The patient is now gay and animated.

On Card V: "This is a bat. It also looks like a peculiar kind of moth. Some of these things suggest an island. I can't tell you why unless it is the isolation this picture gives me. . . . This picture has rather low interest to me." He is asked to explain the reference to isolation: "There was loneliness to that picture. I wonder if that is related to the indication that that is a picture of a bat. That in turn goes back to the story of Fledermaus and the description of the bat: nocturnal and lonely, the despised non-bat, non-mouse and doesn't belong with either. A biological hermaphrodite—not in the sexual sense—a hybrid? I don't quite like that picture. That I think is the reason for my rejection of it and my low interest. It has emotional connotations for me. I don't like it." On Card VI, after first seeing a pelt stretched out to dry and wondering why they hadn't cut off the testicles he sees at the bottom of the card, and next seeing the head of a turtle at the top, he says: "Here is a pair of hands (lower projections on side). I want to take hold of them. Once I did I wouldn't know what to do with them. I just want to take hold of them (demonstrates)." He goes on to see a reptile which also suggests to him the foreskin of a penis, a fancy woman's stole, and then, at the bottom, a pair of buttocks: "Now I begin to see the reason for not cutting the testicles off. . . . I am beginning to get a little headache." In explaining this last inference, he contaminates the skin and buttocks responses: "Because I see this as buttocks, it is natural to, a person could be squatting to defecate and naturally you would see testicles hanging down."

On Card VII he sees two men explaining something to each other and pointing in opposite directions, each trying to convince the other of his point of view and the relation is good: "They are in rapport with each other. They don't, either one, want to offend the other. There is a kindliness about this picture, concern for each other's feelings." In inquiry the patient points out the response in the upper two thirds of the card and adds: "Someone has neglected to show their feet or else they are very tiny. There is some defiance of the law of gravity but I am not interested in that because the emotional content of that picture is high and the headache is gone again. It was just a light one." He is then asked what indicates their rapport: "Their concern with each other. They are two good friends." He is again asked what indicates that: "By pure chance that picture shows feeling in the eyes. Why did I see it I can't tell you but I see that clearly. There is a bond of affection between these two men and I am conscious I am hiding something when I say that: they look like men but one of them is a woman. That is all I can give." And on Card VIII he sees the two popular animals clinging to rock structure in which there is an evergreen tree and surmises they are climbing up a cliff; during the inquiry he says: "The animals for no good reason all seem to be chameleons." Asked what makes them look like that: "Chameleons are changeable; they change their color. (What about that?) Because I am changeable! (I don't follow you.)

Because I have just led myself into a trap, that's all! (The patient is visibly irritated.) I walked right into that! To go one step further—so I am climbing, trying to get some place, I am a chameleon, changeable, indecisive. I'll go a step further: I betray people after having won their affection. You got a lot out of that one, Doc!" Patient is quite agitated now.

Throughout these responses we see obvious image magic, participation, confusing reality and fantasy. For instance: "They look like men but one of them is a woman." The responses are projected pathologically and are taken as omens or magical signs of what he is—sometimes favorable signs and sometimes unfavorable, as in his being changeable. The trap he walks into is a trap defined by loss of self-boundaries and by failure of defenses, particularly of the defense of denial through which he attempts to make himself sexually potent, *en rapport*, strong and independent. His regressive confusion also reaches one of its climaxes when he wants to take hold of the pair of hands on Card VI, evidently having a total experience, affectively and motorically, of wanting to hang on. The rapid coming and going of his headache in association with his denials through image magic further indicate archaic body participation in the response process.

Extreme responses of this sort are not rare in clinical testing. Sometimes they even turn up in the test records of supposedly normal or only moderately neurotic subjects. There is every reason to expect them to turn up in any large-scale assessment program. Moderate and transitional forms of primary-process encroachment are even more frequently observed and can be taken as partial indications of instability of psychic structure, that is, of the extent to which either the ego's use of the primary process tends to slip over into being overwhelmed by it, or the ego is busily staving off pathological regressions. Transitional forms of response will be cited from the record of a young psychiatrist. He was not without significant adjustment problems but capable of effective work and interpersonal rapport. On Card IV: "I see a very cruel, menacing-looking figure here. The head (upper middle): It's even got a moustache and a big nose, narrow and slanting—not slanting —slit-like eyes, eyebrows arched and wrinkles in the forehead. These are sort of hands (upper side projections), very skinny hands, out in a rather menacing, grabbing position and he is standing erect here; here are his feet and legs (lower side projections) and maybe this is a cape that is hanging down (lower middle); it looks like it is hanging in front rather than behind. I don't know how these fit in." Asked what makes it look menacing: "The arms and the eyes slanted and the eyebrows went down. . . . It seemed to be looking right at me and the arms were out as if it could be used for grappling." There is some blurring of self-boundaries here, particularly in the reference to the figure "looking right at me." But apart from that—and that emerges only late in the inquiry—one is struck by the response's relatively detached though interested treatment, its progressive articulation, its built-in self-criticism in terms of details that do not fit in well. The ego remains to a great extent active, and we see overt manifestations of the elaborative and synthetic phase of the creative-response process. It is in some ways a struggle for the subject and in at least one way a not entirely successful struggle, but still a far cry from the responses of the first two subjects.

On Card VI: "Again I get the same first response, of this being some sort of an animal flying along but it sure doesn't look much like it (whole blot). Let's see what else. Oh! This looks like a tank (side detail, seen sideways). Here are the treads. This (a projection) is hard to fit in: this seems like a cannon they carry on a tank, pointing backwards and they have a blanket over it like it is not in actual combat, in mothballs, so to speak, and the different colors of shading make it so that it is camouflaged. Hm: Here are two people standing side by side with their faces turned out this way and arms held out (each half of blot, held upside down.) It is sort of a dainty pose as if they were doing some dance like the minuet and the foot were daintily pointed out here, although they are rather large, ragged-looking people to be doing something like that. The fact that they are almost joined together except for the white line suggests some sort of anomaly like Siamese twins, and here is a little horn on their heads. This thing down here (usual upper projection) to put it all together, could be two people doing the same thing but on a weathervane, mounted on a post and these people turn the way the wind blows. Again, this, just by itself, could be a sort of flying animal, feelers, and wings and head (upper detail). I thought at first it had just gone through something and made a hole and all of this (rest of card) was the debris that was falling off. The animal itself seems to have survived pretty well." Asked what makes it look like debris: "I could see the animal and couldn't figure out what the rest of it would be and it seemed to be flying fast so I thought maybe it had just gone through something, like through a wall or something."

Again, some blurring of the self-boundaries is not eliminated in the final response formulation, some of his quick initial impressions tending to dominate his subsequent efforts to synthesize. Even so, throughout he obviously attempts to articulate, relate, synthesize, note discrepancies from realistic conformations. Maintenance of interest, distance, and capacity for self-criticism is not impaired. One may conjecture a number of significant dynamic problems from the few responses cited from this record—problems concerning self-esteem, passive-compliant defense against hostile impulse, fear of damage, etc. And in some respects one sees that somewhat fluid forms of experience are not unusual in his psychic functioning. At the same time one sees an active, inventive, self-observant ego steadily at work. By implication, higher ego functions are fairly stably established; they are not overwhelmed in the response process and do not give way to image magic, participation, emotional chaos, or archaic projections and introjections.

It would be a mistake, however, to limit our attention to projective tests only. An intelligence test indispensably helps assess the extent to which secondary-process functioning may be maintained in its own right. Because they are relatively structured, impersonal, and consistent with conventional logical requirements and techniques, intelligence-test items invite or demand of the individual that he respond in an entirely nonregressive manner. Assessment of individually administered and verbatim recorded intelligence-test results, such as those of the Wechsler Adult Intelligence Scale, including assessment of the distribution of subtest scores, clarifies to what extent there is something partial, temporary, and controlled about the regressive aspects of the projective-test responses. Of course, we can and do carry out such assessment on the basis of the projective-test responses themselves. We rely, for example, on the Rorschach scores: the *form level*, with its indication of adequacy of reality testing; the use of *color* and *shading* and the control of them through *form*, with their indications of cognitive regulation and articulation of affective experience; the *human-movement* response, with its indication of freedom of fantasy, interpersonal awareness and other imaginative, personalized and organized ideation; etc. And we also observe the test's qualitative aspects, such as differentiation and synthesis within content and form, and optimal emotional distance from response, in order to assess the relative power of the secondary process. In other words, the secondary process is not crowded out of the projective tests. The progressive, elaborational, synthetic phase of creative work is called for as much, if not more, in a projective test as in a free act of creation.

But because projective tests plumb deep, they sometimes dramatize the less stable stages or levels of personality organization. They may obscure adaptive potential. This is a well-known diagnostic difficulty in clinical work. It crops up in training too; for it is a cliché that students learning to use the Rorschach Test and giving it to friends or fellow students seem to be surrounded by schizophrenics. There are many factors that appear to account for these usually misleading results. But whatever the explanation, these findings indicate the importance of using tests calling for more structured and stable forms of secondary-process response. My experience with a variety of more or less normal subjects, such as applicants for secretarial positions, state policemen, college students, pregnant women, and applicants for psychiatric residencies, has repeatedly confirmed the impression that a relatively efficient, well-organized intelligence-test performance must be given considerable weight in assessing adaptive potential. Clinically, this finding is often of great value in distinguishing between incipient and fully psychotic conditions. It is when primary-process expressions intrude into the intelligence test that we are almost certainly dealing with a full psychosis. Psychosis is indicated when, from a formal point of view, the intelligence-test responses become fluid, concrete, and disrupted in their communicative aspects, and when, from a content point of view, they express more and more material that is drive-relevant rather than reality-relevant. Thus, when a reasonably intelligent patient says that a fly and a tree are alike in being inarticulate or in that they can both be destroyed, when cryptic references to venereal disease intrude into the answer to the question *why does the state require people to get a license in order to be married?* and when a patient defines *obstruct* as a detour because an obstruction need not prevent you from getting where you are going if you can make a detour, we see primary processes intrude where they do not belong. We see pathological regression of the ego (pervasive, uncontrolled, enduring) to a more primitive level of function—in other words, structural pathology.

Many of these considerations also apply to the assessment of subjects through interviews and in therapeutic situations. It is, for example, a steady preoccupation of the psychoanalyst to assess the balance of primary and secondary processes and shifting levels of organization in the patient. Loewald (1956) has recently discussed important theoretical aspects of this assessment. One of the points he stresses is the regression in the service of the ego required of the analyst to comprehend the level from which the patient is communicating and hence to comprehend and respond effectively to the communications. He extends significantly the emphasis placed by Fenichel (1941) on the requirement that the analyst oscillate between an experiencing and an observing (conceptualizing) position. Of course, Freud recognized very early that the free play of the analyst's unconscious and preconscious processes was indispensable for his effective interventions. There is every reason to transpose this view to the analysis of test results. In developing the possible implications of content, and coordinating these; in experiencing the subject's style of verbalization as conveying information concerning drives, affects, controls, aspirations, and assets; in being able to comprehend both the more realistic and articulated aspects of responses and their more archaic referents; in all these operations, the test interpreter must be able to move freely over his own range of levels of organization. And in the end he must do a piece of synthetic and elaborational work in which he sifts, interrelates, and weights the implications of his experience of the material. Unless his assessing is piecemeal and carefully prescribed by a manual, that is, unless he is working automistically for specific research purposes, the assessor of human motives is called upon to do a creative piece of work, like the therapist and like the artist.

Implied in all these observations and considerations is that we do the object of our study, whether a patient or a subject being assessed, an injustice if we are too dazzled by content, by dynamics, by motives, and do not pay close attention to formal aspects of functioning and their structural and economic implications.

IMPLICATIONS FOR PERSONALITY
ASSESSMENT RESEARCH

I have already mentioned the importance of including as crucial variables intraindividual and interindividual differences in capacity for regression in the service of the ego. These differences include specific conditions favoring and hampering such regression, the dynamic areas and extent of regression, and the style and quality of ultimate syntheses. I have also indicated a way of thinking about test results in personality assessment, and I have pointed to the advantages particular tests offer personality assessment. I do not imply that existing and popular psychological tests, such as the Rorschach, TAT, and Wechsler Adult Intelligence Scale, are the ideal tools for assessment—although I and many others have come to value them highly for this purpose. Rather, it is the problems these techniques pose to the subject being assessed that are of interest, for assessment must include these problems if it is to be penetrating. Subjects should be required to create, synthesize, and communicate something, be it in a play construction, a joke, a plan for group action, a painting, a TAT story, or a self-interpretation of that story—or many of these. Subjects should be required to function under a variety of conditions other than those usually obtaining in their normal waking state, such as internal states of sleepiness, tipsiness, or high affect, and external conditions of varying degrees of ambiguity. Also, subjects should be observed developing identifications, intimacy, and empathy with others in a variety of group situations. To a significant extent these inner and outer conditions can be experimentally manipulated. A particularly valuable way to enrich the study of such regressive and creative processes in the assessed subjects is to have at least some of them undergo psychoanalysis. When one considers the usual scope of assessment programs in time and expense, this does not seem an extravagant proposal. The psychoanalytic findings in individual subjects should help answer many crucial questions in the interpretation of assessment data, or, if not that, they will certainly raise crucial questions which might otherwise pass unnoticed.

By intention I have slighted questionnaires. I recognize that skillfully constructed questionnaires contribute to assessment research. I believe, however, that all too often assessment suffers because it excessively emphasizes questionnaire results. Questionnaires are obviously tempting: Many subjects may be quickly studied, and the results lend themselves so nicely to quantitative treatment. Research workers often hasten to have numbers to report in order to be "objective," although in so doing they often slight their subjects and their own resources. They hastily restrict themselves to what is conscious, readily available, and easily verbalized. Admittedly, it is not so easy to objectify and quantify creativity, humor, variations in states of consciousness, and varieties of conscious experience. Extensive phenomenological investigations must come first. Reliability checks and quantitative comparisons should be carried out only in due time. Holt's (1956) on-going research, in which he is objectively assessing primary-process manifestations in Rorschach responses, represents a significant methodological advance in this regard. While we may usually look down on the conception of scientific rigor in the writings of many psychiatrists and psychoanalysts, we must respect many for their patience, integrity, and courage in the face of bewildering complexity and ambiguity while they go on mapping out horizontal and vertical psychic territories. They take the individual very seriously. Mass correlations of questionnaire results seem wasteful by comparison, even though they may appease scientific conscience by offering concrete results soon. The impatient scientist may invite his audience of colleagues to identify with him and approve his product —correlations—in order to lighten his burden of guilt at not having been creative. There is a risk of greater guilt in taking one's time, studying subjects intensively even if it limits the size of samples, looking into complex and elusive problems, and trespassing established boundaries of method and subject matter, but one then stands a better chance of assessing central factors and creating something memorable.

REFERENCES

Bellak, L. A study of limitations and "failures": toward an ego psychology of projective techniques. *J. proj. Tech.*, 1954, *18*, 279-293.
Bergler, E. A clinical approach to the psychoanalysis of writers. *Psychoanal. Rev.*, 1944, *31*, 40-70.

————. On a five-layer structure on sublimation. *Psychoanal. Quart.*, 1945, 14, 76-97.

Erikson, E. H. *Childhood and society.* New York: Norton, 1950.

————. Growth and crises of the "healthy personality." In C. Kluckhohn, H. Murray, and D. M. Schneider (eds.), *Personality in nature, society and culture*, 2nd ed. New York: Knopf, 1953. Pp. 185-225.

————. The problem of ego identity. *J. Amer. Psychoanal. Assoc.*, 1956, 4, 56-121.

Federn, P. *Ego psychology and the psychoses.* New York: Basic Books, 1952.

Fenichel, O. Ego strength and ego weakness. In *The collected papers*, 2nd. series. New York: Norton, 1954. (Originally published in 1938.) Pp. 70-80.

————. *Problems of psychoanalytic technique.* (Trans. by D. Brunswick.) Albany, New York: Psychoanalytic Quarterly, Inc., 1941.

Freud, S. *The interpretation of dreams.* In *The basic writings of Sigmund Freud.* New York: Modern Library, 1938. (Originally published in 1900.) Pp. 179-549.

————. Wit and its relation to the unconscious. In *The basic writings of Sigmund Freud.* (Trans. by A. A. Brill.) New York: Modern Library, 1938. (Originally published in 1905.) Pp. 631-803.

————. The relation of the poet to day-dreaming. In *Collected papers.* Vol. IV. London: Hogarth, 1948. (Originally published in 1908.) Pp. 184-191.

————. The unconscious. In *Collected papers.* Vol. IV. London: Hogarth, 1948. (Originally published in 1915.) Pp. 98-136.

————. *Group psychology and the analysis of the ego.* London: Hogarth, 1948. (Originally published in 1921.)

————. *The ego and the id.* London: Hogarth, 1947. (Originally published in 1923.)

————. *The problem of anxiety.* New York: Norton, 1936. (Originally published in 1926.)

Hartmann, H. Ich-Psychologie und Anpassungsproblem. *Int. Z. Psychoanal.*, 1939, 24, 62-135. [Translation, Ego psychology and the problem of adaptation (abridged). In D. Rapaport (ed.), *Organization and pathology of thought.* New York: Columbia University Press, 1951. Pp. 362-396.]

————. Comments on the psychoanalytic theory of the ego. In *The psychoanalytic study of the child.* Vol. II. New York: Int. Univ. Press, 1950. Pp. 74-96.

————, Kris, E., and Loewenstein, R. M. Comments on the formation of psychic structure. In *The psychoanalytic study of the child.* Vol. II. New York: Int. Univ. Press, 1946. Pp. 11-38.

Holt, R. R. Implications of some contemporary personality theories for Rorschach rationale. In B. Klopfer, M. D. Ainsworth, W. G. Klopfer, and R. R. Holt, *Developments in the Rorschach technique.* Vol. I. New York: World Book, 1954. Pp. 501-560.

————. Gauging primary and secondary processes in Rorschach responses. *J. proj. Tech.*, 1956, 20, 14-25.

Kris, E. *Psychoanalytic explorations in art.* New York: Int. Univ. Press, 1952.

Levey, H. B. A critique of the theory of sublimation. *Psychiatry*, 1939, 2, 239-270.

————. A theory concerning free creation in the inventive arts. *Psychiatry*, 1940, 3, 229-293.

Loewald, H. On the therapeutic action of psychoanalysis. Unpublished manuscript, 1956.

Olden, C. On adult empathy with children. In *The psychoanalytic study of the child.* Vol. VIII. New York: Int. Univ. Press, 1953. Pp. 111-127.

Piaget, J. *Judgment and reasoning in the child.* New York: Harcourt, Brace, 1928.

————. *The child's conception of the world.* New York: Harcourt, Brace, 1929.

————. *The child's conception of physical causality.* London: Routledge & Kegan, Paul, 1930.

————. *The language and thought of the child,* 2nd ed. London: Routledge & Kegan, Paul, 1932.

Rapaport, D. On the psychoanalytic theory of thinking. *Int. J. Psychoanal.*, 1950, 31, 161-170.

————. The autonomy of the ego. *Bull. Menninger Clin.*, 1951a, 15, 113-123.

————. *The Organization and pathology of thought.* New York: Columbia University Press, 1951b.

————. Consciousness: a psychopathological and psychodynamic view. In *Problems of consciousness,* Trans. of the Second Conference, March 19-20, 1951, New York, Josiah Macy, Jr. Foundation, 1951c, Pp. 18-57.

————. On the psychoanalytic theory of affects. *Int. J. Psychoanal.*, 1953a, 34, 177-198.

————. Some metapsychological considerations concerning activity and passivity. Unpublished manuscript, 1953b.

————. The structure of psychoanalytic theory. Unpublished manuscript, 1957.

Schafer, R. *Psychoanalytic interpretation in Rorschach testing,* New York: Grune & Stratton, 1954.

Sharpe, E. F. Similar and divergent unconscious determinants underlying the sublimations of pure art and pure science. *Int. J. Psychoanal.*, 1935, 16, 186-202.

Sullivan, H. S. *Conceptions of modern psychiatry*. Washington: William Alanson White Psychiatric Foundation, 1947.

Werner, H. *Comparative psychology of mental development*, rev. ed. New York: Follett, 1948.

IRVING L. JANIS

Yale University

6 *The psychoanalytic interview as an observational method*

This chapter will attempt to give a general account of the main values and limitations of psychoanalytic research from the standpoint of developing scientific knowledge about human motivation. I shall begin by calling attention to the characteristic difficulties that prevent many behavioral scientists from assessing correctly the potential gains that can come from the use of psychoanalytic interviews as a source of observational data. In discussing these difficulties, I shall say a great deal about the *present status of psychoanalytic research,* focusing upon the strengths and weaknesses of the intensive case-study method as it is currently employed by practicing psychoanalysts. Then I shall state my views concerning *potential developments in the future.* This second topic will be discussed in the context of examining two fundamental questions that are pertinent for integrating the findings from psychoanalytic interviews with those obtained by means of other observational methods: (1) How can the methodological weaknesses of psychoanalytic research be corrected? and (2) How can the scope of psychoanalytic inquiry be sufficiently broadened to provide new information and insights concerning unconscious motivational processes in normal social behavior?

A MAJOR GAP IN RESEARCH TRAINING

During the twentieth century clinical psychoanalysis has been the major source of theory concerning personality dynamics. This simple historical fact seems to be quietly accepted nowadays by most psychologists and social scientists. In subdued but deferential tones, recent college textbooks in psychology allude to the importance of psychoanalytic hypotheses. But they give at best only a sketchy account of the main theoretical constructs and usually remain quite silent about the details of the observational techniques and findings of psychoanalytic case-study research.

A rather anomalous situation has been developing in the postgraduate curriculum of most major universities currently engaged in training professional psychiatrists, psychologists, and social scientists. Among trainees in such fields, Freudian concepts and terminology have become common parlance. This condition exists even in research seminars for those who plan to specialize in fields that may be more or less remote from clinical psychology and psychiatry, such as experimental psychology, child development, attitude change, ethnology, social pathology, and political behavior. In seminars on such topics, a considerable amount of discussion is ordinarily devoted to psychoanalytic concepts concerning unconscious motivation, conflict, anxiety, and defense. But there is, nevertheless, a serious gap in the academic training of almost all research workers in the various fields of human behavior, because they do not have the opportunity to learn how to apply the observational methods of psychoanalysis, nor are they likely to have access to the raw data from psychoanalytic interviews. Very little training is available in the use of Freud's free-association technique as a research tool. Except in postdoctoral seminars and clinical conferences conducted by training analysts who are preparing psychiatrists to become certified psychoanalytic practitioners, practically no systematic instruction is offered concerning the way in which data obtained in psychoanalytic interviews can be used to discover, develop, and validate psychoanalytic hypotheses.

This gap in postgraduate university training is all the more remarkable because during the past twenty-five years there has been a growing preoccupation among behavioral scientists with problems of methodology. Already there is a sizable literature on the problems of drawing inferences from psychoanalytic case data. Here I refer to the contributions of Benjamin (1950), Ellis (1956), Frenkel-Brunswik (1954b), Hilgard (1952), Kubie (1947, 1952), and others.

Typically, the instructor in psychology or in some related field will scrutinize with his students various introductory and theoretical writings on psychoanalysis, without ever examining Freud's pioneering case studies of the adolescent hysteric, "Dora" (1905b); the first child analysis, "Little Hans" (1909a); the obsessional patient, referred to as the "Ratman" (1909b), and the patient with a persistent infantile neurosis, referred to as the "Wolfman" (1918). Nor are they likely to read any other basic case studies by Freud's co-workers or followers, such as the illuminating report on the analysis of a phobic child by Berta Bornstein (1949). But most trained psychoanalysts seem to agree that unless one studies such case reports, one can hardly begin to understand how the theoretical concepts and propositions of psychoanalysis grow out of the extraordinary clinical data obtained from the classical free-association interview.

This deficiency becomes painfully apparent in the writings of that growing species of psychologists who have a "double orientation" in psychoanalysis and experimental psychology. At most American universities, to be "oriented" in the latter field usually means not only that one has acquired a high degree of familiarity with current behavioral theories of learning, perception, and motivation, but also that one has a solid background in the research methods used to develop and test such theories. In contrast, to be "psychoanalytically oriented" all too often means that one has merely learned something about the *theoretical superstructure* without having any clear conception of the nature of the *empirical foundations* on which it is based. And yet, of all the theoretical concepts in the human sciences, those of psychoanalysis are probably the most difficult to comprehend without a thorough knowledge of the observations in which they are grounded.

It is extremely difficult for the present-day novice to gain a working knowledge of the observable responses in which psychoanalytic constructs are anchored unless he undergoes a personal analysis and then himself conducts psychoanalytic interviews under the supervision of a control analyst. (Cf. Fenichel [1941] and Freud [1933]. In part, the difficulty can be attributed to the inherent complications arising from the use of a depth interview technique which relies upon empathy and related subjective processes for understanding the unverbalized motivations of the interviewee. But it seems to me that much of the difficulty stems from the ambiguous and incomplete formulations which characterize the psychoanalytic literature.

The numerous abstract and metaphorical terms which Freud introduced into his writings on the nature of human motivation are notoriously lacking in precise definitions, and he very seldom took the trouble to specify how his constructs were linked with observables. Most of Freud's brilliant discoveries and theoretical insights are embedded in the ambiguous language of literary analogies. Even such basic terms as "repression" and "superego" are likely to be inadequately comprehended if everything one has read about these concepts is worded in the metaphorical terminology of "censors," "mental systems," "forces," and "agencies" operating inside a "psychical apparatus." Thus, on the one hand, a trained analyst can draw upon his own analytic experience for comprehending the key psychoanalytic concepts, and he can interpret them in terms of variables that can be assessed by observing a patient's verbal and nonverbal behavior during therapeutic sessions. But, on the other hand, after more than six decades of psychoanalytic research, the observational criteria have not yet been adequately formulated and are seldom referred to in the published literature, even though frequently a topic of oral discussion between supervising analysts and their trainees.

In a recent symposium on "psychoanalysis and scientific method," the main discussants express considerable disagreement about the research value of Freud's theoretical constructs, but they are in essential agreement in their criticisms concerning the lack of empirical referents in the formulation of the key constructs. Else Frenkel-Brunswik, a proponent of psychoanalysis and an outstanding contributor to psychoanalytic research, says this:

*Guided by some relatively fragmentary initial empirical observations,
Freud seems to have proceeded rather directly to the building of a hypothetical theoretical structure, with empirical interpretations lagging
somewhat behind; in the definition of such theoretical constructs as
superego, ego, and id, the major emphasis is on their structural relationships to one another rather than on their relationships to observation.*
(1954, p. 297)

The comments by B. F. Skinner, the well-known experimental psychologist, point toward a rather different conclusion but contain elabo-
rations of the same theme:

*The dynamic changes in behavior that are the first concern of the psy-
choanalyst are primarily changes in probability of action. But Freud
chose to deal with this aspect of behavior in other terms—as a question
of "libido," "cathexis," "volume of excitation," "instinctive or emotional
tendencies," "available quantities of psychic energy," and so on. . . .*

*In his emphasis upon the genesis of behavior Freud made extensive
use of processes of learning. These were never treated operationally in
terms of changes in behavior but rather as the acquisition of ideas,
feelings, and emotions later to be expressed by, or manifested in, behavior* (1954, p. 303).

In the absence of precise specifications of the observable perceptual,
symbolic, motor, and interpersonal behavior to which Freud's various
hypotheses refer, it is no wonder that many "doubly oriented" psychologists become bitterly surprised at the way their painstaking experimental investigations of so-called "unconscious" phenomena are
appraised by leading psychoanalysts. Such experimental research is
likely to be regarded by the latter as wholly irrelevant or trivial; the
hypotheses tested are often alleged to be the product of the typical
misunderstanding and naiveté that characterizes the beginner who
has not yet had any training or experience in psychoanalytic technique.

Probably it is partly because of the lack of opportunity to obtain
training in psychoanalytic techniques that so few psychologists study
the methodological aspects of psychoanalytic case research. During the
past two decades, many quasi-legal and professional obstacles have been
set up by the "official" psychoanalytic organizations in the United

States with the intent of restricting the practice of psychoanalytic therapy to the medical profession. Because it is impossible for anyone without an M.D. degree to become a member of the American Psychoanalytic Association, all lay-analysts, including many prominent clinicians trained in European Institutes, are generally regarded as "illicit" practitioners. This is an elementary political fact in the everyday professional world—and underworld—of clinical practice in psychotherapy. It has influenced American universities to avoid giving trainees in clinical psychology any courses on the application of psychoanalytic techniques to the treatment of emotional disorders. But this practical consideration offers no rationale whatsoever for the anomalous unfamiliarity with the psychoanalytic case-study method among research workers in psychology and the social sciences. As Benjamin, Grinker, Kubie, and other analysts have repeatedly pointed out, much misdirected time and energy is devoted to studying, developing, and evaluating all sorts of laboratory techniques and standardized tests that are intended to investigate "unconscious" processes by research workers who know hardly anything at all about the prime methods from which most present-day knowledge of psychodynamics is derived.

Fortunately, the lack of sophistication concerning the technical aspects of psychoanalysis is beginning to be corrected by a trend that has grown up in recent years mainly because of the efforts of a few leading training analysts who are aware of the need to provide adequate psychoanalytic instruction for experimentally oriented psychologists and for other research specialists in the human sciences. Certain of the major psychoanalytic institutes have begun admitting "research candidates" into their regular curriculum for medically qualified candidates, thus providing a small number of psychologists, biological scientists, and social scientists with the opportunity to obtain a didactic personal analysis, to participate in case seminars, and, in some instances, to conduct psychoanalytic treatment of control cases under the supervision of a training analyst. As a participant in one such training program, the present author became acutely aware of the differences between the training in psychoanalysis available to university graduate students and that offered to professional psychoanalytic trainees.

CONFLICTING STANDARDS AND TRADITIONS

Among the small percentage of research workers who have acquired, in one way or another, substantial training in the psychoanalytic case method, as well as in experimental research methods, a rather marked dilemma is likely to arise. Metaphorically speaking, there is a conflict between part of his "professional ego," which inclines the research worker to make use of his psychoanalytic orientation, and his "scientific superego," which demands adherence to the general methodological standards used in more rigorous fields of research. Consider, for example, the inner turmoil and embarrassment created in a research psychologist who conscientiously tries to make use of his "double orientation" in conducting a graduate seminar on personality dynamics or social psychology. From time to time the instructor will probably ask the group to examine specific empirical studies on such topics as attitude change, level of aspiration, rigidity of set, experimental neurosis, avoidance conditioning, induced frustration, social perception, and the like. In his role as instructor, he will try to convey to the students the essential features of sound research in his field by helping them to discern what is methodologically "good" and "bad" about the specific studies under discussion. Thus he may often point up the reasons for adhering to one or another of the fundamental norms of research workers in experimental psychology by calling sharp attention to the way in which deviations from the norms can give rise to misleading or erroneous conclusions. For illustrative purposes he may take pains to show that one experimenter's findings are open to question because of the sampling errors which can distort or obscure any comparisons between experimental and control groups; he may single out another study to show that an investigator's findings remain inconclusive because of failure to obtain reliable measurements or to apply the appropriate tests of statistical significance. Moreover, he will generally find himself striving to teach his students to be alert, not only to the most common errors in research design and statistical analysis, but also to defects in the way the research is reported. Thus he is likely to emphasize over and over again the importance of describing the procedures and the findings in such a way that (a) other investigators can replicate the findings by repeating the entire experiment; and (b) knowledgeable readers can examine critically the author's inferences from the findings to determine for themselves whether or not there are alternative interpretations warranting further theoretical analysis or further empirical investigation.

But then one day, after having sharpened his own and his students' knives, as critical dissectors of research, the instructor finds himself confronted with the task of trying to convey the need for equitable judgment to those students who are starting to view with a butcher's eye the field of psychoanalytic research. At first the conscientious instructor may find it easy to describe in general terms how Freud's free-association technique can be used to study unconscious processes that would otherwise remain almost completely inaccessible to scientific investigation; and he may go on to explain how intensive case studies employing this technique can be used to make new discoveries (or to confirm the discoveries of other psychoanalysts) concerning hidden motivational conflicts and dynamisms that account for hitherto unexplained behavior. Soon, however, the instructor will reach the point where he must hunt about for cogent documentation and illustrations of the personal convictions he has been expressing. And so he begins to search over the past six decades of psychoanalytic literature for case studies that meet the elementary standards of scientific reporting with respect to (a) describing the interview observations that are used to support the author's hypotheses, (b) stating explicitly the inferences that are drawn from the observations, (c) relating the inferences to other relevant observations made by other investigators using comparable observational methods, (d) formulating testable conclusions, and (e) indicating the qualifications imposed by the limitations of the available data.

As he engages in this search, looking over a generous sample of the major psychoanalytic journals and monographs, the instructor is likely to find many publications that could be used to illustrate effectively the *potential* scientific value of the provocative material to be found in psychoanalytic writings. His problem, however, is to select material which will be taken seriously as "evidence" by students who are becoming well trained in scientific method but who have not yet become familiar with the traditions of the psychoanalytic movement. Bearing in mind the fact that the young scientists under his tutelage will have had no firsthand experience with psychoanalytic phenomena, he would feel it to be a disservice to begin their methodological orientation in psychoanalysis with typical examples of deficient clinical reports. Such reports formulate tentative hypotheses as unqualified universal propositions and then refer to the propositions as "demonstrated" or "proved" after citing as crucial supporting evidence nothing more than a few anecdotes about the behavior of one, two, or some unspecified number of neurotic patients, culled from either the author's memory or from clinical notes which the author set down and subsequently examined in some unsystematic or unspecified way. In choosing psychoanalytic case material to present to his students, the instructor would want to use only those reports in which the observed verbal behavior of the patient is described or summarized. He would like to eliminate any clinical report that fails to give clearcut indications of which statements are about the interview data, which are propositions inferred from the data, and which are purely speculative remarks. He could not expect an audience trained in elementary scientific standards to be very receptive to any publication in which all three types of statements are formulated as though they are all matters of fact, especially if the statements are intermingled to such a degree throughout the entire report that even a thoroughly experienced analyst would have to use considerable ingenuity and imagination to guess which refer to empirical observations and which do not.

As the instructor continues his search for adequate publications to recommend to his students, he may find himself looking with an increasingly jaundiced eye at the psychoanalytic literature, noting the shortcomings with respect to the standards of scientific reporting, the casual manner in which many authors leap to universal generalizations from a single case, and, above all, the frequent failure to take account of the usual methods for trying to prevent the observer's conscious, preconscious, and unconscious sources of bias from influencing his observational reports. Prizing the valuable insights and discoveries afforded by psychoanalytic case studies, the instructor tends to ask himself how far he can allow himself to go with respect to overlooking gross methodological defects in the recording, analysis, and reporting of interview evidence.

As this dilemma becomes more and more acute, the instructor will become increasingly motivated to assuage his scientific conscience. Sometimes the attempted solution results in such a marked shift in values that it changes the instructor's primary professional affiliations. Here I am referring to those university-trained psychologists who partially abandon the scientific tradition by adopting special pleading for bold clinical insights. Their starting point is the commonly accepted premise that sometimes a scientific investigator should not be expected to restrict himself to drawing rigorous deductions from operationally defined postulates and from critically appraised facts; rather, he should be expected to permit himself freedom to make effective use of his intuitive and imaginative capacities. This rationale is obviously quite justified when applied to making judgments in connection with either inventing new theoretical concepts prior to designing a research study or arriving at practical decisions in clinical work. But it is sometimes offered as a general apology for abandoning the usual objective criteria for testing and validating intuitive or imaginative hypotheses. For some psychologists, scientific standards seem to apply to the study of all phenomena except "the unconscious"; psychoanalysis is thus kept immune from methodological criticism by an implicit assumption that it has a unique intuitive access to truth. To accept the latter assumption is equivalent to adopting a quasi-religious attitude of the kind which Freud vigorously attacked wherever he encountered it, both inside and outside the psychoanalytic movement. (Cf. E. Jones, 1955.) Among university psychologists, those inclined toward the cult of the "two truths" are, of course, few in number, because the inherent contradictions are likely to be exposed whenever their double standard becomes apparent to their university colleagues or students.

Even the most methodologically sophisticated instructor will sometimes be tempted to accept verbal formulas which temporarily alleviate but do not resolve the conflict. Perhaps the most popular solution is the doctrine that psychoanalytic interviews can be used to arrive at excellent hypotheses and theoretical leads, but can provide no acceptable evidence for testing or validating them. In the extreme, this view holds that the only value of the psychoanalytic interview lies in the fact it yields some interesting and significant propositions (never mind the fact that they come from observational data) which are worth reformulating and testing (by research workers who are not psychoanalysts) using objective methods (nonpsychoanalytic procedures that are "respectable"). Only when extrapsychoanalytic testing is done, according to this view, can psychoanalytic propositions about unconscious determinants of behavior be regarded as scientifically acceptable; otherwise, the propositions derived from psychoanalytic interview data are simply unverified guesses, i.e., speculative statements that are in essentially the same class as quotations from the more insightful metaphysicians and poets. The proponents of this view may be growing in numbers because, I suspect, they rather seldom encounter anyone who is prepared to challenge them. And unchallenged, their main assumption sounds quite attractive, viz., that the observations of a patient's verbalizations in the situation of interaction with the analyst might often provide fruitful theoretical leads but can never provide reproducible empirical data that are open to consensual validation by independent (trained) observers.

In current psychological research a number of objective research methods are being developed—including direct behavioral observations of spontaneous activities, experimental implantation of conflict by hypnotic procedures, tests of perceptual distortion, and various measures of latent attitudes—some of which should be capable of contributing highly reliable and valid data for testing many psychoanalytic hypotheses. Many psychologists maintain that such methods offer the *only* means for obtaining acceptable evidence bearing on unconscious phenomena; nevertheless, they seem to agree that psychoanalytic discoveries are of great potential scientific value and that considerable time and energy should be devoted to validating them. For those who accept this position, there are some embarrassing questions which remain to be answered. For instance: How does it happen that a method which yields supposedly worthless evidence continues to be a useful source of supposedly worth-while scientific discoveries? Granted that the process of discovery can be sharply differentiated from the process of verification and that one is free to arrive at new hypotheses from any source: How does this particular source of hypotheses happen to have such a high degree of success? How can one maintain that the numerous propositions about human motivation, reported by psychoanalysts on the basis of free associations from their patients, are *not* based on at least partially acceptable empirical data, if one claims to value the inferences because a reasonably high percentage will turn out to be validated by (acceptable) objective methods? How is it possible for a nonempirical or invalid method of inquiry to do much better than chance in predicting verifiable cause and effect relations? Such questions as these are perhaps the simplest antidote against the inclination to relegate the products of the psychoanalytic case method to the realm of uncanny prophecies.

IMPROVING THE CASE METHOD

In recent years, a number of psychoanalysts have begun to examine critically the techniques and traditions of psychoanalytic case research from the standpoint of improving their methods and increasing the scientific status of their findings. For example, Lawrence Kubie (1947, 1952) has constructively examined some major methodological deficiencies in psychoanalytic case reports, calling attention especially to the consequences of failing to keep adequate records of interview sessions. John Benjamin (1950) has also discussed numerous methodological problems in the validation of psychoanalytic theory and has concluded that the psychoanalytic case method is "more *subjective than it need be*." He points out that there are some obvious limitations which need to be taken into account, such as the fact that the interplay between the analyst's interpretations and the patient's associations introduces an effect of the observer upon the observed. For the purpose of increasing the objectivity of the case method, he offers two main suggestions: (1) "that better protocols of psychoanalytic interviews than are now available would strengthen both the heuristic and the verificatory aspects of the . . . method" and (2) that "the method itself be carefully examined for possible techniques which could increase its relative objectivity and accessibility to critical scrutiny without sacrificing its unique heuristic qualities." (Benjamin, 1950, p. 144)

In line with the above comments, it could be said that there are additional methodological shortcomings, repeatedly emphasized by some of Freud's scientific critics, which also make psychoanalytic research findings more questionable than they need be. Some of the important difficulties center on the fact that even the most thorough psychoanalytic investigations are based exclusively on patients who have been able to obtain intensive therapy. Not only are the samples limited to one or a handful of cases, but the entire series of research studies bearing on any given psychological problem are likely to be limited to persons who represent only a very small substratum of the total urban population. It is a well-known fact that during the 1950's the vast majority of psychoanalytic patients in the United States have been well-educated neurotics who can afford to pay an analyst at least $15 or $20 per session, four or five times every week, for two or more years.

There is an obvious need for deliberate and concerted effort to replicate the initial findings of each psychoanalytic investigation with a wide variety of additional cases from different social strata. The feasibility of such replication seems to have increased during the past decade. At present there are thousands of neurotic patients undergoing treatment with well-trained analysts. Despite the high concentration on upper-income levels, the total population of analysands includes several hundred low-income patients, many of whom are being charged minimal fees at psychoanalytic clinics. And there are also hundreds of relatively "normal" persons, who, as psychiatric candidates, are undergoing psychoanalysis for training purposes (cf. Knight, 1953). Professional census statistics, presented by Knight in his Presidential Address to the American Psychoanalytic Association at the end of 1952, indicate that during that year there were 996 postdoctoral students affiliated with eleven "official" psychoanalytic institutes in the United States. The current crop of students, according to Knight, differs greatly from that of the 1920's and 1930's:

. . . *perhaps the majority of students of the past decade or so have been* "normal" *characters . . . not so introspective, inclined to read only the literature that is assigned in institute courses. . . . [with] interests [that] are primarily clinical rather than research and theoretical. Their motivation for being analyzed is more to get through this requirement of training than to overcome neurotic suffering in themselves or to explore introspectively and with curiosity their own inner selves. (Knight, 1953, p. 219)*

Since most psychoanalytic practitioners are affiliated with national and/or international professional organizations, it should not prove to be extraordinarily difficult to mobilize the research potential of those psychoanalytic observers who have the requisite methodological training. In the future, as research training becomes more extensive, it should be possible to alert those psychoanalysts with research interests to the need for objective replication as well as discovery; they would thus be motivated to keep systematic records and to pool their data occasionally so that at least a few research studies may have the benefit of the collaboration of several analysts who are separately making comparable interview observations, using mutually agreed-upon criteria for investigating the same clinical or theoretical problem. For the long run, then, it seems realistic to expect that repeated observations can be made which will provide replications of observations bearing on the causes and consequences of unconscious conflicts, motives, memories, and fantasies. Although large and representative samples may be unobtainable, it should be possible to have crucial replications carried out more or less independently by numerous trained psychoanalytic observers in many different parts of the world, with samples including persons of different cultural and ethnic backgrounds from diverse socioeconomic strata.

In addition to the difficulties of gathering reliable facts from adequate samples, there are several special problems of case reporting. Some of these have been alluded to in Kubie's and Benjamin's general comments about the need for greater objectivity; they are of central importance for attaining what Kris (1947) has referred to as "semantic clarification." Among the most crucial problems are those of giving accurate and unambiguous summaries of the extensive interview data on which the psychoanalytic case findings are based.

In order to test certain of the most complicated psychoanalytic propositions, it will undoubtedly be necessary to develop reliable quantitative techniques of semantical-content analysis that can be applied systematically in interview protocols. (Cf. Auld and Murray, 1955; Dollard and Auld, 1955; Janis, 1943; Lasswell, 1938.) Before such an enterprise can lead to successful means for testing significant hypotheses, however, a great many major obstacles must be overcome, the most important of which involve the problems of translating major psychoanalytic constructs into objective terms that are unambiguously connected with the raw data of psychoanalytic observations. To begin with, the most feasible content-analysis procedures probably will be those which enable the analytic investigator to test *short-term predictions* concerning his patient's verbal behavior. For example, many hypotheses concerning the differential effects of a given type of analytic intervention on transference attitudes, fantasies, and defenses can be tested by (a) systematically studying the content of the patient's associations in the two or three sessions following each instance when the given type of intervention was used, and (b) comparing the content-analysis results with those obtained in similar sessions following comparable instances when other types of intervention were used. After content-analysis techniques have been developed for the study of short-term changes in behavior, it will probably be much easier to work out appropriate modifications to apply to longer series of sessions and thus to extend the systematic investigations to *long-term* changes.

Even when the observer is merely trying to summarize some of the most elementary data concerning unconscious phenomena obtained from psychoanalytic interviews, a number of special requirements should be regarded as essential for indicating the status of the evidence. In continuous case seminars conducted at psychoanalytic institutes, sharp disagreements sometimes occur among experienced analysts, as well as among the trainees, regarding such questions as the following: What evidence, if any, shows the analyst to be correct in surmising that a patient's politely worded complaints about him at the beginning of the session are indicative of unconscious hostility? Can a patient's fragmentary recollections of a childhood sexual experience in the associations given to a dream be regarded as a genuine memory? Intense debates are occasionally provoked if a reporting analyst happens to make grossly incomplete observational statements which refer more or less vaguely to only a fragment of the evidence from which he has made his inferences. His judgment is likely to be quesitoned, for example, if he makes the mistake of confining his remarks to such generalizations as, "The patient was outwardly friendly and deferential but made criticisms of the analyst which reflect latent negative transference," or "His associations led to the recovery of a memory of childhood masturbation." In the course of a seminar dispute, the reporting analyst usually amplifies his remarks by citing a great many detailed observations, and sometimes his evidence is sufficiently clear-cut to convince everyone present that he had, in fact, encountered a genuine instance of negative transference or that his patient was recalling an actual childhood event.

Despite exposure to numerous seminar experiences of this kind, however, most psychoanalytic writers continue to fill their published case reports with vague and ambiguous statements, taking no cognizance of the need to describe what was actually observed with sufficient clarity and in sufficient detail to convey the status of their case evidence to fellow analysts (even omitting from consideration the problems of communicating the positive and negative features of the evidence to a more general audience of students of psychology, psychiatry, and the social sciences).

Perhaps the simplest way to illustrate the gross ambiguities that occur in psychoanalytic case studies is to consider a typical statement concerning the "reconstruction" of a childhood memory. An analyst may assert, for instance, that his psychoanalytic investigation indicates the patient had undergone a specific type of traumatic experience at a certain period of childhood. In making such an assertion, the analyst may mean any of at least six different things so far as the nature of his evidence is concerned:

1. The patient *spontaneously recalled* the specific event during one or more psychoanalytic sessions, and, in addition to displaying *behavioral and verbal consistency*, the patient also produced or described *independent external evidence* (e.g., a contemporary newspaper clipping, or a family letter) to verify the event. (Cf. Maria Bonaparte's, 1945, famous example of the use of independent evidence in verifying a primal scene memory.)

2. No external verification was available, but the patient *spontaneously recalled* the event during one or more analytic sessions while displaying consistent *behavioral signs* of genuine recollection and, at other times in the analysis, gave numerous associations which were *internally consistent* with respect to the specific content of the "memory." (Cf. the comments about laughter, blushing, transitory somatic symptoms, and signs of internal consistency with respect to the patient's productions during psychoanalytic sessions in the discussion by Ferenczi [1916]).

3. No external verification of the event was available, and the patient did not spontaneously recall it but gave *confirmatory postintervention associations,* such as the recollection of "new memories which complete and extend the construction" after the analyst had communicated his conjectures about the event on the basis of the patient's (preintervention) associations. (Cf. Freud's, 1932, account of the criteria for confirmatory associations in judging the validity of psychoanalytic interpretations.)

4. No external verification of the event was available, the patient did not spontaneously recall it, and after the analyst had communicated a reconstruction of the memory, the patient's (postintervention) associations were too ambiguous to be regarded as confirmatory; nevertheless, there were numerous *specific "derivatives" in the preintervention associations,* from which the analyst inferred that the patient actually had undergone and retained the experience, even though it remained inaccessible to awareness. By "derivatives" is meant verbalizations that are derived from repressed memories and impulses, symbolically expressed by means of "associatively connected ideas that are less objectionable to the conscious ego" (Fenichel, 1945, p. 17). (Cf. also Freud's illustrations of the way free associations are used to infer those crucial childhood events which "are as a rule not reproduced as recollections, but have to be divined—constructed—gradually and laboriously from an aggregate of indications." (Freud, 1918, p. 524)

5. No positive evidence was obtained with respect to any of the various criteria referred to in paragraph 4; nevertheless, after a careful retrospective examination of his detailed case notes, the analyst judged —on the basis of his knowledge derived from the psychoanalytic literature and from his own experience with similar cases—that it was plausible to postulate the given traumatic experience (as a hypothetical "construction") because it appeared not only to account for otherwise unexplained psychoanalytic observations but also *fitted in consistently with all known facts about the patient's life history and personality development.* (Cf. the comments by Isaacs, 1939, concerning the way analysts attempt to confirm or modify their conclusions about the meaning of a patient's story about past events by observing the consistencies and variations in the patient's repetitions of the story during successive phases of the analysis.)

6. No evidence at all can be cited, but when he thought retrospectively about the treatment of the patient, the analyst had a *general clinical hunch or impression* which inclined him to postulate the particular childhood memory; although the analyst made no attempt to examine the case notes in detail (or had not recorded any), he had a general sense that the postulated memory fit in well with his global recollections of the psychoanalytic case material. (Cf. the discussions by Brierly, 1951, and Reik, 1949, on the importance of "empathy" and "intuitive" processes.)

The above six categories are not exhaustive but merely represent some typical combinations of the following *eight criteria* which appear to be the main criteria used to evaluate any psychoanalytic observer's hypothesis asserting that the patient had experienced a given childhood event: (1) spontaneous recall of the event during one or more analytic sessions; (2) independent external evidence of the event; (3) consistent behavioral signs of the genuineness of the recollections bearing on the event; (4) internal consistency of the recollections bearing on the event; (5) specific (symbolic) "derivatives" of the event in preintervention associations; (6) confirmatory associations after the analyst's intervention focused attention on the inferred event; (7) over-all consistency of the inferred event with respect to the entire set of case-history data; (8) the observer's global clinical impression of the plausibility of the inferred event. The eight criteria can occur, of course, in many other combinations in addition to those described in the six categories. The latter were selected to highlight one simple fact about psychoanalytic findings, which is sometimes difficult to grasp from reading psychoanalytic reports, namely, that *the supporting evidence can range from being very substantial to very flimsy.* The first category (p. 164), for example, comes close to meeting the criteria of reliability and validity that most legal experts and historians require for deciding that an alleged event had actually occurred. At the other end of the scale, however, the last category would be evaluated by most analysts (as well as by most research workers in other fields) as useful only for arriving at new hypotheses about a patient's unconscious processes, but of such questionable reliability and validity that it offers very little empirical weight to the analyst's conjectural reconstruction. In other words, an analyst's over-all recollections and impressions of his unrecorded psychoanalytic observations would be regarded, at best, as increasing the empirical probability of the reconstruction by a barely noticeable difference over what it would be if the analyst had merely indulged in crude armchair speculation based solely on the obvious clinical diagnostic facts regarding the onset and development of the patient's emotional disorder, without taking any account whatsoever of the patient's free associations.

The criteria discussed above are formulated with reference to the problem of reconstructing childhood memories; but similar criteria (with some modifications in wording, especially concerning the nature of external verification) would apply to other major types of constructions inferred from psychoanalytic data: e.g., unconscious fantasies, the latent content of dreams, and the infantile impulses and defenses that enter into transference reactions and that determine the "meaning" of symptoms.

Ultimately, with other improvements in the methods of psychoanalytic case-study research, more refined categories for specifying the status of the evidence will undoubtedly be developed to take account of differential degrees of reliability and validity.

The general scientific status of psychoanalytic findings undoubtedly would be quite different today if—after the first few decades of major discoveries—participants in the psychoanalytic movement had paid more attention to legitimate scientific criticisms concerning problems of sampling, replication, and accurate reporting. After all, during the many years since Freud made his last case study, there must have been tens of thousands of persons all over the world who have had psychoanalytic treatment, from whom the data could have been obtained that is needed for testing and developing Freud's verifiable hypotheses. Perhaps the next few decades will bring much greater research productivity and a growing realization that the mere reinforcement of an esoteric oral tradition, however valuable for purposes of clinical training, nevertheless contributes little in the direction of achieving the major scientific goals toward which Freud directed his entire life work.

EXPANDING THE SCOPE OF PSYCHOANALYTIC RESEARCH

Up to the present time, the contributions to psychological theory made by psychoanalytic case research have been concentrated mainly in two areas: (1) the development of the human personality from infancy through adolescence and (2) the dynamics of unconscious motives, defenses, and conflicts underlying the neuroses and other personality disorders. In recent years psychoanalytic interview observations have been restricted almost exclusively to problems of psychopathology and therapy. From the standpoint of developing general psychological principles, the primary value of this research is that it furnishes data which help to account for *developmental sequences* and *individual differences* in personality characteristics and adjustive or maladjustive behavior. Psychoanalytic case studies have revealed a great deal about the structure and genesis of *personality predispositions* (e.g., deeply ingrained emotional habits derived from childhood experiences) which incline a person to have high or low tolerance for specific types of frustrations, which make for high or low ability to cope with the usual demands of the adult social world and which make for psychological symptoms that are amenable or unamenable to psychological treatment. In the context of studying how chronic predispositions are developed, much attention continues to be devoted to situational events in childhood, notably traumatic experiences and recurring crises which appear to play a significant formative role in neurotic personalities. But situational events in adult life are rarely investigated by psychoanalysts except insofar as they function as "precipitating" or "contributing" factors in the onset of symptoms among pathologically predisposed personalities.

Freud's earliest work was not so sharply restricted to investigating predispositional aspects of abnormal behavior. Many of his researches were directed toward understanding various types of reactions to environmental situations which he selected for investigation because of their general psychological interest, quite aside from any connection with psychopathology. Included in his studies on the psychology of dreams, for instance, were inquiries concerning the normal changes in fantasy activity which take place under conditions of sleep, from which he inferred mediating processes involving a reduction in internal censorship. (Cf. Freud, 1900.) Similarly, normal psychological reactions evoked by various classes of social stimuli occupied Freud's attention in his studies of grief (1917), humor (1905a), idealization of leaders, social conformity, and related topics (1921). In his monograph on *Wit and the Unconscious* (1905a), for example, Freud was attempting to discern a mediating psychological process that occurs in all normal adults —in this instance, one that could account for the pleasure produced by certain types of interpersonal communications (jokes, wit, the comic). However, on the negative side, it must be said that Freud frequently failed to give an adequate account of the psychoanalytic interview evidence which he presumably used to evaluate his insightful hypotheses. Except for his detailed monograph on the psychology of dreams, (1900), in which he draws upon data from his clinical practice, Freud's writings on normal processes rarely refer to any specific evidence from psychoanalytic investigations of his patients. In his contributions on humor, group behavior, and other normal aspects of adult life, he rarely cites anything more than some anecdotal examples from his own pioneering efforts at self-analysis or from his incidental (nonpsychoanalytic) observations of friends and acquaintances in daily life. Other psychoanalysts who discuss these same psychological problems seem to follow Freud's example with respect to omitting detailed presentation of pertinent case-study material from their patients. Only very fragmentary material bearing on the problems of normal personality dynamics can be found in those reports that attempt to describe or summarize the data obtained from psychoanalytic interviews.

In published case reports, detailed accounts are sometimes given of current situational factors in relation to the patient's nonpathological fantasy productions (e.g., hypnogogic reveries) and parapraxes (e.g., slips of speech and forgetting of names). But here again, the central interest is much the same as in studies concerning the role of the current reality situation in the production of abnormal symptoms: Most carefully examined is the type of case material on "the psychopathology of everyday life," which helps to illuminate the nature of the pathological processes involved in neuroses, character disorders, or psychoses. The only other situational stimuli of adult life that have been extensively discussed in psychoanalytic case reports are those pertaining to the interaction between analyst and patient (problems of effective therapeutic technique and the psychology of transference and counter-transference). Even in this limited area much of the interest has been centered on understanding the relation between interview stimuli and changes in neurotic attitudes and symptoms. Thus psychoanalytic interview data continue to be reported almost exclusively for the purpose of increasing knowledge about psychopathology or about ways of modifying the personality predispositions which give rise to psychopathological disorders.

A large number of important scientific problems outside the field of psychopathology remain to be investigated by the psychoanalytic method. Social scientists in many different fields of research have repeatedly suggested that the scope of psychoanalytic inquiry could be fruitfully broadened to include relatively neglected aspects of interpersonal relations, creativity, and normal emotional reactions in which unconscious factors may play just as important a role as in neurosis. (Cf., for example, H. D. Lasswell's *Power and Personality*, 1948; J. Dollard, 1938, on social class factors; N. C. Leites, 1948, on studies of national character; C. Kluckhohn, 1949, on psychocultural hypotheses.)

Within the psychoanalytic movement itself there seems to be a growing recognition of the need to broaden the scope of psychoanalytic case studies, especially in connection with the problems of elucidating the "conflict-free functions of the ego" and the role of successful "sublimations" in coping with restrictions of the social environment. (Cf. H. Hartmann, 1951.) Specialists in psychoanalysis as well as in bordering disciplines are beginning to devote more attention to intensive case-study materials bearing on the environmental conditions of adult life which affect stress tolerance and the "creative" and "healthy" features of normal adjustment. (Cf., E. H. Erikson, 1950, and R. White, 1952.) A few pioneering psychoanalytic studies concerning the effects of environmental events have appeared. For example, Sterba (1946, 1947) has described the way his patients reacted to two outstanding news events: the Detroit race riots in 1943 and the death of President Roosevelt in 1944. Glover (1942) has summarized the comments obtained from a group of British analysts concerning how their patients reacted to the Munich war-scare crisis in 1938 and to the air blitz of 1941;

Melitta Schmideberg (1942) has described her patients' reactions to the evacuation of London and to the dangers of the air blitz; Helene Deutsch (1942) has discussed her patients' reactions to surgical operations. Many valuable hypotheses concerning unconscious and preconscious aspects of normal reactions to environmental events are contained in these reports, but the pertinent case material is generally compressed into a few summarizing statements or given only in the form of illustrative anecdotes.

At the present time, it seems warranted to repeat once again the suggestion that detailed case reports should be devoted to a broader scope of inquiry in the field of human behavior. Perhaps this suggestion will have a better chance of being implemented if accompanied by examples which call the attention of psychoanalytic investigators to the potential value of studying various nonpathological aspects of their analysands' reactions. Probably the most useful material will come from studies which focus on those environmental variables known from other fields of research to have significant psychological or social effects. In the current life situation of persons undergoing analysis, important events occur from time to time which may provide unique opportunities for studying variables of general scientific interest, even though the occurrences may have relatively little or no connection with the patient's neurosis or with his therapeutic process. By observing the impact of such environmental variables upon the patient's fantasies and free associations, an analyst may be able to discover *latent motivational processes* which are not likely to be revealed by other methods of investigation.

To give a specific illustration: Suppose that during psychoanalytic treatment a patient (or a psychoanalytic trainee) suddenly finds himself promoted to an executive or policy-making position (e.g., in a business organization or a hospital), and, for the first time in his career, he is given considerable administrative power and responsibility. By observing how the analysand reacts to his new position, the analyst has the opportunity not only to see whether or not the patient is "wrecked by success" and to learn more about his personality strengths and weaknesses; but he may also discover something about the psychological effects of the demands and prerogatives associated with the administrative role. The analyst's observations could contribute a great deal toward the understanding of mediating processes which help to explain how the assumption of a power position gives rise to marked shifts in ideological beliefs, alterations in appraisals of strategic persons within the power hierarchy, and changes in the individual's self-conceptions, personal values, and aspirations. Certain of the effects noted in the particular case may be uniquely determined by the patient's specific combination of social skills, group affiliations, ideological preferences, and personality predispositions; but at least a few of the individual's psychological changes are likely to be generalizable in the sense that they might prove to be typical of a delimited group of persons who share a common social background or who possess a specifiable constellation of personality characteristics. Some of the individual's reactions might even prove to have such a high degree of generality that the psychoanalytic data could help to explain what happens to the motives, values, and covert attitudes of a very high percentage of administrators or other power holders in modern society.

If a sizable number of analysts were to investigate comparable instances of upward power mobility in one of their patients, it would be possible to discover and partially test a number of significant hypotheses about regularities in the impact of power roles on certain types of personalities, on the average individual in a given subculture, and perhaps even on the average individual in Western civilization. (Cf. the discussion above, pp. 160-162, concerning the possibilities of building up large samples of psychoanalytic cases and of replicating case-study findings in subjects from various social strata in different countries.)

In general, the fields of social psychology, sociology, and political science could be greatly benefited by the use of depth interview data from psychoanalytic case studies concerning the effects (preconscious and unconscious) or many different types of social stimuli. The following examples, each of which pertains to a limited aspect of normal interaction, will serve to illustrate some of the nonpathological features of social behavior that may be illuminated by psychoanalytic data:

1. What are the long-term changes displayed by persons who, during an analysis of three or four years' duration, enter a new environmental situation involving a marked shift in social role or status? Among the specific topics warranting longitudinal case study, in addition to the example of changes in power status just discussed, are the effects of (a)

entering the ranks of independent wage earners after being an econom-
ically and socially dependent student; (b) becoming a recognized member of a large industrial or professional organization; (c) attaining a
leadership position within a dissident (or counterelite) minority fac-
tion that is attempting to influence the policies of a political organization; (e) being appointed to a key juridical position within the community.

2. What are the immediate and subsequent motivational effects of
various types of influential communications to which people are frequently exposed in daily life? Aside from the special problems of studying the impact of the analyst's communications, there are opportunities for observing how analysands react when a powerful impression has
been made on them by persuasive communications from persons in
their own primary groups or from the mass media. For example, an
analysand may become agitated by urgent requests for his time and
energy from a close friend who wants help or from a superior who
wants greater work output. Guilt, resentment, empathy, and other reactions to such stimulation may clearly emerge during analytic sessions
and may illuminate some of the complex motivational factors which
determine whether interpersonal influences will be accepted or rejected.
Similarly, there are unique opportunities to observe the ego processes
that enter into attitude change when the analysand, while on the
couch, is mentally and emotionally working over a stirring news an-
nouncement, an affect-arousing propaganda broadcast, or an insight-
producing movie (e.g., concerning such provocative topics as the Su-
preme Court decision on racial desegregation, or the prospects of avert-
ing the devastation of a future atomic war). By taking account of the
patient's comments, deliberations, and ruminations about the communications, together with his related affective reactions and chains of free
associations, one should be able to discern some of the more subtle
dynamisms that explain how social communications can create new
cognitive beliefs, modify social prejudices, and provoke ideological
conversions.

3. What are the short-run and long-run effects of various "oppor-
tune circumstances" and "incentives" which are commonly assumed to
foster original thinking and high productivity among persons in scientific, technological, and managerial positions? Included in this area

would be problems concerning psychological effects pertaining to the success or failure of (a) administrative policies which are designed to foster high intellectual achievement among research workers, engineers, military planners, legal experts, or other intellectually skilled groups (e.g., What happens to the motivations of an inventor or author who is granted unusual forms of autonomy—"freedom" to choose his own work assignments, to decide upon his own work schedule, or to determine the frequency and content of conferences with co-workers and consultants?); (b) patterns of group organization which are intended to facilitate effective collaboration on intellectual problems requiring creative group solutions (e.g., What types of emotional and adjustive responses facilitate or interfere with intellectual productivity under different conditions of participation in interdisciplinary scientific or technological teams? What types of leadership practices increase or decrease cooperation among persons having initially divergent group identifications and divergent ideological commitments?)

4. Under what conditions are adjustive responses to external dangers and socially induced stresses facilitated, and under what conditions are such responses impaired to such a degree that panic or temporary emotional disorganization occurs? This category includes numerous sources of disruptive stimuli associated with the dangers of pain, body damage, and physical annihilation. Incidentally, in some of my own research on these problems, I have had the opportunity to make use of psychoanalytic-interview data on reactions to surgery in order to arrive at a series of general hypotheses concerning psychological stress. (Cf. Janis, 1958). There are also other types of stress situations, involving acute social dangers and socially imposed frustrations, which could be investigated as they arise in the current life situation of persons undergoing psychoanalysis. (E.g., What situational factors increase or decrease the individual's ability to cope effectively with loss of economic security, with the threat of downward social mobility, and with similar social dangers?)

The above four general topics obviously do not begin to exhaust the nonpathological aspects of human life which warrant intensive psychological study. They are offered only to suggest a variety of examples which may help to concretize the proposal that the psychoanalytic case method should be more frequently and more systematically directed toward understanding the cognitive and motivational processes which mediate the normal behavioral impact of significant environmental variables.

The suggestion that the effects of situational events in adult life should be carefully studied is based on the simple assumption that such events can play a more or less important role, in interaction with predispositional variables, as determinants of changes in adult attitudes and behavior. This suggestion does not carry any implications with respect to the debatable issues raised by Kurt Lewin (1935), Karen Horney (1937), and numerous anti-Freudian critics concerning the relative causal importance of *current* reality factors as compared with predispositional factors which are the product of *past* experiences. Studies of the impact of current events do not necessarily minimize the importance of past experiences. On the contrary, researches concerning the sustained effects of exposure to wartime dangers and to many other types of adult experience often highlight the crucial importance of latent reaction tendencies which are the residues of childhood experiences (cf. Glover, 1942; Janis, 1951, 1958; Schmideberg, 1942).

Of course, when an important event occurs in the life of a patient, the analyst often does not obtain clear indications of how the patient's daily activities have been affected and, in the absence of information from outside sources, he can only guess at how the patient's overt behavior has changed in relation to other people. The analyst would therefore have to confine his case studies on the effects of environmental variables largely to the changes in emotional reactions, attitudes, fantasies, and other such aspects of behavior that are directly observable during psychoanalytic sessions. The opportunity to obtain case-study data of general scientific interest can not be expected to arise in the treatment of every psychoanalytic patient. Moreover, the practical demands and therapeutic objectives of professional clinical work might sometimes prevent the analyst from obtaining systematic interview records of even those rare sessions which contain important data pertinent to understanding the psychological impact of a current environmental event. Nevertheless, it is likely that many more case-study contributions in this field would be forthcoming if the majority of practicing analysts (including those in private practice as well as those who are affiliated with a research-oriented clinic or university department) were to become more aware of the possible ways of using their daily interview sessions for research purposes.

Because the potential research contribution of clinical practitioners is becoming increasingly recognized by postgraduate medical schools and psychiatric institutes, excellent instruction in research methods is now becoming available for many psychiatric trainees, some of whom will subsequently go on to receive psychoanalytic training. Moreover, since several of the major psychoanalytic institutes have begun making their training available to research specialists in psychology and related fields, there is some reason to expect a substantial increase in the number of well-trained investigators who will be adequately equipped to conduct psychoanalytic case research.

VALUE OF PSYCHOANALYSIS FOR STUDYING
MEDIATING PROCESSES

In terms of the stimulus-response vocabulary frequently used in current behavioral research, the most general explanatory propositions concerning the dynamics of environmentally induced behavior can be schematized as taking the following form: For all human organisms (or for some general class of predisposed people), the occurrence of a given stimulus situation or event will tend to evoke temporary or sustained changes in internal processes—including changes in motivational states, attitudes, fantasies, and other response-produced stimuli—which mediate a delimited class of observable reactions. By carrying out research that is oriented toward formulating and testing hypotheses about mediating motivational variables, the likelihood is increased that the data will contribute to more precise propositions that specify the observable factors (environmental stimuli and indicators of personal dispositions) which are necessary conditions for the occurrence of a given type of observable behavior. (Cf. the discussion of mediating variables and constructs in the writings of Brunswik, 1952; Hempel, 1952; Spence, 1948; and Tolman, 1949.)

Research on mediating processes usually begins after an S-R or antecedent-consequent relation has been established on the basis of behavioral observations. Sometimes the mediating symbolic or affective responses are available to consciousness and hence may be investigated by a variety of standard research techniques, including focalized interviews and attitude questionnaires. But, when attempting to study some of the more subtle aspects of human motivation, one must expect to find that the mediating internal responses will prove to be partially or wholly unconscious.

The main advantage of psychoanalytic observations, compared with other observational methods, is that during the interviews a variety of verbal associations, affective changes, and other behavioral manifestations can be observed which facilitate inferences about unconscious emotional impulses, attitudes, anticipations, fantasies, and other mediating response-produced stimuli not ordinarily available to consciousness. After all, most psychologists feel that the objective personality tests, projective techniques, and other observational devices currently available cannot be compared with the intensive procedures of psychoanalysis as a method for investigating the deepest layers of the human personality and for obtaining detailed personal information concerning the impact of past and present events on the inner life of the individual. (Cf. Hilgard, 1952.) While many other observational techniques can be used to study the same basic antecedent-consequent relations, they do not afford as great an opportunity for microscopic study of unconscious and preconscious processes.

More specifically, psychoanalytic case research has the following main assets: The technique of free association elicits observable verbal responses in which fantasies, wishes, and conflicts are expressed that are not subject to reliable self-observation and that are ordinarily withheld from the observation of others. Both the form and the content of each patient's verbal responses can be investigated in the light of empirical generalizations and theoretical assumptions based on prior psychoanalytic observations of other cases. Furthermore, the observations of each analysand are made during hundreds of sessions, so that if a given emotional or symbolic response appears to be a reaction to a given inner or outer stimulus, the relation can be checked by obtaining comparable observations from many sessions with the same subject. In the course of two or more years of psychoanalytic sessions, the observer becomes thoroughly familiar with the personality of the subject; thus he can more easily distinguish those reactions which are highly dependent upon the occurrences of external stimuli from those that are not.

It is the combination of these particular features that gives the psychoanalytic case method its unique status in the human sciences. With regard to studying the impact of environmental events, the essential point is that the analyst is sometimes in a position to observe repeated instances where (a) the given patient is currently exposed to a specified type of impressive situational event; (b) he gives clear-cut indications (which meet the minimal criteria for accepting retrospective verbal reports) that in his daily life he is displaying manifest attitudes and actions which are overt reactions to the event, and (c) while talking about the event he also displays various affective responses and sequences of verbal associations which are indicators of internal mediating processes. Thus a large sample of behavioral instances may be obtained from which to infer a causal sequence for the particular individual.

An obvious weakness of a single case study, which has already been mentioned, is that it can provide no indication whether the findings apply to all other, many other, a few other, or no other human beings. But it seems to me that the problem of obtaining objective replications probably can be solved, along the lines I have indicated in this paper. Consequently, I will venture the prediction that in the long run, psychoanalytic-research contributions to the general problems of explaining how "normal" adults react to environmental changes will prove to have as much or perhaps more value for the human sciences than those devoted to clinical problems and psychopathology.

REFERENCES

Auld, F., and Murray, E. Content analysis studies of psychotherapy, *Psychol. Bull.*, 1955, 52, 377-395.

Benjamin, J. Methodological considerations in the validation and elaboration of psychoanalytic personality theory. *Amer. J. Orthopsychiat.*, 1950, 20, 139-155.

Bonaparte, Marie. Notes on the analytic discovery of a primal scene. *Psy-*

choanalytic study of the child. Vol. I. New York: Int. Univ. Press, 1945. Pp. 119-127.

Bornstein, Berta. The analysis of a phobic child. Some problems of theory and technique in child analysis. *Psychoanalytic study of the child.* Vols. III-IV. New York: Int. Univ. Press, 1949. Pp. 181-226.

Brierly, Marjorie. *Trends in psychoanalysis.* London: Hogarth, 1951.

Brunswik, E. The conceptual framework of psychology. *Int. encycl. of unified sci.* Vol. I, No. 10. Chicago: University of Chicago Press, 1952.

Deutsch, Helene. Some psychoanalytic observations in surgery. *Psychosom. Med.,* 1942, 4, 105-115.

Dollard, J. The life history in community studies. *Amer. Sociol. Rev.,* 1938, 3, 724-737.

————, and Auld, F. *Development of quantitive methods for detailed study of psychotherapy hours.* 1955. Report on Project M-648, U.S. Public Health Service Grant. (Mimeo.)

Ellis, A. An operational reformulation of some of the basic principles of psychoanalysis. In H. Feigl and M. Scriven (eds.), *The foundations of science and the concepts of psychology and psychoanalysis.* Minneapolis: University of Minnesota Press, 1956. Pp. 131-154.

Erikson, E. H. *Childhood and Society.* New York: Norton, 1950.

Fenichel, O. *Problems of psychoanalytic technique.* (Trans. by D. Brunswick.) Albany, N.Y.: Psychoanalytic Quarterly, Inc., 1941.

————. *The psychoanalytic theory of neurosis.* New York: Norton, 1945.

Ferenczi, S. Transitory symptom-constructions during the analysis. In *Sex in psychoanalysis.* Boston: Badger, 1916.

Frenkel-Brunswik, Else. Meaning of psychoanalytic concepts and confirmation of psychoanalytic theories. *Scientific Monthly,* 1954a, 79, 203-300.

————. Psychoanalysis and the unity of science. *Proceedings of the Amer. Acad. Arts and Sci.,* 1954b, 80, 271-350.

Freud, S. *The interpretation of dreams.* (Trans. by J. Strachey.) New York: Basic Books, 1955. (Originally published 1900).

————. Wit and its relation to the unconscious. In *The basic writings of Sigmund Freud.* (Trans. by A. A. Brill.) New York: Modern Library, 1938. (Originally published 1905a.)

————. Fragment of an analysis of a case of hysteria. In *Collected papers.* Vol. III. (Trans. by A. Strachey and J. Strachey.) London: Hogarth, 1943. (Originally published 1905b.)

————. Analysis of a phobia in a five-year-old boy. In *Collected papers.* Vol. III. (Trans. by A. Strachey and J. Strachey.) London: Hogarth, 1943. (Originally published 1909a.) Pp. 147-289.

————. Notes upon a case of obsessional neurosis. In *Collected papers.* Vol. III. (Trans. by A. Strachey and J. Strachey.) London: Hogarth, 1943. (Originally published 1909b.) Pp. 296-383.

————. Mourning and melancholia. In *Collected papers*. Vol. IV. (Trans. by J. Riviere.) London: Hogarth, 1946. (Originally published 1917.) Pp. 152-170.

————. From the history of an infantile neurosis. In *Collected papers*. Vol. III. (Trans. by A. Strachey and J. Strachey.) London: Hogarth, 1943. (Originally published 1918.) Pp. 473-605.

————. *Group psychology and the analysis of the ego.* (Trans. by J. Strachey.) New York: Liverright, 1949. (Originally published 1921.)

————. Constructions in analysis. In *Collected papers*. Vol. V. (Trans. by J. Strachey.) London: Hogarth, 1952. (Originally published 1932.) Pp. 358-371.

————. *New introductory lectures on psychoanalysis.* (Trans. by W. J. H. Sprott.) New York: Norton, 1933.

Glover, E. Notes on the psychological effects of war conditions on the civilian population. Part III. The blitz. *Int. J. Psychoanal.*, 1942, 23, 17-37.

Hartmann, H. Ich-Psychologie und Anpassungsproblem. *Int. Z. Psychoanal.*, 1939, 24, 62-135. [Translation, Ego psychology and the problem of adaptation (abridge). In D. Rapaport (ed.), *Organization and pathology of thought.* New York: Columbia University Press, 1951. Pp. 362-396.]

Hempel, C. *Fundamentals of concept formation in empirical science.* Int. encycl. of unified sci. Vol. II, No. 7. Chicago: University of Chicago Press, 1952.

Hilgard, E. Experimental approaches to psychoanalysis. In E. Pumpian-Mindlin (ed.), *Psychoanalysis as science.* Stanford, Calif.: Stanford University Press, 1952. Pp. 3-45.

Horney, Karen. *The neurotic personality of our time.* New York: Norton, 1937.

Isaacs, Susan. Criteria for interpretation. *Int. J. Psychoanal.*, 1939, 20, 148-160.

Janis, I. L. Meaning and study of symbolic behavior. *Psychiatry*, 1943, 6, 425-439.

————. *Air war and emotional stress.* New York: McGraw-Hill, 1951.

————. *Psychological stress.* New York: Wiley, 1958.

Jones, E. *The life and work of Sigmund Freud.* Vol. II. *Years of maturity, 1901-1919.* New York: Basic Books, 1955.

Kluckhohn, C. Mirror for man. New York: McGraw-Hill, 1949.

Knight, R. Present status of organized psychoanalysis in the United States. *J. Amer. Psychoanal. Assoc.*, 1953, 1, 197-221.

Kris, E. Problems in clinical research (Round table). *Am. J. Orthopsychiat.*, 1947, 17, 210-214.

Kubie, L. Problems in clinical research (Round table). *Amer. J. Orthopsychiat.*, 1947, 17, 196-203.

————. Problems and techniques of psychoanalytic validation and progress. In E. Pumpian-Mindlin (ed.), *Psychoanalysis as science*. Stanford, Calif.: Stanford University Press, 1952. Pp. 46-124.

Lasswell, H. D. Provisional classification of symbol data. *Psychiatry*, 1938, 1, 197-204.

————. *Power and personality*. New York: Norton, 1948.

Leites, N. Psychocultural hypotheses. *World Politics*, 1948, 1, 102-119.

Lewin, K. A *dynamic theory of personality. Selected papers*. New York: McGraw-Hill, 1935.

Reik, T. *Listening with the third ear*. New York: Farrar, Strauss, & Cudahy, 1949.

Schmideberg, Melitta. Some observations on individual reactions to air raids. *Int. J. Psychoanal.*, 1942, 23, 146-176.

Skinner, B. F. Critique of psychoanalytic concepts and theories. *Scienctific Monthly*, 1954, 79, 300-305.

Spence, K. The postulates and methods of behaviorism. *Psychol. Rev.*, 1948, 55, 67-78.

Sterba, R. Report on some emotional reactions to President Roosevelt's death. *Psychol. Rev.*, 1946, 33, 393-398.

————. Some psychological factors in Negro race hatred and in anti-Negro riots. In G. Roheim (ed.), *Psychoanalysis and the social sciences*. Vol. I. New York: Int. Univ. Press, 1947. Pp. 411-427.

Tolman, E. G. Discussion: interrelationships between perception and personality. *J. Pers.*, 1949, 18, 48-50.

White, R. *Lives in progress*. New York: Dryden Press, 1952.

HENRY A. MURRAY

Harvard University

7 *Drive, time, strategy, measurement, and our way of life*

Despite a firm commandment to the contrary, we often find that psychology, like charity, begins at home. Anyhow, this is the way it was with me when I faced the topic of the present conference. I began at home with an inquiry into the motives that impelled me to accept this flattering invitation to discuss motives. No proof here that I am an armchair introspectionist of the old school. My friend Edward Tolman —never anything but new school—has assured me that he *always* identifies empathically with the rat at a choice point, and asks himself: What would *I* do in such a crisis?

And so, without shame, I intraverted my attention and measured, first of all, the volume, temperature, and pressure of my cortical resources. Was my head bursting with such hot intellectual news that it could no longer be confined? No. I calculated that what I could deliver on May 2 would be premature—at best, an incubator baby with no more than a beat or two of viability. But this is not the point. The four points I want to make on the basis of what I have just said are these: one, that we psychologists should take account, not only of needs to receive or to acquire some kind of vital thing, coming from *lack-tension,* but of needs to secrete or to transmit some kind of vital thing, coming from *pleni-tension.* Since, in this case, we are dealing with the external secretion, expression, presentation, or transmission of ideas, I am implying—and this is my second point—that we should include *mental needs,* as well as somatic, material, and social needs, in our inventory of human motivations. Mental aims—say, to observe events and acquire representations of the environment and of cause-and-effect relations, and to make plans —are generally treated as subaims in the service of the body or in the service of social interests; but in some persons—scientists and writers, for example—they occupy a superordinate position. My third point is that among the significant variables which await adequate definition is the *phase* of needful, or motivational, activity with which one is dealing, especially the propsective and decision-making phase as contrasted with the phase of actuation, or endeavor. I use the symbol *nd* to stand for a needful decision (which may or may not be executed), and *ne* to stand for a needful endeavor. The motives that are operative in arriving at a decision with regard to some proposed enterprise in the future may be different from the motives that will be operative during the actuation of the enterprise. A final point is this: that the *temporal position* and the *duration* of the time segment which is fixed or suggested for an enterprise in the future is likely to be one of the most influential variables in determining a decision. And in this connection we might note to what extent our present motivations are committing us to distal actions and to what extent prospective time gets filled and then, once filled, excludes the exercise of other dispositions.

Now, to return to my self-analysis of motives at the choice point. Was it the unusual honor conferred on me and the thought that here was an opportunity to raise my status in the fellowship of scientists? Was it the all-powerful need for recognition and prestige, for esteem and self-esteem? No. Strong as it is in me, this ambition could be better served by staying home, because, to my knowledge, I passed the point of diminishing returns some time ago. As stated most tactfully— after pages of exceeding praise in the latest and best book on theories of personality (Hall and Lindzey, 1957)—my conceptions are passé, because they have failed to generate research. Was it duty, then, that impelled me to accept? No, because John Croesus Harvard expects every man to do his duty at Cambridge, Massachusetts.

To be sure, money was a factor. I can always find a way of spending it when I get it. But enough of this. Let me jump to the conclusion of this overdrawn examination of my needs and say that what swayed me most strongly to my decision was a compound of several motives at the core of which was my affection for Gardner Lindzey. There is but one impeding prospect. He detests listening to speeches; at my last spout in his presence—three months ago—he lit a symbolically grand cigar, turned his back, and went to sleep. Somehow he held on to the cigar. Faced by the probability of a recurrence, the only strategy that occurred to me was to make him the hero of my talk.

Now, you may suppose I have wasted a good deal of time in getting to the starting line of serious considerations. But, as a matter of fact, I have already illustrated pretty nearly all the points which constitute the first third of my discourse—this third being addressed to at least four of the issues which our host set forth for us. In short, the following conclusions can be drawn from the report of my self-analysis: (1) that I am in favor of exploring the conscious motivations of others to the limit of practicality, and, since these can be revealed only by direct methods, (2) that I am in favor of direct methods; (3) that it is important to specify the situational context within which a motive will operate; and (4) that one cannot understand a single human decision or a single human endeavor above the level of somatic needs without including in one's survey a number of different needs as well as a variety of other variables, some of which have not yet been explicitly identified.

Variety of Needs. Let me say a few more words pertinent to the last point—the self-evident fact that a number of different needs are very frequently involved in a single course of action. Allport has set forth the principle of functional autonomy (1937), which, so far as I can see, is valid, though it seems to be exemplified far less often than its opposite, which I shall term the principle of functional subsidiation. Autonomy of short-range impulses and needs is the original state of things in childhood; but with age larger and longer systems are developed, so that motives which were once autonomous become subordinated to a few major purposes. Anyhow, the point I want to make is that in arriving at a decision to accept or reject an opportunity to engage in a certain kind of activity, a competition of needs and disneeds ensues, and the decision will depend on the relative urgency and/or enduring potency of those which might be favored by a "yes" and those which might be favored by a "no." Very rarely is a decision of this sort based upon the operation of a single need.

Method of Examining Conscious Motives. This conclusion, instead of discouraging a psychologist, suggests an excellent procedure for the examination of conscious motives. Hand a subject a series of paragraphs each of which presents a number of alternative kinds of activity or each of which presents a complex situation that calls for some action on his part. The subject is directed to write down his decision in each instance. After his series of decisions have been given, an interview is conducted in which the subject is pressed to offer *all* his reasons for each decision. The psychologist keeps asking "Why?" until he has arrived at a number of motives which are not susceptible of further analysis. Later, the same kind of interview can be conducted, but, in this session, based on actual decisions the subject has made in the course of his life as revealed, say, in his autobiography.

A corollary of the above stated proposition is this: it is rarely possible to measure the momentary strength of any one *human* need or motive in terms of such criteria as intensity or duration of *all* the activity that occurs between the limits of a single temporal segment of behavior. Even when the major aim of the endeavor can be discriminated, it is usually envisaged as the possible fulfillment of several needs, and in the course of that endeavor, other irrelevant minor needs are likely to intrude as well as certain words and phrases or slips of speech, or certain expressive gestures, which are indicative of still other covert and commonly suppressed, needs. After observing a subject's behavior in a lifelike experimental situation—let us say, a stressful situation—he may be interviewed in some detail about the sources of experienced satisfaction and dissatisfaction. This method provides another kind of crucial index of a person's needs and disneeds. Questionnaires, followed by interviews relative to major experiences and determinants of contentment and distress, are likely to be even more rewarding.

Validation among the Facts of Life. I am assuming all along that the ultimate concern of the personologist is to explain and, under specified conditions, to predict activities of everyday life, rather than the different ways in which people—college students very often—perform the role of "experimental subject." It would be possible to construct a fairly coherent science of human nature in terms of a kind of sub-culture bounded by the walls of laboratories, and we seem already to have gone quite a way in this direction; but I hardly think that this could be the conscious intention of more than a very few psychologists. Most of us simply want to know as much as possible about the conditions of arousal, the sensitivities, the intensities, and the interrelations of the motives that are operative in the on-going lives of people of our world. We cannot be satisfied with validations of one test by another test. Sooner or later validations must be sought among the facts of life. I admit that such data are very difficult to acquire in a systematic, scientific way—in fact, they are largely out of the question for members of most departments of psychology under the existing system of small packages of research for undergraduate honors as well as for M.A. and Ph.D. degrees. But this difficulty should not compel us to abandon the ideal, which, consistently in my view, is a small but sufficient number of detailed, comprehensive formulations of individual personalities. This year at the Harvard Psychological Clinic we have a pool of seventy subjects who were administered a battery of questionnaires and inventories, on the basis of which twenty-five subjects were selected for special study, selected in such a way that the lowest and the highest representatives on five different dimensions were included. As usual for us, the basic behavioral data will consist of autobiographies, past-history inventories, fantasy inventories, questionnaires relating to desires and aspirations as well as to common overt activities, reports and estimates by acquaintances; a number of casual as well as a few precisely recorded observations; a moving picture with soundtrack of an interpersonal discussion of the subject's philosophy of life; and, as an ending to this series of procedures, a number of interviews in which the psychologist asks for (a) concrete illustrations of the kinds of activities in which he is most interested, (b) an hour-by-hour account of two or three representative days, and finally, (c) reasons, or motives, for some of the described forms of behavior. So much for data relevant to conscious motivations and recurrent proactions and reactions.

One great difficulty in assessing the strength of needs manifested in such data is that the external pressive situation, whether momentary or enduring, is different in each case, and, furthermore, that the subject is capable of reporting only the beta situation, the situation as he interprets and evaluates it. The alpha, or actual, situation is likely to be distorted by the very needs one is endeavoring to estimate. Nevertheless, no other varieties of information are more pertinent than these to a personologist's concerns.

Ratings based on data obtained in such ways have provided Lindzey and Newburg (1954), Davids and Murray (1955), and others with rank orders to be used in testing the validity of various "projective" indices of certain variables of personality—anxiety and alienation, for example. But more of this later. I must now turn to the second third of my paper, which deals in a rough way with covert states and needs, those which are rarely, if ever, *fully* manifested publicly and rarely, if ever, *fully* avowed in an ordinary interview or questionnaire, either because the subject is unwilling to confess them or because he is unable.

ASSESSMENT OF COVERT STATES AND NEEDS

There would be nothing at all to write here (1) if every normal subject had an equally perfect knowledge and understanding of his past and present motivations and could accurately estimate their intensities relative to other subjects; (2) if the whole psychoanalytical theory respecting normal, beneficent repression were utterly invalid; and (3) if every normal subject, fully conscious of all that his personality contained, were ready to admit fully—under all circumstances and to any psychologist who asked him—every actuated and unactuated disposition of his nature—every deviant sexual impulse, every delinquent act or crime, every lie, every shameful stratagem or treachery, every hatred, every touch of malice or ignoble envy, every hurt or vanity or season of inflated pride, every extravagance of rivalrous ambition, et cetera, et cetera. If all people were as conscious, judicious, and open as this, the injunction "Know thyself" would be unnecessary: every person would be capable not only of writing a complete and accurate formulation of his own personality, but of predicting the nature of a future psychotic episode or breakdown, and, furthermore, be willing to admit whatever unpopular ideologies happened to appeal to them—communism, fascism, atheism, et cetera, et cetera. These remarks in defense of the reasonableness of a good many years of scientific effort devoted to the study of covert dispositions were prompted, as you might guess, by the now famous statement of my old friend and colleague, Gordon Allport, to the effect that normal subjects will tell you by the direct method precisely what they tell you by the projective method. "You may therefore take their motivational statements at their face value, for even if you probe you will not find anything substantially different." (Allport, 1953, p. 110).

Direct Methods Alone Insufficient. I am not sure how conscientiously, patiently, deviously, and subtly Professor Allport has probed; but I am sure that the probings of my collaborators as well as my own probings have yielded very different findings and conclusions than those which he reports in the excerpt quoted. As I have already stated, however, I heartily agree with his main point, which is that direct methods should never be abandoned. Their abandonment would be fatal to a major focus of concern, namely, to the *relation* between overt and covert, avowed and unavowed, conscious and unconscious, voluntary and involuntary processes. Dr. Lindzey—who enjoys boxing matches—encouraged his invited speakers to take firmly, if not belligerently, one side or the other on one or more of the issues he proposed; but unhappily— for I love a good argument—I cannot oblige him in this instance, since there would be no relation to study if one restricted oneself to either overt or covert processes and hence to either direct or indirect methods. Now, let us consider the question of indirect methods, particularly, if you will pardon me, story compositions, such as one obtains by the MAPS or TAT.

Before discussing story compositions, however, let me point out that composition—the composition of scientific books, literary composition, the composition of works of art, not to speak of the composition of integrated plans of action (a process that I call ordination)—none of these endeavors, so far as I know, has any conceptual place in academic psychology. When we speak of higher mental processes we mean cognition. I suspect that cognitive processes are "higher" because they de-

scribe what we psychologists are up to—an excellent example of ego-
centric projection. But Dante's composition of the *Divine Comedy*,
Shakespeare's composition of *Hamlet*, or a subject's impromptu composition of a story is not officially recognized by our science. It certainly involves higher mental processes, but it is not cognition as we define
cognition. It involves emotion—say, "emotion recollected in tranquillity"
—but the word "emotion," or "affection," does not include magnificent
arrangements of themes and counterthemes, of words and phrases. It involves intention and striving, but "conation," as defined in textbooks, is
not the word for it. This elimination from our theoretical systems of all
writers—be they artists, moralists, or scientists—is as good an illustration
as one could find of constricted cognitive projection, that is, the making
of theories in one's own image.

Indirect Methods—Story Composition. But let me return to story compositions, the TAT and Gardner Lindzey, who has done more than
anyone to give this procedure a firm footing within the framework of
academic psychology (Lindzey, 1952). While he was laboring to set
forth clear-cut principles of interpretation and clear-cut criteria for this
or that variable of personality, endeavoring, in short, to make the TAT
respectable as a precise and objective instrument, I was annoying him
no end by suggesting that we change the pictures, by constructing TAT
2 and now TAT 3, and a host of other methods to reveal covert images
and motives. I was using procedures of this sort less as tests of known
motives than as means of discovering new complexes, new integrates
of submerged motives, and as means of testing in a preliminary way
propositions respecting the operation of different varieties of projection.

What I learned from Lindzey was that a psychologist should not rely
on any presuppositions about which TAT variables are likely to be
indicative of a given personality variable. If the heroes of stories are disposed to be dominant (directive, coercive) in their dealings with other
characters, one cannot assume that dominance is either a conscious or
an unconscious motive in the author of these stories. One must take
two aggregates of subjects, one aggregate known (in some way) to be
extremely high in overt and/or covert dominance and one known to be
extremely low, and then search their TAT protocols for significant
differential criteria. It might turn out that the introduction of a wild
animal, unexpected and unexplained, is a dependable index of domi-

nance. This, as you know, is the method that McClelland and others (1953) have been using with such generally reliable results.

Its value can be illustrated by a brief history of our attempts to measure hedonic level or, more specifically, degree of depression in an aggregate of thoroughly assessed subjects. First, Goldings and Jones, rating protocols in terms of the everyday signs of discontent and dejection, obtained significant correlations in the high .40's. Then all the different determinants of depression in these and other story compositions were classified and counted, and it was found that three determinants recurred with sufficient frequency to permit statistical calculations. Confining his attention to these three, Brian Welch discovered that depression resulting from the loss of a loved person (e.g., rejection, infidelity, desertion, or death) was highly correlated with a low hedonic level in everyday life; that depression resulting from guilt after a transgression was also positively correlated, but to a lower degree; and that depression following the failure of some endeavor was *negatively* correlated with a low hedonic level. Thus we learnt that it was the happy contented person—in our small and special population—who, when confronted by a gloomy picture that seems to call for some tragic theme, was more likely to compose a story in which the hero fails in his attempt to attain a goal. In short, unhappy stories of this type were told by happy authors, which seems paradoxical at first, but, on second thought, is not difficult to explain. When Welch took account of these and other findings, correlations mounted to .60 or above. Then the protocols were examined in a minute detail, and it was found that if one scores in terms of combinations or clusters of protocol variables, instead of summing scores on single variables, one obtains still higher correlations—in the .70's, and .80's. To take the slightest example I can find, the protocol variable *guilt*. This is not scored at all unless there is *either* (a), an explicit statement that the hero feels guilty, or (b) some form of moral self-condemnation—one of these two *and* the fact that the hero's feelings of moral unworthiness continue entirely unrelieved through the *outcome* of the story. If a ray of hope is indicated in the last sentence of the story, no score is given to this variable.

These results are not yet ready for publication. The entire procedure will be repeated this summer, using stories told by a new aggregate of thoroughly assessed subjects. What evidence we have, however, indicates that an unhappy person may compose a number of happy stories; but none of them will contain the critical—one might say the *secret* —signs of happiness. And the same goes for happy subjects. They may compose, by conscious intention, several melancholy, tragic stories; but, measured by the new criteria, these stories have a false ring, and thereby the subject unconsciously informs us that over the years he is consistently happy rather than unhappy in his being.

For this possible discovery, Welch and I are indebted to the empiricism taught me by Gardner Lindzey. The tentative conclusion which might be drawn here is that what counts is the *form* of the temporal components of a story, rather than the sum of the scores of discrete variables. This is gestalt psychology, if you will, applied to the thematic units of a story composition, just as I am suggesting that it might advisedly be applied to units of overt behavior. So much for the second third of my remarks. The last third is neither a third in weight nor a third in duration. It is more accurately a fifth, though not the kind of fifth that some of us enjoy most. It was tacked on at the eleventh hour in order to demonstrate that, if pushed to it, I could stick to my word, which happens in this case to be the succession of words entitling this address.

OUR WAY OF LIFE

The significance of decisions which commit a man to a certain form of action in prospective time is exampled by the fact that Professor Lindzey called for the title of my talk long before I had decided what to talk about; and so whatever words I chose in compliance with his request would inevitably hold my mental processes a month hence to a fixed path. Out of the id jumped, "Drive, Time, Strategy, Measurement, and Our Way of Life," and, without fussing, this is what I sent my host as title. The fussing started a few weeks later when it came time to interpret that peculiar string of words and somehow to squeeze out of it something that was both juicy and pertinent to the general topic of these lectures. The juice which came out eventually—acid as lemon without sugar—is in the nature of a fantasy, illustrative of one of my earlier points, namely, that we psychologists make theories about the nature of man in our own image, and perhaps, reciprocally, that theories about human nature make us in *their* own image.

Ascensionism. It all started from my reading, some weeks back, that Santayana once observed that Americans are possessed by an obscure compulsion which will not let them rest, but drives them on faster and faster—not unlike a fanatic who redoubles his effort when he has lost sight of his aim. It seemed there was some truth in this, and so I gave the notion room and board, and one night it conjugated with another boarder that had been round for quite a while, an idea I call ascensionism. To explain this, a short digression is required. It will not take us outside the topic of the conference, but now I shall be operating on a grander scale, looking down the ages of the Western world and appraising, in a crude way, a particular compound of motives, very similar to the compound which, under the title of Icarus complex, some of us have been assessing in a variety of fairly precise ways in individual personalities.

Ascensionism may be defined as an integrate of the need for achievement and a relatively much stronger need for awed attention, for spectacular glory, for sensational prestige, which may or may not be linked with a component of sexuality, the special aim of this compound being to ascend vertically, in a physical, social, or intellectual sense. It is illustrated in the physical sphere by the child's desire to stand erect, later to climb furniture, trees, and other structures; but, more especially, by dreams and fantasies of flying. In primitive religions, particularly in Greek mythology, there were scores of gods, demigods, and heroes who ascended to high places—the summit of Mt. Olympus, say, or some paradise in the upper regions of the sky. Here the goal was combined with imagined social ascensionism, since high places of this sort were occupied by the spiritual elite—aristocratic deities, choirs of angels, or a whole society of elected saints.

Now, in ancient Egypt it was pretty well agreed that only the Pharaoh, the Divine King, was fit to ascend to heaven and to sail down the Milky Way—Nile of the sky—in a boat that was specially built for him. Later, in Greece, the prevalent belief, as Socrates expressed it, was that the soul, not only of the ruler but of all free and virtuous men, was destined to return to its original abode in heaven. Not until the advent of Christianity, however, was the possibility of resurrection opened up to every man and woman—every man and woman who repented and believed, particularly if he was meek and poor, a member of the proletariat. This last feature was eventually modified by proud and well-to-do, middle-class Protestants in such a way that proud and well-to-do middle-class Protestants would be favored in the selection process. Anyhow, for centuries people in the Western world were looking up to heaven with a passionate longing that is scarcely appreciated today, and the hypothesis I am suggesting is that with the decline of religious zeal after the American Revolution and the advent of democracy, there was a secularization of this desire for vertical achievement, for prestige through election to an elevated and exclusive group, and what came out of it was the Horatio Alger myth—the craving for upward social mobility by means of material success. Since, under these circumstances, all the upward motion must occur before death, in fact, several years before death, in order to allow some time for the enjoyment of whatever elevation one is capable of achieving, speed is of the essence. And this is the cardinal point in my hypothesis—the marriage of greed and speed, and their embrace of the machine as the surest and quickest means to paradise—a villa in Florida or California, let us say.

Drives and Tensions. Leaving out all details, I suggest—in conformity with other authors—that this ambition to ascend, which was once religious and zealous but now secular and zealous, is the obscure compulsion which will not let us rest, as Santayana said; and, further, that the concept of human nature which comes out of it is a concept of perpetually recurrent *drives*, or tensions, each hurrying the organism down some alley to some terminus where the promise is held out of a speedy reduction of that awful tension. The problem of learning, then, comes down to the question of how, in the shortest *time*, *strategies* are acquired by means of which an organism can reach the goal place in the shortest *time*. *Measurements* are made of learning time and travel time and of the amount of food that is acquired at the terminus. Besides food, one can also measure amount of money, size of property, number of utilities manufactured, number of friends, degree of social elevation, et cetera, et cetera. It's enough to give us psychologists the impression that we're Newtonian physicists, since we are dealing with the same essential variables—energy, mass, distance, time. Anyhow, the formula is this: strong drive (ambition) and the selection of efficient strategies (intelligence) combine to bring a rodent or a human being in the shortest possible time to the highest and largest material rewards, and these measurable things constitute, at least in caricature, *our way of life*. This, in brief, is the essence of the meaning that was squeezed out of my title—drive, time, strategy, measurement, and our way of life.

Extrinsic Rewards. Now, it is permissible for a psychologist to ask, How valid is this formula? and it is permissible for anyone who is fond of life to ask, Is this a "good" formula to live by? Hence I am assuming that I have the privilege of asking both these questions, but not, since my allotted time is nearly spent, of setting out to answer them. Let a few remarks suffice.

Note, first, that the acts studied by learning theorists are considered to be *instrumental*, that is, they are not intrinsically satisfying, but performed—perhaps laboriously and painfully—for the sake of something else. They are extrinsically rewarding. Then note that the word "satisfying" and all its close synonyms—pleasure, contentment, happiness—have been pretty thoroughly eliminated from modern terminology, despite the fact that signs and reports of satisfaction are no less dependable than signs and reports of anxiety, anger, depression, and several other inner states. It is still respectable to speak of pain avoidance but not respectable to speak of pleasure seeking. Thus, neither means nor ends are conceptually connected with satisfaction, intrinsic satisfaction; and this fact suggests the possibility that for many of us a goal consists in the reduction of some distress, the cessation of something negative and painful, rather than the addition of something positive and enjoyable. That this is experientially valid in numberless cases is irrefutable, it seems to me; but does it cover everything? Take eating, for example. If cessation of hunger were the only object, we should be content, say, with a slab of ice cream on top of a bowlful of chicken hash, mixed with consommé and bread crumbs, over which a couple of Martinis had been poured. I surmise that even those who have the habit of gobbling their dinners without consciousness of taste would be repelled by such a hodgepodge, however capable it would be of speedily reducing hunger pangs. No, everyone knows, as well as they know anything, that the intrinsic satisfactions associated with eating, with courtship and sexual intercourse, with conversation, with "play" in the true sense, with the enjoyment of literature and the arts, with all types of creative activity, and with many other activities are dependent on such qualities as tempo, order, harmony, variety, novelty, and such experiences as spontaneity, zest, surprise, suspense, and resolution—in short, on form and style, things that cannot properly be represented in quantitative terms, but are, nonetheless, as real and as determining as anything that numbers can express.

These considerations bring us to the possibility that we psychologists have shunned the study of activities that are intrinsically satisfying and beneficent, first, because the Puritan ethic, with its low evaluation of the art of life and its high evaluation of persistent effort for the sake of some ultimate reward, still operates in us and in our countrymen; and second, because this ethic of materialism has been transferred from the sphere of morality to the sphere of science; and third, because it appears to be impossible to translate the formal determinants of intrinsic satisfactions into numbers and equations, and thereby to include them into the only kind of science with which we are familiar. Let us stop here and so to bed.

REFERENCES

Allport, G. W. *Personality: a psychological interpretation.* New York: Holt, 1937.
——. The trend in motivational theory. *Amer. J. Orthopsychiat.,* 1953, 23, 107-119.
Davids, A., and Murray, H. A. Preliminary appraisal of an auditory projective technique for studying personality and cognition. *Amer. J. Orthopsychiat.,* 1955, 25, 543-554.
Hall, C. S., and Lindzey, G. *Theories of personality.* New York: Wiley, 1957.
Lindzey, G. Thematic Apperception Test: interpretive assumptions and related empirical evidence. *Psychol. Bull.,* 1952, 49, 1-25.
——, and Newburg, A. S. Thematic Apperception Test: a tentative appraisal of some "signs" of anxiety. *J. consult. Psychol.,* 1954, 18, 389-395.
McClelland, D. C., Atkinson, J. W., Clark, R. A., and Lowell, E. L. *The achievement motive.* New York: Appleton-Century-Crofts, 1953.

RAYMOND B. CATTELL

University of Illinois

8 *The dynamic calculus: a system of concepts derived from objective motivation measurement*

In understanding a brief exposition of a topic which is a complex crossroads of many issues, an audience is often helped if the speaker quickly sketches in his antecedents and his main prejudices or, perhaps I may be permitted to say, his convictions, in the field of psychology generally. A recurring theme in my own work has been that a good theory arises only out of quantitative and exact experiment, but that there is no virtue in measurement unless it is organically related to known personality structure. A second conviction or prejudice is that we have far more theory in psychology than is good for effective experimental advance. As a person initially working in the physical sciences, I believe that psychology has a lot of alleged theory that is not theory in the true sense of the physical sciences, and that in fact a great deal of it has flourished for no better reason than to further the psychologist's belief that he must "keep up with the Joneses," the Joneses in this case being physics, chemistry, and other sciences of some maturity. My position is therefore rather like that of Dr. B. F. Skinner. Indeed, I wish that more psychologists who are interested in theory for esthetic or social rather than scientific reasons would express their needs by writing a novel or some other imaginative fiction, that they might return with purged minds to make clear, sufficient, and unexcessive inferences from the data and their relationships.

In accordance with this position, my contribution to this symposium will, I am afraid, be undecorated by polysyllabic "isms," alleged to be theories. Instead, it will deal with a series of strategically planned and closely interlocking experiments; with operationally defined concepts arising from them; and with tentative notions that should properly be called hypotheses rather than theories. The ideas involved in these hypotheses may, indeed, turn out to be newer, stranger, and more complex than those we are accustomed to encounter in many theories. But their hallmark is that they admit of more positive operational definition, and invite experimental treatment. In this respect, and in the close interdependence of the concepts in a single scheme, my treatment is certainly—as stipulated for this symposium—highly *systematic*, but in the true hierarchy of scientific development I do not think it is entitled to the dignity of being called a theory. The true meaning of theory in science has been a set of complex relations, embracing *concepts*, which in turn integrate the existing findings in a number of well-established scientific *laws*. And where, may I ask, are the dependable scientific laws in the field of motivation? What I have to offer is not even a set of laws, but a set of replicated and replicable experimental findings, which promise an avenue to laws and perhaps a firm foundation on which to erect genuine theory in the future.

Like any respectable systematist, I must begin a little pedantically by stating how one delimits the topic of motivation from other psychological areas and themes. In my 1946 book on personality I attempted an operational definition of "dynamic" to which I must refer you, since there is not time to reason closely upon it here. The definition was concerned essentially with the differentiation of cognitive, temperamental, and dynamic behavior *modalities*, and stated that ability traits are patterns in behavior the individual score levels of which have the peculiarity of changing readily with change in the complexity of the stimulus situation. Motivational traits are patterns the individual score levels of which are affected most sensitively by changes in the *incentive* strength in the environmental situation. I then proceeded to define environmental complexity and incentive independently, so that there is no circularity left in the argument. Of course, all *behavior* is motivated behavior, but a dynamic trait is a pattern abstracted from behavior which remains responsive to incentive, whereas the ability and temperament modality traits do not. This definition respects common use of language and merely crystallizes existing semantics, enabling distinctions to be made where common sense otherwise might leave differences of opinion. Motivation thus covers in common parlance the study of interests, drives, attitudes, values, conflict, defense dynamisms, and such dynamic structures as the ego, the superego, and the self sentiment. The words dynamic and motivational are initially treated as synonyms, though I believe that later a valuable distinction can be made which adds clarity to certain experimental findings.

PRECONDITIONS FOR THE STUDY OF MOTIVATIONAL STRUCTURE

Now the scientific, theoretical grasp of dynamic phenomena which we seek requires, as I have just stated, the discovery of dynamic laws, and this discovery of dynamic laws can be derived from, and only from, *observations dealing with changing strength of motives and changing structure of motives.* From our general knowledge of scientific method we realize that all knowledge of structure has to be obtained from observing covariation of parts. This may be carried out either in the framework of simple classical experimental design or, more powerfully, by means of modern multivariate experimental designs, involving correlation of many variables and such analytical tools as factor analysis. Any attack upon structure assumes that if two manifestations of motivational behavior vary together in a high degree they must spring from the same common source, or have a high degree of causal connection. In fact, as John Stuart Mill pointed out long ago, *demonstrated covariation is our only proof of causal connection or functional unity.*

Until this multivariate analysis in search of unitary patterns is completed it is vain to talk about experiments on particular drives, "the mechanism of projection," the superego, or other motivational terms. No matter how sophisticated our brass instruments or our tests are, if we have fallen into the intellectual immaturity of assuming that wherever there is one word there is one thing, we are doomed to failure and confusion. The next man who comes along is quite free to refer the verbal concept to a different operation and to come out with different conclusions. Even if he uses the *same* single test operation, linked to the same verbal definition, he can still come out with different conclusions, for not once in a million times is the variance in the whole factor construct accounted for by the variance in any *single* operational measurement. It is necessary, in fact, to measure the same factor and to know with what validity we are measuring it.

Measurement, we have said, must be related to the structure—of the thing measured—for any definitive experiment on a concept. But before this concept can be located, there has to be a phase of blind measurement to reveal the structure which we shall use in meaningful measurement. In an unfamiliar dark room your hands touch many things before they land on the switch on the wall and the switch on the lamp, but the second time in the room you may operate directly on the two switches which produce the significant relation with which you are concerned. So here, though our ultimate aim is to experiment with relations among unitary motives, we have first to go through a phase of blind measurement of a wide range of *specific, arbitrary* motives or interests, to *find* the unities. For it is on these specific *ad hoc* measurements that our correlations, designed to reach unitary structure, must be based.

I have to describe therefore, *two* distinct phases of investigation, carried out in proper sequence. In the first of these we ask, "Just how do you propose validly to measure the strength of *any* motive whatsoever?" We ask this because it is from such measurements on a collection of widely sampled specific attitude-interests, perhaps chosen only with vague hunches, that we can hope to find the unitary structures. In other words, just as the perception of unitary patterns in a mosaic of colored tesserae presupposes the sensory ability to see color, so the discovery of dynamic structure presupposes that we have achieved some validity in objectively measuring the strength of motive in some specific, pin-pointed attitude or interest. If we can measure the intensity of individual attitudes or motives we can then pass on to the second, structuring phase of research, in which we study the correlations, or other relations, among many attitudinal behavioral responses, with a view to factoring out the unitary dynamic traits in the total structure.

Parenthetically, I would not propose that our initial choice of concepts and variables should lean too heavily on any supposed knowledge of motivation derived from clinical observation, employing the unaided human eye and erratic human memory. If the ultimate findings *should happen to* agree with those of, say, psychoanalysis, all well and good, and we can then take over the nomenclature of psychoanalysis for those constructs which find experimental support. To ensure the *possibility* of such conceptual continuity we should always arrange that common "marker variables," identical with some frequently used by the clinician, go into each experiment. But there should initially be such a degree of independence of experimental-factor-analytical, and clinical variables that the form of the larger shapes due to emerge will not be prejudiced in any way. The betting at present can scarcely be that any clinical scheme will be *largely* verified; if only because no two of the many clinical theories of structure agree!

However, let us note a certain degree of kinship between our experimental approach and that of the clinician. With regard to the two great scientific methods—that of classical, univariate experiment and that of modern, multivariate, factor-analytic experiment—the clinician has unknowingly been applying largely the second. The so-called "clinical method" observes the covariation of intensity of interests and symptoms with changing stimulus intensities and thus draws conclusions about the existence of unitary traits, e.g., the superego, by concluding that there is *covariation in a certain set of manifestations*. Although he observes covariation without the aid of measurement or explicit mathematical analysis, one would certainly expect some similarity of end results. We should not, however, expect the clinical concepts to reach the precision of statement and the quantifiability that are possible through the formal multivariate method in factor analysis.

MEASUREMENT OF SINGLE MOTIVATIONAL VARIABLES

With this unavoidable and crucial preamble on method, we can inquire what progress has been made in the first phase of motivational measurement, i.e., what advance has been made in measuring the intensity of a single motive, as a basis for the later structural analyses. What, indeed, are the general manifestations of the degree of intensity of a motive? The procedure of science in attempting to penetrate into any new area is usually to accept the common semantic definition of the area of manifestation and then to pry into it with more intensive methods. This method we have followed in the field of motivation, accepting as a sign of motive strength anything which a reputable psychologist has ever claimed to reflect the intensity of need. Thus we have taken conventionally the subject's conscious verbal statement about how much he wants to do something or other. But this has been taken only as one among many manifestations. We have also considered a variety of physical signs, such as are involved in the psychogalvanic-reflex and blood-pressure changes; many learning phenomena which learning "theorists" have considered to be signs of the strength of motive; a variety of defense mechanisms which have been regarded among clinicians as reflecting strength of motive; and a wide range of misperception and misbelief devices such as are involved in what are popularly called projective tests. For those who like to think that some *one* variable is the criterion, our researches have also included as measures of motivation the amount of money people spend on the given interest, and the amount of time they are willing to devote to it. In our thinking, however, there is no *a priori* single criterion, and everything which psychologists have called signs of motive strength is also eligible to be called a criterion. Indeed, such signs constitute a collective criterion.

Having thus delimited the field of manifestation in which our quarry lies, how do we finally hunt it down? Since these manifestations are by definition signs of motive in general, we need theoretically to take only one representative motive or interest, measure it on all these variables, and then intercorrelate the scores, finding which devices have the highest agreement with the pool. Actually, to establish the *general* validity of these devices, the experiment has been repeated with several motives sampled from the field of human interests.

To understand the ensuing reasoning one must notice a little more closely the actual operations in these investigations of measures of motive strength. Typically, about two hundred subjects are measured on a single attitude-interest, say, interest in taking part in athletics. A measure is made on each of twenty to fifty "devices" (as we may best call the motivation-manifestation tests used), each oriented to this one interest. The devices are intercorrelated and the mean correlation of each with (a) the pool, (b) the centroid, and (c) the group of devices considered to be *criteria* is worked out.

Some seventy extremely varied motivational-measurement devices have now been tried out in this way. Indeed, we have been able to interrelate as many as fifty-four in one experiment. (Cattell and Baggaley, 1956.) They have been tried on a sufficient variety of attitude-interests to know that their validity is not peculiar to any one form of interest. Interesting as these devices are, I must pass them over at the moment and leave you to read about them in the literature (Cattell, 1957). Research upon them has incidentally produced several generalizations of importance for the particular specialty from which the devices were derived, e.g., perception, learning.

One specific finding that has far-reaching importance for psychological generalization is that the standard, verbal, *opinionnaire* method of measuring attitude-interest strength correlates only about .3 with the pool. Thus the measure accounts for less than one tenth of the variance in what psychologists agree to be the area of motivation-strength manifestation. It is consequently not surprising that the conscious verbal assessment of motivation strength has so often given erroneous social and political predictions. But it *is* surprising that, in an era when the psychologist has been revealing on all sides the discrepancy between motive and conscious verbal logic, the attitude testers should have uncritically accepted verbal response measurement. All the generalizations we at present possess about attitudes, their organization, and their change under various influences, insofar as they are based upon the opinionnaire method of measurement, should be tagged in one's mind as suspect and makeshift. Indeed, the present vast mass of generalization loosely said to apply to "attitudes" is actually true of only a very special and restricted fraction of any total attitude-interest strength.

Incidentally, I think it would help in this advance into objective motivation measurement if we threw away the phraseology about "direct and indirect" attitude measurement. There is far more to a

truly objective motivation measurement than cooking up indirect statements. Someone should tell the attitude-survey specialists that what
they have thought of as direct attitude testing has always been, to
depth psychologists, the merest verbal froth on the ocean of motive.
A direct measure is surely one which gets at the heart of things, and
this the verbal attitude measurement surely does not do. Consequently,
if such terms must be retained, to soften the revolution that is really
taking place, it is the objective measurement which should be called
direct, and the conscious, superficial, deceptive, verbal statement, which
we know misses nine tenths of the variance, that should be called *indirect or peripheral.*

It has been implied above, and will now be more explicitly brought
out, that the specific structural unit of measurement in most of this
investigation has been the attitude. That is to say, the motive is defined as the strength of interest in a course of action particularized regarding situation and goal, e.g., "In my junior year I want to participate in more football games." Now, I suggested initially above that
the validity of a given device for measuring the strength of an attitude-
interest so defined might be measured by its correlation with a *pooled
score* from a stratified sample of all devices measuring what have commonly been called motivation-strength manifestations. Such validation
might have been acceptable years ago, but we are now accustomed to a
more sophisticated approach; before proceeding with such an approach
we always ask the important psychometric question: "Is the semantically
delimited pool itself a unity?"

Consequently, in the three main studies now completed on the examination of the validity of motivation-strength measurement devices we
have sought first to answer this question, typically intercorrelating from
twenty-five to fifty-four different devices and then factoring, to see
whether, indeed, there *is* a single power that can be called strength of
motive, or whether there are independent motivational *components* in
the total strength of a motive. This is a very fundamental issue, and
the answer has come out very clearly in favor of the latter view. We have
repeatedly obtained *six* motivational-component factors, each characterized by a particular set of high variables, and by a recognizable pattern in others of lesser loading. These factors have been labeled alpha
through zeta, and the particular variables which load them may be

studied elsewhere (Cattell, 1957) and in the three specimen factors in Table 1, below. The patterns were first found in a series of factorings on young male adults by Cattell and Baggaley (1956), and were replicated on a sample of men and women by Tapp (1958). An extensive study is now in progress under John Radcliffe to explore these motivational-component factors in objective motivation tests applied to eleven-year-old children.

Although we started with no prejudice in favor of psychoanalysis, it has seemed to us that the three major factors in this set, designated alpha, beta, and gamma, are more reasonably interpreted in psychoanalytic terms than in any other (see Table 1). In fact, we have specifically hypothesized that factors alpha, beta, and gamma are, respectively, the individual's id, the ego, and the superego contributions to any of his interests. The remaining three factors, delta, epsilon, and zeta seem to correspond, respectively, to (a) a contribution to interest from specific unconscious complexes, (b) a purely physiological interest component which is probably identical with that measured in most animal-motivation experiments, and (c) a factor in some way connected with reminiscence phenomena.

At this point in the research on the objective measurement of motive some of our fellow investigators, pledged to their sponsors to come out with a single attitude measurement, felt themselves to be in the embarrassing position of foster parents who went to adopt a child and came away with six. Nature apparently says that we must always measure six distinct motivational components when we wish to know the strength of an attitude-interest and that no single measurement will really suffice to describe the true state of affairs. However, we observed that the clear, simple structure position which we had discovered for the six presented them as definitely *oblique* factors. Consequently, there *might* exist a conceptual possibility of handling this diversity under some simpler second-order factor concept, if a single second order should be found to subtend all six.

A careful determination of angles and factoring of five of these primary motivational components, in fact, yielded *two* major second-order factors. Though our hope of a monotheistic solution among the gods of motivation theorists thus vanished, it must be admitted that the two big second-order factors made good psychological sense. The

Table 1[1]   Motivation Component Factors

Reference No. in Section 5	Direction	Name of Measuring Device*	Corrected Loading †	Uncorrected Loading

Motivation Factor Alpha: the Id Component in Interests

41	(Much)	Autism: misbelief	.93	(.64)
44	(Much)	Rationalization: misbelief	.99	(.76)
50	(Much)	Distortion of reasoning: ends for given means	.85	(.66)
49	(Much)	Distortion of reasoning: ways and means for given ends	.70	(.56)
14	(Much)	Decision time response	.82	(.56)
16	(Much)	Fluency on cues to course of action	.73	(.46)
1	(Much)	Preference: opinionnaire	.57	(.49)
29	(Much)	PGR deflection per cent to threat	.62	(.20)
39	(Much)	Fantasy: choice of fantasy topic	.68	(.48)
17	(Much)	Fluency on consequences, good	.56	(.27)
17	(Little)	Fluency on consequences, bad	−.58	(−.31)
42	(Much)	Naive Projection: wrong information	.47	(.33)
39	(Much)	Fantasy: choice to explain	.38	(.29)
7	(Much)	Memory for associated material (Unoriented)	.37	(.22)
38	(Much)	Fantasy: time spent on rumination	.28	(.20)

Motivation Factor Beta: the Realized Ego ‡

32	(Downward)	Response of diastolic blood pressure to threat	−.95	(−.27)
2	(Much)	Information on means to ends	.66	(.33)
22	(Much)	Learning effort for sake of interest	.58	(.23)
9	(Much)	Memory for rewards of course of action	.99	(.37)
32	(Downward)	Response of systolic amplitude to threat	−.56	(−.16)
10	(Much)	Competitive inhibition (auditory)	.70	(.24)
29	(Negative)	P.G.R. deflection to threat	−.64	(−.29)
32	(Negative)	Area of pulse wave to threat	−.70	(−.33)
55	(Much)	Expectancy effort	.26	(.11)
18	(Little)	Fluency on justifications	−.32	(−.20)
1	(Negligible)	Preference (opinionnaire)	.07	(.06)

* Measurement devices ranked in order on number of studies agreeing, as well as on absolute size of loadings.

† Loadings corrected for attenuation, from actual loadings in parentheses.

‡ Further labelled: Adjusted Ego component; Integrated desires.

[1] The three tables in this chapter are taken from *Personality and Motivation Structure and Measurement*, by Raymond B. Cattell. © 1957, by World Book Company, Yonkers-on-Hudson, New York.

Motivation Factor Gamma: Ideal Self or Super Ego

7	(Much)	Easy memory path to associated material	.73	(.50)
32	(Much)	Response of area of pulse wave to threat	.80	(.23)
32	(Much)	Response diastolic blood pressure to threat	.91	(.21)
39	(Much)	Choice of fantasy topic (b)	.85	(.54)
39	(Much)	Choice of fantasy topic (a)	.26	(.19)
46–50	(Much)	Distortion of reasoning	.50	(.34)
15	(Much)	Decision time adjustment	.42	(.29)
1	(Much)	Preference (conscious opinionnaire)	.21	(.25)
32	(Much)	Response of systolic amplitude to threat	.49	(.12)
55	(Much)	Expectancy effort	.46	(.23)
41	(Much)	Autism: misbelief	.24	(.17)
2	(Low)	Information on means to ends	−.11	(−.05)
54	(Possibly, low)	Capacity for perceptual integration	−.64	(−.22)

two primary components connected with the conscious self, namely, the ego-strength and superego-strength factors, which are usually psychologically considered to be integrated in a single *self sentiment*, appear together in a single second-order factor. With equal definiteness the primary motivational components which represent *un*integrated factors, namely, those of the id, of complexes, and the factor of physiological origin, appear in the other second-order factor. These two factors, however, appear to be very little correlated. These relations are shown in Figure 1. Thus it would seem that two factors constitute the irresolvable limit for simplification of motivational components. However, it would be legitimate, in seeking a single score, to add the strength on these two factors arbitrarily, with equal weight, for a single individual. One can then say that this is his total strength of interest in the given course of action, discounting the extent to which it springs, respectively, from integrated and unintegrated sources.

At this point of investigation, therefore, my own answer to Dr. Lindzey's apt question regarding the role to be assigned to ego processes, and to directing mechanisms in general, between the motive and its expression, is that any motive is divisible into clearly discernible and measurable components, which have different proportions in different interests. Only the ego and superego are strictly directive, for the id is presumably unintegrated and diffuse. Thus in every motive there is presumably some degree of controlled, and some degree of unintegrated and uncontrolled, spontaneous interest.

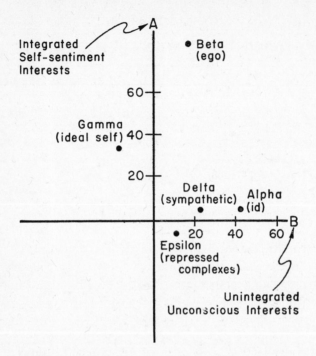

Figure 1. *Relation of second-order to primary motivation-component factors.*[2]

The question of how important conscious and unconscious (or, at least, integrated and unintegrated) motives are in various dynamic predictions cannot yet be answered; but it now becomes a matter opened up for experimental investigation. However, before such investigation with motivational-component-factor batteries proceeds, it seems to me vitally important that as many as half a dozen independent investigators check this factor structure. In addition, they should penetrate further into the psychoanalytic interpretation by adding to these device markers new crucial variables which meet their conception of how id, ego, and superego factors *should* manifest themselves. A systematic discussion of interpretations to guide research is given elsewhere (Cattell, 1957).

[2] Figures 1 and 2 are from *Personality and Motivation Structure and Measurement*, by Raymond B. Cattell. © 1957, by World Book Company, Yonkers-on-Hudson, New York.

INVESTIGATION OF DYNAMIC STRUCTURE

With this clarification of what is done when we measure the strength of any *single* attitude-interest, the stage is set for the second phase of investigation, in which a large variety of attitudes or motives with different content are measured and correlated to determine the dynamic personality structure residing in them. I shall spend the next few pages, therefore, in describing these experiments in the structuring of attitudes. Attempts to measure structure among attitudes by correlation are by no means new, but previous to the present systematic experiments they have been vitiated (at least as far as concepts defined here are concerned) by two circumstances. First, the measurements have been made only in terms of conscious, opinionnaire-type, self-revelatory evaluations of motive strength. These devices have low validity and emphasize only one special factor. Second, the choice of attitudes has usually had to be dictated by some largely practical, industrial, or political interest, or by psychometric, scaling preoccupations, as in the work of Cantril, Gallup, Stagner, Lentz, Dexter, Carlson, Ferguson, Guttman, Coombs, and Eysenck, rather than by *interest in the structure* of individual personality and motivation in itself.

By contrast, the series of investigations to follow have specifically aimed at the dynamic structure of the typical individual and have been concerned with making a sampling of attitudes more meaningful to the clinician and the personality theorist. Political and social attitudes, instead of being 90 per cent or 100 per cent of the variables, have been 5 per cent or 10 per cent, and the wide spectrum of human interests has been more fully represented in our studies by attitudes concerning wife and home, children, career, health, hobbies, religion, neurotic symptoms, community neighborhood duties, economic concerns, sexual, and vague but libidinally important sensuous interests, etc. Each of the attitude variables included—each of the bricks sampled, as it were, from the dynamic structure to be investigated—has been represented and measured as "strength of interest in an attitude." But it should be understood that an *attitude* is here defined somewhat differently from attitude in opinionnaire method.

An attitude is here defined in the stimulus-response paradigm:

"In these circumstances	I	want	so much	to do this	with that."
(Stimulus situation)	(Organism)	(Need)	(Intensity)	(Direction)	(Object)

That is to say, the attitude is defined as a response to a continuing life situation, particularized by a specific course of action, which the individual wishes to carry out in regard to an object. This action is not conceived as being "for" or "against" the object; for such a stereotype, so common in past attitude measurement, is often oversimplified or meaningless. But there is a continuum of strength from zero to high positive (or from negative to positive, according to circumstances) in the strength of the individual's desire *to carry out the given course of action*, responsive to the situation.

Each attitude, as one proceeds to experiment on it, is therefore initially described, in the experimental write-up, by breaking it down in the above verbal paradigm. For example, an attitude might be designated by: "I want to buy my wife the things that will make her household work easier," or "I want to see America get more protection against the terror of atomic bombs," or "I want to increase the size of my bank account." In doing this, it will be seen that we have not actually written in the "circumstances," which are part of the paradigm, since they are held constant in all attitudes as "the circumstances in which the person is living at that time," but they *could* be physically and socially described if necessary. The moving parts with which we are experimentally concerned lie in the rest of the paradigm, which always defines a course of action, desired with a given strength. Because each attitude is always thus initially *verbally* defined, one must not make the error of assuming that the actual measurements below are made by an opinionnaire statement. The measurement of any one attitude in all that follows is made by a battery of six subtests consisting of objective devices (e.g., autism, information, P.G.R. response to threat to interest) which have proved most valid in the sense of being most highly loaded in the two major factors just described, the integrated and unintegrated.

A verbal convention to distinguish "dynamic" from "motivational" must be made at this point. Since we shall now encounter factors among attitudes instead of among devices, as above, I am proposing to call the six factors among devices in any *single attitude*, as above, the *motivational-component factors*, whereas we shall refer to the factors obtained in factoring a wide variety of attitudes (each measured on a composite of the two main motivation-component factors) as *dynamic structure factors* or dynamic factors. The first and most dramatic finding in the factoring of a set of variables chosen to represent the total personality sphere of interests is that they seem to reinstate the main drive factors which for the last twenty years in psychology have had the dubious status of being scientifically indefensible but practically indispensable. Nine drive patterns, including sex, fear or escape, self-assertion, curiosity, etc., have repeatedly been found in these researches as independent factors, marked by uniform emotional content. (Cattell, 1950; Cattell and Cross, 1952; Cattell, 1957; and Cattell and Baggaley, 1958). They have been found in the sense that each groups together a set of attitudes having a common ultimate biological goal, despite complete difference of cultural content and acquired mode of expression among them. However, this interpretation as drives or ergs must remain for a while strictly tentative and hypothetical, for it still remains to be shown that these groupings correspond to *innate* sources of energy; for such proof further investigation of these factor scores by the usual genetic experimental designs (Cattell, Blewett, and Beloff, 1955) is necessary.

The main reason at present for hypothesizing that these interest patterns represent innate patterns is that they correspond so closely to the concepts reached by Freud, McDougall, and Murray, and to behavior seen in higher mammals, similar to ourselves, which obviously cannot be ascribed to cultural roots. Nevertheless, I have suggested that we use the new term *ergs* for these entities, in order not to get involved in all the old vendettas about "instincts," "propensities," and "drives." These latter terms never correspond to patterns which have been exactly demonstrated, even in animals. Moreover, they carry an aura of ill-defined connotations differing with each user, whereas an erg simply means, i.e., is operationally defined as, a pattern of factor loadings among dynamic trait measurements. The term "erg" is of course derived from the Greek root meaning work or energy, since the essential feature common to these patterns is that they are sources of reactivity or work; that is, the organism expends energy in proceeding toward a particular biological goal. Among the ergic patterns which our investigations have unearthed are the following: Mating, Gregariousness, Parental Protectiveness, Exploration, Escape to Security, Self-Assertion, Narcistic Sex, Appeal, Rest Seeking, Constructiveness, and Self-Abasement. In Table 2 some of these ergs are presented, together with the individual measures and factor loadings comprising them, and they may be studied more fully in the recent systematic presentation (Cattell, 1957).

Table 2 Ergic Factor Loading Patterns

Loading

Attitudes Defining the Sex Erg

I want to fall in love with a beautiful woman.	·5
I want to satisfy my sexual needs.	·5
I like sexual attractiveness in a woman.	·5
I like to see a good movie now and then.	·4
I like a novel with love interest and a ravishing heroine.	·4
I like to enjoy smoking and drinking.	·4
I want to see more good restaurants serving attractive food.	·3
I want to listen to music.	·3
I want to travel and explore the world.	·3

Parental Protectiveness

I want to help the distressed, wherever they are.	·5
I want to insure the best possible education for my children.	·5
I want my parents never to be lacking the necessities of comfortable living.	·4
I want to save my wife unnecessary drudgery.	·4
I want to see, for everyone, the danger of death by accidents and disease reduced.	·4
I want to see the congenial way of life of my native country preserved.	·4
I do *not* want (need) the help and advice of my parents.	·4
I do *not* want to drive myself beyond reason (or to fight).	·3

Exploration (Curiosity)

I like to read books, newspapers, and magazines.	·5
I want to listen to music.	·5
I want to know more about science.	·4
I like to satisfy my curiosity about everything going on in my neighborhood.	·3
I want to see more paintings and sculpture.	·3
I want to learn more about mechanical and electrical gadgets.	·3
I like to see a good movie or play.	·3
I am not interested in being smartly dressed.	·3

Escape (Fear, Need for Security)

I want my country to get more protection against the terror of the atom bomb.	·5
I want to see any formidable militaristic power that actively threatens us attacked and destroyed.	·5
I want to see the danger of death by accident and disease reduced.	·4

I want to see those responsible for inflation punished. .4
I want never to be an insane patient in a mental hospital. .4
I want to see a reduction of income tax for those in my bracket. .3
I want to take out more insurance against illness. .3
I want to become proficient in my career. .3
I want my country to have power and influence in the world. .5
I like to take part in political arguments. .3

However, not all the factors in dynamic traits appear to be ergs. There are, additional to the ergic patterns, others which clearly cannot be characterized as having, in all loaded attitudes, a common emotional quality and a common biological goal. Instead, they show a common *sociological or cultural origin*, with emotional and cognitive complexity. To perceive what these patterns might be, let us go back to first principles with regard to patterns of covariation in phenomena of any kind. In general, a correlation cluster can be accounted for by two or three different sources of variance, overlapping in their effects in the cluster area. However, we are dealing here with a *factor*, not a cluster, and it is theoretically possible that a factor pattern could be generated by a single constitutional source, on the one hand, in what I have called a *constitutional trait* (Cattell, 1946) or a single environmental source; on the other, in what I have called an *environmental mold trait*. The latter will bring together items of behavior which have in common *learning from a single source*.

As we inspect the attitudes brought together in the nonergic patterns it becomes evident that they represent *common learning* and, indeed, *environmental mold traits*. Typically, one can see as the central source a single social institution, such as the family, or a career, or a particular form of organized recreation, and so on. Accordingly, it seemed best to designate the second kind of pattern by some such term as an acquired attitude pattern, i.e., an acquired dynamic pattern. I shall henceforth refer to it as a *sentiment*, in lieu of any other suitable generic term. A sentiment is thus a pattern of common variance in attitudes, presumably acquired by the ordinary rules of learning, involving repeated common reward for the attitudes involved. For example, if a person attends a church repeatedly there is repeated reinforcement of several attitudes which in ergic origin are quite diverse—for religion satisfies many needs—but which have the fate of being learned and exercised in common in the institution which we call the church. An individual who goes to church with high frequency, compared with an individual who goes to church with low frequency, should therefore stand higher simultaneously on *all* the attitudes concerned. Continued through the sample, this fact will generate a single factor sentiment. It is probable that there are, in learning experience and resulting statistical pattern, *three* distinct types of sentiment formation (Cattell, 1957, p. 556). To cover all acquired dynamic patterns, and to distinguish them from ergs, the term *engrams* has been suggested. The classification would therefore be as follows:

Dynamic, Structure Factors

Ergs		Engrams	
Viscerogenic Ergs; sometimes called primary drives	Nonviscerogenic Ergs (Murray, 1938); sometimes called secondary drives	Sentiments	Complexes

It should be noted that ergic and engram patterns can be demonstrated both in analysis of individual differences and in P-technique (Cattell, 1954) analyses, i.e., of day-to-day functional covariations within one person (Cattell and Cross, 1952; Cattell, 1957). Illustrative of the sentiments (environmental mold traits) that we have identified are the Self-sentiment, Sentiment to Career, Sports and Games, Mechanical Interests, Religious Sentiment, Patriotic Sentiment. Three of these are presented in Table 3, together with measures and factor loadings that are associated with them.

Table 3   Some Sentiment Factor Patterns

Loading

Sentiment to Profession (Air Force)*

I want to make my career in the Air Force.	.70
I like the excitement and adventure of combat flying.	.63
I want to get technical education such as the Air Force provides.	.58
I enjoy commanding men and taking the responsibilities of a military leader.	.44
I do not want to take more time to enjoy rest and to sleep later in the mornings.	—.41

* Here, as in other tables setting out factors, the signs of the loadings are given as they occur for all the positively directed ("I want") attitudes in the original list of variables. For the reader's convenience in reading the list of salients the qualifying "not" is inserted whenever the loading has gone negative. The attitudes thus read consistently as they stand and need no change.

I like being up in an airplane. .41
I want to satisfy my sense of duty to my country by enlisting in its most important defense arm in threatening times. .39
I want to become first rate at my Air Force job. .36
I do not want to spend more time at home puttering around. —.36

Religious Sentiment

I want to feel that I am in touch with God, or some principle in the universe that gives meaning and help in my struggles. .6
I want to see the standards or organized religion maintained or increased throughout our lives. .6
I want to have my parents' advice and to heed their wishes in planning my affairs. .4
I want my parents never to be lacking the necessities of comfortable living. .3
I do not want to see birth control available to all. .2
I want more protection against the atom bomb. .2
I want my country to be the most powerful and influential. .2
I want to help the distressed, wherever they are. .2
I do not want to spend more time playing cards. .2

The Self-Sentiment

I like to have good control over all my mental processes—my memory, impulses, and general behavior. .4
I want never to do anything that would damage my sense of self-respect. .4
I want to be first-rate in my job. .3
I want to take part in citizenship activities in the community in which I live. .3
I want to maintain a reputation for honest and high principles among my fellows. .3
I like commanding men and taking the responsibilities of a leader. .3
I want to satisfy my sense of duty to my country. .3
I want never to be an insane patient in a mental hospital. .3
I do not want to spend more time in sleep. .3
I want to give my wife the good things she should have. .3
I want to spend more time reading. .3

THE SPECIFICATION EQUATION IN DYNAMIC ANALYSIS

So far, I have talked about factoring a large variety of attitudes in order to arrive at the unitary dynamic source traits which operate among them all. Factors are thus revealed which can be identified on the one hand as ergs and on the other as engrams (including sentiments). This resolution is important both because it leads to testable hypotheses about dynamic structure and also because it enables us, by adding scores on the loaded attitudes, to assign a particular score to an individual for each erg and each sentiment strength.

However, the factor-analytic model also enables us to proceed to dynamic analysis in another way. A column of the factor matrix indicates the attitude composition of an ergic or sentiment factor; i.e., it tells us what attitude scores to add to score a particular sentiment or drive strength; but a row presents the analysis of an attitude into its ergic and sentiment components. It breaks down a single given interest into its ergic sources and thus achieves the same goal as psychoanalysis, but with additional quantitative information. This is a special case of what is called in factor analysis the *specification equation*, and I shall call it the dynamic specification equation. Typically, such an equation has factor strengths and loadings (or situational indices), and it can be used on the one hand to tell us how a given attitude breaks down into dynamic sources and on the other to estimate an individual's strength in the given attitude when we know his endowment in the dynamic source traits. Although these (dynamic structure) source traits, from what has been discerned above about their nature, will be represented by E's (Ergs) and M's (Engrams), it will be realized that mathematically they operate similarly and that each can be estimated for any given individual by combining his scores on the particular variables that are high in the given erg or in the given sentiment. In general, the strength of interest of an individual "i" in a course of action "j" may be stated, therefore, in a dynamic specification equation as follows:

$$I_{ji} = s_{j1e}E_{1i} \ldots + s_{jne}E_{ni} + s_{j1m}M_{1i} \ldots + s_{jnm}M_{ni}$$

Here, I is the strength of interest in the course of action, represented in this case for an individual i in the attitude j (that is to say, an attitude defined as the common-habitual response of people to the situation j). The E's represent different ergs, such as fear, sex, hunger; and the M's represent different engrams, i.e., acquired sentiment patterns such as that to religion, to home, to the self-concept, or patterns of interest due to complexes. It will be observed, incidentally, that this general statement regarding the intensity with which an action is performed, or desired to be performed (if actually inhibited), is an alternative psychological statement to the Hullian learning equation. It seeks similarly to account for the strength of a habit, namely, the attitude-response habit, in terms of concepts of drive strength and of a history of reinforcement (in the sense of reward, not classical conditioning).

However, since our main concern is to clarify the motivational structure itself, we must defer any such digression into the learning "theory" field. Indeed, there are many finer points and possibilities in the present dynamic calculus itself which we have no time to expand upon here, and which must be left to special reading and consideration (Cattell, 1950, 1954, 1957; Cattell and Baggaley, 1958). First, one must point out that the above specification equation could be based either upon an R-technique or a P-technique analysis (Cattell, 1952, 1954), and that in the latter situation, where the values are based on factoring within a single person, it will define the particular structure of the attitude uniquely for an individual, whereas in the R-technique situation it will be a statement about the attitude as it exists in common form in the population at large (Burt, 1940; Cattell, 1952). Second, the motivational-component scores used in the factor estimation are ipsative, or performative, scores (Cattell, 1957), not normative scores. Performatizing is necessary in order to cancel out from the motivational-manifestation measurements the influence of individual differences in what may be called "vehicles" or capacity factors, such as strength of memory, perceptual sensitivity, general autonomic reactivity, etc., which influence the raw scores of the various motivational-component measurement devices. Third, the E measurements strictly define *ergic tension* levels at a given moment, as derived from measurements at a given moment. The analysis of this ergic tension into a steady constitutional component, a temporary stimulus situation strength effect, a physiological influence, etc., as measurable components or sources (in the manner shown in the next formula), must be a result of separate experimental and conceptual division. Fourth, there is evidence, into which we have not time to enter here, that the sentiment patterns actually can arise from two distinct kinds of learned covariation. These unitary sources of covariation in sentiments may be called, respectively, the unity of a subgoal and the unity of an object intersection (Cattell, 1957). They can be made clear only by reference to the concept of the dynamic lattice (Cattell, 1950) and the inspection of subsidiation chains (Murray, 1938) in a number of typical sentiments. Figure 2 may help to indicate these two types, but for fuller discussion thereof the subject must be referred elsewhere (Cattell, 1950, 1957). Finally, there is some evidence of patterns, especially in

P-technique work, which suggest that not all acquired factor patterns are sentiments, but that we must admit a second type of acquired pattern which may be called a complex, after the psychoanalytic terminology. For clarity, a common term and symbol then become necessary to cover all kinds of acquired patterns, and for this we have suggested the term *engram*, indicating a learning or memory phenomenon, and to cover generically both sentiments and complexes. The M's in the specification equation therefore represent engrams, or patterns acquired through any kind of *experience*.

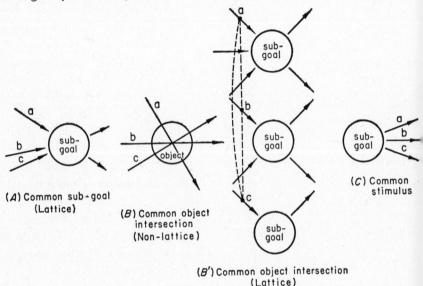

Figure 2. *The three possible non-ergic sources of attitude covariation.*

POTENTIAL CONTRIBUTION FROM THE CONCEPTS DEVELOPED IN DYNAMIC CALCULUS

Let us now take stock of the resources that are put into our hands by the formulation up to this point, and see how they can be used to generate fresh experimental knowledge. On the one hand, we have a model which has been shown to work effectively in representing nature with reasonable accuracy of measurement and prediction. This model contains a number of effective new concepts, as well as a variety of computational possibilities, that have proved useful in both investigation and applied psychology, but which we have not yet fully explored and utilized. These implications can now receive attention.

But before expanding implicit concepts, i.e., examining the gains already in hand, let us take a wider glance to include also potential gains. First we should look at a research harvest which can be foreseen, even though not exactly specified, arising from novel experimental designs previously impracticable. The new designs and goals arise largely from our being able to measure certain entities which could not previously be meaningfully introduced into experimental situations.

The experimental possibility of measuring an attitude without relying on opinionnaire scales promises to give us some claim to ·measuring an *attitude-as-a-whole*, instead of the conscious, partial, and almost certainly distorted verbal manifestation. This greater validity of concept measurement, i.e., greater construct validity, in turn may lead to finding some effective laws about attitudes which we do not now possess. Second, the possibility of measuring two distinct conscious and unconscious, or integrated and unintegrated, components, by definitive factor batteries, makes possible an attack on problems, e.g., on areas of repression, on behavioral effects of unconscious attitudes, which have been theoretically discussed for some time. Third, a whole new realm of experiment begins in the field of learning "theory" when the measurement of the strength of a sentiment structure as a whole becomes possible. Learning theorists frequently overlook the fact that practically all generalizations in learning are at present based on experiments on the acquisition of highly specific and narrow habits and skills. This emasculated theory lacks any basis of reference to the acquisition of complex patterns, and it also ignores that vast field of human and animal behavior which has to do with integrative learning; that is to say, not with success in learning to reach a given goal, but in learning to achieve balance among a set of goals (Cattell, 1950, 1953b).

Obviously, most of the learning which is of interest to personality theorists is not concerned with acquisition of particular skilled habits but is that "emotional learning" which leads to attachment to major cultural institutions or even abstract values. It is this type of learning that now becomes susceptible to measurement and experiment through the ability to measure the strength of sentiments. Furthermore, the measurement of sentiments would enable many theories by sociologists to be put to the touchstone of reality. By grouping the sentiment measurements of individuals, according to various age groups and social classes, it should now be possible to develop and test many hypotheses long existing in a state of suspended animation along the too speculative frontier of theories between social psychology and sociology. The whole of economics hinges on the measurement of values and sentiment strengths, but an effective linking of economic theory with psychological theory has waited upon our capacity to measure the strengths of these major attachments of interest, in various social and cultural groups. Indeed, we have done practically nothing about what the economist calls the "utility" of various goods and services. The very real, dollars-and-cents data on human behavior known to the economist have long provided a challenge which psychologists in motivation theory have conspicuously failed to take up. Sentiment measurement offers one opportunity to meet this challenge.

To anticipate certain broader principles which the present writer plans to develop theoretically elsewhere, let us refer here briefly to the opportunities which these measurements present to the social and cultural psychologist who is interested in classifying cultural stimuli and situations. The loadings, or situational indices, as we call them in the specification equation, actually constitute the emotional (or orectic) meaning of the situation to which the individual is reacting by the given attitude. Social psychology, and indeed individual psychology, have sought a basis for classifying the bewildering multiplicity of cultural stimuli, and social situations, in some way that will permit stimulus-response laws to be found and applied with comparative economy. A substantial loading of situation j in the specification equation on, say, the sex drive, means that changes in ergic tension in sex tend to cause powerful changes in the strength of reaction to the situation and that, by implication, it is a sex-stimulating situation; and so on for other ergs. The profile of obtained factor loadings for a given situation (and attitude response) is therefore properly described as a set of dynamic *situational indices* (Cattell, 1950, 1957) defining the emotional meaning of the situation. Consequently, through grouping a population of situations, by means of a profile-similarity index applied to the loading profiles, using Q'-technique (Cattell, 1957), it should be possible to arrive at a classification, by emotional meaning, of human social situations.

However, among the directions in which we are liberated to experiment, by these new possibilities of conceptual measurement, none is more important than that connected with measuring the E or ergic strength terms in the above specification equation. What does ergic strength mean, in terms of the operations by which we have derived the factor? It is evident both conceptually and from the first experiments using these measures in a clinical case (Cattell and Cross, 1952) that the E terms in the above equation represent the tension level of an erg *at a given moment*, rather than the constitutional or inherent strength of the drive (or other components discussed above.) For example, it was shown in measures made on the above clinical case that the different ergic-drive levels varied in an understandable way from day to day with changes in the individual's life-stimulus situation. Thus the score on the succorant erg, that is to say, the drive connected with protective, pitying behavior, rose steeply and stayed up during the time that a member of the subject's family was seriously ill in hospital. The fear or anxiety drive changed suddenly with stress reports in the consulting-room situation and with the imminence of college examinations, while the narcistic erg was markedly stimulated when the individual began to play a leading role in a stage play.

Hitherto, the measurement of drive level, e.g., of the need for achievement or dominance (Allport, 1937; McClelland *et al.*, 1953), has been an arbitrary procedure, in which both the boundaries of the drive itself and the operations that shall be used to measure its strength have been based on *a priori* definitions and procedures, with resulting lack of comparability of conclusions from one investigator to another. It is true that experimenters with animals have shown some consistency—at least on two drives, hunger and thirst. But this really turns out to be the consistency of a school, not the consistency of scientific investigation; or, as the psychometrist would say, it is merely concept reliability rather than validity. For, as Haverland has shown (1954), the definition of hunger by fiat, which has customarily been by the number of hours that the animal has been deprived of food, has only a moderate relation to the strength of the hunger drive as estimated from a factor. By contrast, the factor pattern, and the beta-weighed estimate of its value that is derived from it, though still not 100 per cent valid, provide an objective, replicable measurement from study to study—one that has a *calculable* level of saturation (validity). An important array of researches relating drive strengths to various psychological, physiological, and sociological conditions has been held up among good experimenters until they could be satisfied that their measurements meant something. Parenthetically, since it has been shown by Haverland (1954), Anderson (1937), and others that our current model works as well with lower animals as with man, we may claim one of the firmer bridges in comparative motivation studies. This model permits researchers to carry out on animals those extreme dynamic experiments which they cannot carry out on human beings, yet reliably to extend the generalizations as far as the measured pattern similarity of dynamic structure authorizes them.

Granted that the E terms represent the final, manifest strength of an ergic tension, it becomes possible to experiment with stimulus situations, and for this the following hypothetical formula has been suggested and discussed elsewhere (Cattell, 1957):

$$E = S\,(C + H + (P - aG)) - bG$$

Where E is the *ergic tension* level, S is the strength of the *stimulus situation*, and the expression within the brackets is the total *need strength*. The expression on the extreme right is the degree of satisfaction or discharge being experienced at the time, which reduces the drive strength generated by the product of the situational intensity and the need strength (in parenthesis). The terms within parentheses, defining the need strength, represent an analysis into a constitutional strength component C, an experiential, historical component, H, arising from past learning affecting this drive as a whole, and a physiological component, P, expressing present independent physiological conditions. G represents the degree of satisfaction or satiation, which operates according to the coefficient "a" (reductively) upon the physiological need state, P, and according to the coefficient "b" (reductively) upon the total psychological need strength. Of course, this is offered only as a hypothesis about the ingredients in the total ergic-tension level, but as a hypothesis that can be checked by investigation, because we have the means of experimentally measuring the strength of a particular erg, in separation from any other erg, so that its relations to the independent variables, S, G, P, etc., can now be reliably experimented upon.

It should be observed that the possibility of measuring the ergic tension level of one particular drive, in separation from the general drive level associated with several ergic sources, creates also the possibility of experimentally investigating and creating a reliable inventory of the particular stimuli which trigger a given erg, either constitutionally or by acquired learning patterns. Thus a path is open to the experimental investigation of what may be called the natural history of drives, their changes with maturation and age, their physiological roots, and the exact manner of their modification by learning. For example, one could map the stimuli which appear to need reinforcement with those which do not, to arrive at some idea of the innately more potent stimulus situations for a given drive.

DEMONSTRATED UTILITY OF THE SPECIFICATION EQUATION

Let us now turn to the conceptual and computational possibilities inherent in the formula that are now known, regardless of further research findings. I propose to deal systematically with these, instead of in the somewhat discursive references just made to merely *possible* experimental ramifications; for one may rightly object that this talk of experimental possibilities is drawing checks upon the future, whereas what we actually have in our grasp is a model verified to a certain point but containing further concepts fully implicit in it. Let us therefore leave the harvest of results which we believe to be experimental possibilities, and return to the implications of the specification equation.

Much debate has occurred in clinical psychology and elsewhere regarding the importance of defining the situational context in which motives operate. For example, the personality theorist is sometimes accused of assuming that "motives" are purely static entities, entirely inherent in the individual. It is sometimes asserted that traits give insufficient regard to the stimulus situation and temporal changes in the trait, whereas in everyday life, when we see some extreme action, we are inclined to ask, "Was this individual extreme or was the situation extreme?" or "Was he in an extreme mood?" Now, the situational indices—the s's in the specification equation—provide a natural and comprehensive way of dealing with the first, and the need strength symbols a way of dealing with the second. The role of the situational indices has already been indicated in a preliminary way in the discussion of a method for classifying the stimulus situations in our culture, but let us bring out this neglected theme of situational indices more fully.

It has been pointed out elsewhere (Cattell, 1957) that the factor loadings, when they deal with personality and ability factors of known psychological nature, accurately describe the extent to which particular temperament traits and mental capacities have become involved in reaction to a given situation. Consequently, I have previously represented what are actually factor-analytic loadings (Cattell, 1950, 1952) in the formula as small s's meaning "situational indices." The situational indices can now be used to describe the situation, in measurements arising from the behavior of the persons in the sample involved in the interaction. For example, if success in handling clinical problems proves to be loaded substantially and positively on "g" and on the emotional-stability factor, then we say that it is a situation making demands on intelligence and emotional stability, or, in other words, that it is "a complex and provocative (or upsetting)" problem. This descriptiveness of the situational indices becomes even more apparent when we move into the area of drives. Everyday language, by its projective habit, in fact, does just what we are proposing to do here, when it describes some natural situation as being, say, awe-inspiring, indicating that both fear and curiosity are strongly stimulated by it. The s's will now be perceived to be a quantitative statement of what has loosely been called the valence or value of a stimulus situation. (Incidentally, this remark does not imply in any animistic way that the energy is somehow "in the stimulus," as the rejected "valence" theories would imply;

it only states that for the given species this stimulus evokes the primary drives with the given pattern of weightings.) As the psychologist pursues this measurement of the dimensions of stimuli further he will see that final, exact work requires that one distinguish and use both the loading, which indicates the *variance* contribution of the given ergic reactivity, and the mean level of evoked tension, which indicates the *average* population reactivity to that situation.

Now, typically, any given stimulus situation evokes a complex orectic reaction, in which some ergs are highly loaded, others are less loaded, and yet others loaded not at all. This reaction provides the profile or pattern of *s*'s of which we have been speaking, and, as I indicated earlier, it should be possible to use the Q'-technique on them, correlating situations one with another and thus grouping them as to dynamic "type" of situation in an objective fashion. If such a true cultural taxonomy of stimulus situations, based on meaning, is soon achieved, there will doubtless arise a valuable field within anthropology and sociology of comparative culture studies based on such quantifiable taxonomies.

So much for the implications of the model in terms of classifying motivational situations and of assigning quantitative potencies or valencies to environmental situations. Now let us swing around and look at situational indices from the standpoint of inferences about the individual, or about individuals in general. The important inference here is that the simultaneous presence of positive and negative ergic loadings, in a course of action arising from a particular stimulus situation, is an indication of conflict. There have been many psychometric attempts to quantify conflict and integration, but they are often remote from clinical realities, and I think that what we have here comes nearest to what the clinician has always been talking about. If for a course of action defined by attitude X, a given erg, E_a, is substantially positively loaded, while another erg, E_b, is substantially negatively loaded, this (according to the very nature of the factor analysis) can mean only that the course of action X gives satisfaction to *a* at the cost of reduction of satisfaction of *b*. There must always be some positive balance of satisfaction in a course a person positively wishes to follow, but with that single reservation we could have almost any pattern of positive and negative loadings over a certain set of ergs in regard to a certain course of action. If the degree of conflict in a dynamic system is to be indicated percentagewise as the fraction of blocked or canceled energy in relation to the total energy in the system, then we arrive at an index of conflict, C, which contrasts the algebraic sum with the arithmetical sum of the ergic loadings. To be exact, the fraction used would be the arithmetic sum minus the algebraic sum divided by the arithmetic sum, as follows:

$$C = \frac{(\Sigma s^{(+)} + \Sigma s^{(-)}) - (\Sigma s^{(+)} - \Sigma s^{(-)})}{(\Sigma s^{(+)} + \Sigma s^{(-)})}$$

This expression simplifies to (twice) the sum of the negative loadings over the sum of all loadings, thus:

$$C = \frac{\Sigma s^{(-)}}{\Sigma s^{(+)} + \Sigma s^{(-)}}$$

Instead of a percentage we can alternatively use the expression which gives weight to the absolute size of the drives in conflict.

So far, we have talked of the percentage of conflict in a system, which could be either a single attitude, or an aggregate of attitudes, as in a major sentiment, or indeed the total personality. If we apply it to the total personality, it will be seen that we are getting, in accepted psychological parlance, a measure of adjustment or integration. In order to be effective, such a measure must obviously include a stratified sample of attitudes from the total life space of the individual. It would be unfair to compare the total conflict of person A with person B if we took only, say, the attitudes concerned with the occupation or the attitudes concerned specifically with the home, since in one case the person might be more integrated in his occupational attitudes and in another more integrated in his home attitudes. This problem of obtaining a stratified sample that will give a good estimate of what is happening in the whole population of attitudes of major importance in life is, of course, a difficult one and perhaps may never be entirely satisfactorily solved. But in principle we shall assume that a reasonable solution can be obtained through obtaining a total conflict or integration index by comparing individuals on an equivalent, stratified sample of common attitudes and interests. With this restriction a formula for adjustment, A, can be written

$$A = 1 - C$$

Now, it is psychologically intriguing to find at this point that whenever we have factored sets of attitudes, which approximate complete sampling of the life space, we have typically approached what mathematicians call "a positive manifold." That is, the majority of the projections of attitude interests upon the factors has been positive, and the positive quadrant of the factor plots has far more variables in it than occur in the other three quadrants. The reader may recall that in the early days of factoring abilities this was so frequent a finding that it became, according to Thurstone, the proper rule for rotation, namely, to rotate to keep a positive manifold. By contrast, when the assault was made on *general* personality analysis, the discovery was made that loadings were no more frequently positive than negative, a curiosity which Burt first pointed out (Burt, 1940). In other words, as I have indicated in discussing the meaning of various general personality dimensions (Cattell, 1950), a given temperament trait, scored positively, is just as frequently a hindrance as a help in any random sample of performances. However, upon extending research from general temperament traits to measurements on specifically dynamic traits we were at first surprised to find that we again met a picture like that of abilities, in which far more projections were positive than negative (though not to the extent found in abilities, where negative loadings are very rare).

That dynamic analysis should yield a positive manifold is seen, on closer examination, to be a necessary corollary of the general Hedonic principle. People tend to acquire only those attitudes and interests which give them a predominance of positive satisfactions over dissatisfactions. If we take the standard, stratified sample of attitudes on which to compare people, then the ratio C in the equation above is bound to be less than 1, so long as the person's total life satisfactions remain positive. It will be seen that the proposed adjustment index, A above, will approach unity in a person perfectly free from conflict, and zero in a person whose energies are totally absorbed in conflict.

This is a first, simplified statement of the proposition, but closer scrutiny will reveal the need for some conceptual clarification and also for special conditions of calculation in the use of the index experimentally. Conceptually, it is necessary to examine the relation of this mathematically based definition to the interrelated definitions of Adaptation, Adjustment, and Integration reasoned out earlier on psychological grounds (Cattell, 1950, p. 261). It will be seen that this index exactly corresponds to the definition of adjustment there given as (metaphorically) "freedom from internal friction." An open mind must be kept, however, until experiment decides whether this exact conception also corresponds to the clinician's conception of *desirable* adjustment.

In terms of calculation from the specification equation, we encounter first the fact that though all ergs are given unit, equal weight by the specification equation we are accustomed clinically to think of some drives as stronger than others. For example,

$$R = .3E_F - .3F_C$$

would suggest that if fear and curiosity are in conflict, an equal fraction (0.3) of each erg being involved, the result will be zero action, i.e. complete mutual inhibition, whereas the clinician may bet that fear, being on an average a stronger drive, will win out. In factor analysis it does not follow, however, that even with a perfect sampling of variables the sums of squares of all the loadings of any one factor (what the mathematician calls the latent root) will equal that of any other factor. The latent roots, indeed, granted that they are based on a stratified sample of life interests, may prove to be the required mathematical expression for calculating "the relative strengths of ergs." These intriguing issues, and complications, which can be given only a glance here, must be left to fuller development elsewhere.

However, there is a more basic item of mathematical treatment on which one must be clear even at a first statement of the dynamic calculus. This is the difference between R-technique and P-technique factor analyses (Cattell, 1952). The former states average values for the whole population sample. The latter gives values peculiar to the individual, and it is therefore from P-technique (factoring of the single person) that the values for C and A must be derived. This would involve a factor analysis of each clinical case, but with electronic computers this is no serious objection if the dynamic calculus propositions prove to be effective. An experimental examination of the hypothesis that the above index essentially describes the degree of dynamic adjustment of the individual is now being made by J. R. Williams, who on a first sample of five patients and five normals found C higher for the patients at $P < .05$ significance, and a correlation of .70 of C with psychiatric, clinical evaluations of the magnitude of conflict in each.

Perhaps a word should be said here about P-technique in connection with current debates on the relative strategic value of detailed studies of *individual* cases versus large-scale experimental investigations. It would be a mistake on the part of clinical psychologists to classify the present writer and other users of factor-analytic techniques as inveterate supporters of large-scale experiment. For significance of loadings and adequate identification of factors, many people and many variables are in some circumstances essential. But in other circumstances the factor-analytic study of a single person may be highly contributory to general scientific principles. The present writer's objections to alleged "intensive studies of individuals" has been only that frequently these are, as in Lewin's and Stephenson's advocacy, concerned with art rather than science. That is to say, they are not designed in a way to make them capable of revealing laws of a completely general applicability. Scientific analysis recognizes that the individual is unique, but he is unique in the sense of a unique configuration of the effects of universal principles. In P-technique we measure one individual on perhaps a hundred variables, repeating the measures as he changes from day to day, for perhaps three months. The factorization of the single *person*, i.e., P-technique, thus yields the unique dynamic structure of that individual. But the laws by which we see that structure acquired and changed are presumably universal laws, and the study of the individual is an avenue to these laws.

The writer's chief criticism of those who advocate an intensive study of the individual is, therefore, that they are not intensive enough! A truly intensive study requires many variables, exact quantitative methods, and the skill to take advantage of multivariate analytical techniques powerful and positive enough to reveal structures. That is to say, it must be scientifically intensive and rigorous enough to obviate the danger that the clinician will project his own subjective interpretations. Such methods, including P-technique, which present a quantitative and objective analysis of individual motives, are still unfortunately insufficiently used by clinicians and therefore given no chance to lift hunches to new scientific levels. But here we have strayed into questions of routine clinical practice and must return to the conceptual development of the model itself.

A third direction of conceptual development implicit in this model, (and, what is more important, in the factual findings already obtained by the model), is the possibility of using it to predict the outcome of conflict. This includes predicting the strength and nature of an adjustive new attitude which may arise from the conflict and eventual integration of two existing attitudes. It will be evident that any sentiment or other acquired dynamic structure in personality can be said to possess a given investment of drive energy, describable by the summed projections of that system upon the ergic coordinates. Now, anyone familiar with algebra will recognize that the profile of loadings for a given attitude, that is to say, its set of situational indices (the row of the attitude in the factor matrix) corresponds to the mathematical definition of a vector, and that an alternative way of representing an attitude is therefore to draw it geometrically, as a vector in the space defined by the coordinate system. This is illustrated in Figure 3. Consequently, the ordinary mathematical rules for the summation of vectors, as in the well-known polygon of physical forces, apply also to the summation of attitude vectors. If one can find a new attitude C, i.e., a new course of action, which, whatever its actual behavioral course of action, achieves the ergic satisfactions of conflicting attitudes A and B simultaneously, then this new attitude C will be highly psychologically acceptable to the individual. It will become invested with the energy of A and B and will be represented by a vector, corresponding to the diagonal of the parallelogram defined by the first two vectors. The problem of conflict solution is first to find this vector and its ergic pattern and then to seek lines of behavior which will yield this particular kind of satisfaction.

A little reflection on this summation will reveal a way out of the confusion created by the customary inelegant description of an at-

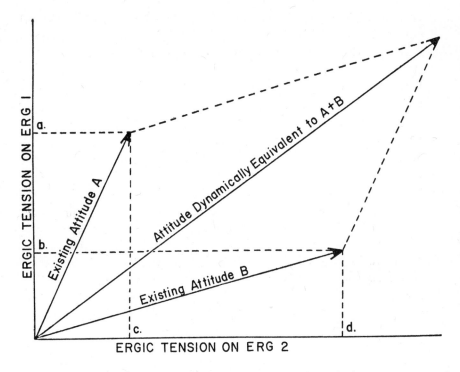

Figure 3. *Vector representation of ergic conflict and resolution.*

titude as "for or against" an object. Our attitude definition is for or against *a course of action,* which is operational and real enough. For or against an *object* may mean almost anything—to avoid it, to destroy it, to be fond of it in any of the thousand varieties of affection, and so on. The "for or against a course of action" is fixed by the course of action and becomes exactly analyzed by the subsequent determination of the vector in ergic space, which *defines the precise emotional quality by its direction,* and *the intensity by its length.* Now, since a sentiment is a collection of attitudes bound by common use of an object or subgoal, the ergic investment in that object can be determined as the vector sum of all those attitudes. If this sum is positive, regardless of its quality, the persons want the object to go on existing, as the means to satisfaction of all these attitudes. If it is negative, the object is a source of dissatisfaction, no matter what the quality. This is the element of reality in the popular "for and against" terminology, and we see that it really applies *to a sentiment, not an attitude.* (Semantics aside, and calling each what you wish, "for and against" has meaning, on the one hand, for courses of action and, on the other, for particular objects—those which are organizing points for collections of attitudes or courses of action.)

The utilities of the dual formulation in attitudes and sentiments, with the vector summation of the former to the latter, and the representation of both on ergic coordinates, are very great. These potent applications ramify into many phases of social psychology, group dynamics, and sociology. For example, the attitudes of members of a group toward their group may be summed to give the total synergy (Cattell, 1950, p. 387) of the group as a group. However, so long as we are concentrating mainly on the assessment of motives in individuals, the more important inference is in the summation of intrapersonal conflict. I am suggesting that even before conflict takes place, typically through a new situation forcing hitherto nonconflicting attitudes into a relation of conflict, we can predict what the outcome of such a conflict will be. The attitude with the larger energy investment, that is to say, with the greater vector length, will be the one expressed, if only one is to be maintained. Alternatively, if a new solution by confluence (Cattell, 1950, p. 215) is reached, the attitude defining the new behavior must fall within the ergic satisfaction pattern defined by the calculable resultant of the two vectors.

So far in this discussion of a "calculus of conflict" our model has been concerned with only the total resultant or final outcome. It compares an initial equilibrium position with another reached after upset, and claims to throw no light upon the particular psychological processes and temporary mechanisms which mediate the conflict. For example, nothing has been said about whether the conflict is or becomes conscious or unconscious; yet there is reason to think, from clinical observation, that such differences may be important for the outcome. All that our analysis shows, when it reveals "conflict" by the coexistence of positive and negative loadings of ergs on a particular attitude-interest, is that some sort of stable compromise—a dynamic equilibrium between the conflicting forces—has been reached. This is the best solution that the individual can find in terms of the largest possible total satisfaction, even though it involves the suppression or repression of one drive in the interests of another. However, the clinician, from the patient's introspections, may conclude that this stable state has been reached either in terms of a successfully achieved repression, or in terms of a constantly recurring conscious conflict with willed suppression of the dissatisfied drive. Apparently, our methods of analysis, as so far stated, would not disclose any difference.

However, the dynamic calculus does possess a source of evidence on this matter. So far we have dealt largely with dynamic structure factors, having set aside the motivational-component factors described at the beginning, as something concerned only with the measurement devices and their interrelations. But in theory, though it has not yet been put to experiment, it would be possible to measure any dynamic structure factor in terms of the devices in one motivational-component factor only. Thereby we should find what a given attitude or sentiment means in terms of the ego, id, and superego components in it. Does attitude X, in fact, sustain itself largely from conscious or unconscious components? By introducing this cross analysis we restore the conscious and unconscious dimensionality in which the psychoanalyst is accustomed to think, and thus gain access to a fuller predictive power, by virtue of our knowledge of the different correlates and outcomes of conscious and unconscious conflict.

Although no experimental investigation has yet been made, we may hypothesize certain systematic relations as indicated above between the dynamic-structure and motivation-component systems. Initially, it will be remembered that the motivational-component system and the dynamic-structure system are totally independent. One is a system of factors among motivational-manifestation measuring devices, on any single attitude measurement, and the other is a set of factors from factoring a great variety of diverse attitudes and interest contents. They are primarily "cross classifications"; yet hypothetically we should expect certain relations. Principally, it would be expected that if the measures of varied attitudes are made in the ego-component devices the dynamic factors corresponding to established, reality-tested sentiments would come out more clearly, i.e., with larger variance, whereas if one used devices shown to be more saturated in the id component of all interests, the dynamic interest factors we have called ergs should achieve greater emphasis in variance. The effect is strictly analogous to looking at a picture with some objects painted largely in red and others largely in green, now with red glasses and now with green glasses. Investigation of this selective emphasis by motivational-component test device is still to come.

In this connection something more specific may be said about the *self-sentiment,* which is such an important and constant finding in our dynamic structure factorings. This pattern is distinguishable from the self-assertive erg, though *both* affect some attitudes; e.g., "I want to increase my salary," "I want to stand well with my neighbors" simultaneously. The self-sentiment is a pattern of attitudes centering on the self-concept, and manifesting interest in the physical, social, and moral preservation of the self according to desired standards (Cattell, 1950, p. 244; 1957, p. 524). However, a conceptual problem remains in reconciling this entity with two others found in general personality-factor data, namely, the Self-Sentiment "Power of Control" factor in objective tests (Cattell, 1956) and questionnaires, labeled Q_3 (Cattell, Saunders, and Stice, 1957), and the second-order General Integration Factor (Cattell, 1957, p. 317). Our tentative solution is that the present dynamic structure factor represents the strength of the individual's desire (aspiration) to achieve behavior fitting the self-concept, whereas Q_3 represents the extent to which he *feels he has* achieved it, and the Integration factor measures the extent to which he has actually achieved it. The exact correlational relations among these patterns are set out elsewhere (Cattell, 1957, p. 317, 527), but it suffices that the dynamic factor has the highest correlation with Q_3 (about 0.6 when corrected for attenuation) of any dynamic factor, and that Q_3 correlates also with the dynamic Super Ego factor. The experimental connections thus come out initially as theory would require, but much remains to be cleared up by subtly conceived and metrically exact research with these factors.

If clinical psychology and personality theory are right in assigning so large a role in the resolution of conflict to the self-sentiment, we should expect to find it loading certain attitudes in factor analysis accordingly. For example, it should be *pervasive,* with "a finger in every pie," and this wide prevalence of slight loadings seems to be found. Again, it should in conflicts of ergs and sentiments, tend to throw its weight with the sentiments, and this also we find in the major second-order dynamic factor, headed by the self-sentiment, followed by other stable sentiments, e.g., religion, and, opposed in loading to sex erg, self-assertion (aggression) and anxiety (Cattell, 1957, p. 56). However, after these factor-analytic clarifications of patterns, the time will come for manipulative experimental designs to see how the self sentiment factor behaves in the actual temporal process of attitude conflict.

In this discussion of integration, conflict, and the summation of attitudes in more confluent solutions, we have several times hovered around the use of the word "energy." Now, mental energy is a concept which no clinician, or student of personality dynamics, seems to be able to avoid entirely, yet it is at the same time one which no respectable psychologist can operationally define in a way which justifies continued use of it. In concluding this account of a model—and I should remind you, an already substantiated model—for a dynamic calculus, I should like to ask whether it also gives us a chance of catching and bringing back alive so rare a quarry as this elusive concept of energy.

Let me remind you that the value I_j, in our first and basic specification equation defines the *strength* of interest in a given course of action. Strength is, in terms of the diagram, the length of the vector, abstracted from its direction. Consequently, any one attitude can be compared with any other in terms of the strength of interest in it, regardless of the quality of this interest, since the length represents quantity and the direction quality. So far then, we have achieved a concept which can be abstracted from the particular direction of reactivity, as the energy concept requires. But whether this length remains in other respects the psychological equivalent of a physical force or of a physical energy, i.e., a force multiplied by the distance through which it acts, remains to be investigated. The decision, if it can be made, hinges both upon consideration of the nature of the behavioral battery through which the measurements are made, and upon experimental findings showing the further behavior of people whose scores upon the test are accurately known. For example, is it possible that two people with equally strong intentions to act in a certain way, i.e., of equal strength of attitude, will behave differently when the wear and tear of work intervenes? If individuals A and B score identically on attitude strength, but A carries the same intensity of application through a greater distance than individual B, then energy must be I_j, multiplied by distance, analogously to the physicist's definition of work or energy. On the other hand, it may be argued from the nature of the tests which come out with high loadings in strength as now measured (for example, a test of the ability to memorize in the field of the interest indicated) that I_j is *already* a work measurement.

The question can be raised but not solved. I am sorry if I disappoint you by leading you to the walls of a citadel only to say that there is now no time to assault it. Fascinating though the prospect may be of at last devising an operational approach to the concept of mental energy, I think you will agree that there must be several years of experimental consolidation of our lines of communication up to this point, before we can attack this great theoretical issue with some prospect of success.

Meanwhile I believe all research on this area would do well to keep sharply in focus the nine pregnant questions which Professor Lindzey has propounded to the speakers in this survey of motivation. They seem to me to illuminate very clearly the target for present-day research; and, as we all know, there is nothing so important in research as asking the right questions. It is for all participants in this enterprise to judge how far I and the other contributors have given the right answers. But if your judgment on this matter is to mean anything it must be guided by the further answers derivable from your own active research on the points and concepts at issue.

REFERENCES

Allport, G. W. *Personality: a psychological interpretation.* New York: Holt, 1937.

Anderson, E. E. Interrelationship of drives in the male albino rat. I. Intercorrelations of measures of drives. *J. comp. Psychol.*, 1937, 24, 73-118.

Burt, C. L. *Factors of the mind.* London: University of London Press, 1940.

Cattell, R. B. *The description and measurement of personality.* New York: World, 1946.

————. r_p and other coefficients of pattern similarity. *Psychometrika*, 1949, 14, 279-298.

————. *Personality: a systematic theoretical and factual study.* New York: McGraw-Hill, 1950.

————. *Factor analysis: an introduction and manual for the psychologist and social scientist.* New York: Harper, 1952.

————. The principal invariant personality factors established in objective tests. Adv. Public. No. 1, Lab. of Person. Assess. & Group Behavior. Urbana: University of Illinois, 1953a.

————. On the theory of group learning. *J. soc. Psychol.*, 1953b, 37, 27-51.

————. P-technique. A new method for analyzing the structure of personal motivation. *Trans. N.Y. Acad. Sci.*, Ser. II, 1954a, 14, 29-34.

————. *A universal index for psychological factors.* Adv. Public. No. 3, Lab. of Person. Assess. & Group Behavior. Urbana: University of Illinois, 1954b.

————. *The O-A Personality Factor Batteries.* Champaign, Ill.: Instit. Person. & Ability Testing, 1956.

————. *Personality and motivation structure and measurement.* New York: World, 1957.

————, and Baggaley, A. R. *The salient variable similarity index-s for factor matching.* Adv. Public. No. 4, Lab. of Person. Assess. & Group Behavior. Urbana: University of Illinois, 1954.

————, and ————. The objective measurement of attitude motivation: development and evaluation of principles and devices. *J. Pers.*, 1956, 24, 401-423.

————, and ————. The objective measurement of motivation. II. Determination of dynamic personality structure. *Austral. J. Psychol.*, 1958, 10.

————, Blewett, D., and Beloff, J. The inheritance of personality: a multiple variance analysis determination of approximate nature-nurture ratios for primary personality factors in Q-data. *Amer. J. Human Genet.*, 1955, 7, 122-146.

————, and Cross, P. Comparison of the ergic and self-sentiment structures found in dynamic traits by R- and P-techniques. *J. Pers.*, 1952, 21, 250-270.

————, Saunders, D. R., and Stice, G. F. *The 16 P.F. Questionnaire,* rev. ed. Champaign, Ill.: Instit. of Person. & Ability Testing, 1957.

————, and Tapp, J. A check on the nature and interpretation of the alpha, beta, gamma, delta motivation component factors in adult attitude-interest. (In press.)

Haverland, E. The application of an analytical solution for proportional profiles rotated to a box problem and to the drive structure in rats. Ph. D. Thesis, University of Illinois Library, Urbana, Ill., 1954.

McClelland, D. C., Atkinson, J. W.; Clark, R. A., and Lowell, E. L. *The achievement motive.* New York: Appleton-Century-Crofts, 1953.

Murray, H. A., *et al. Explorations in personality.* New York: Oxford University Press, 1938.

GORDON W. ALLPORT

Harvard University

9 *What units shall we employ?*

Man's nature, like all of nature, seems to be composed of relatively stable structures. The success of psychological science, therefore, as of any science, depends in large part upon its ability to identify the major structures, substructures, and microstructures (elements) of which its assigned portion of the cosmos is composed.

EARLY INADEQUATE UNITS

The Humors. From the fourth century B.C. to the seventeenth century A.D. the life sciences—indeed all the sciences—were badly frozen because they had chosen unproductive units of analysis—the Empedoclean elements of earth, air, fire, and water. These units and these alone are the "root of things"—so said Hippocrates and Galen, so said all the sages of the Middle Ages and Renaissance, including both Christian and Islamic scholars (see Sherrington, 1953). Personality theory, such as it was, was written entirely in terms of the four temperaments arising, men said, from the humoral distillations of the four cosmic elements—black bile (*melancholic*), yellow bile (*sanguine*), blood (*choleric*), and phlegm (*phlegmatic*). *Quatuor humores in nostro corpore regnant* sang the thirteenth-century medical poem. This rigidity of analysis endured at least until the time of Harvey, whose discovery of the circulation of the blood in 1628 cast doubt upon the whole humoral doctrine (see Allport, 1937).

The Faculties. Freed at last from this incubus, psychology perversely entered a second ice age by adopting the conception of "faculties"— units scarcely more productive than the humors. The faculties set forth by the Thomists, by Christian Wolff, by the Scottish school, and by the phrenologists have a certain common-sense appeal, but they do not satisfy modern theorists.

Instincts and Drives. Under the influence of Darwin, personality theorists traded faculties for instincts. The ensuing era, lasting approximately sixty years, cannot be called an ice age, for it brought with it McDougall's elegant and consistent defense of instincts and their derivatives, the sentiments. More than anyone else, McDougall fixed our attention upon the possible existence of uniform motivational units. Freud reinforced the search, though unlike McDougall, he himself offered no clear taxonomic scheme. During this era innumerable instincts were discovered, postulated, invented. In 1924 Bernard reported that more than 14,000 different instincts had been proposed, and that no agreement was yet in sight. Sensing disaster in this direction, psychologists started fishing in fresher waters. The doctrine of drives (a limited form of instinct) continued to hold the behaviorist fort, and still to some extent does so, but most psychologists nowadays seem to agree with Hebb (1949) that to equate motivational structure with simple drives or biological needs is a wholly inadequate procedure.

DIFFICULTIES AND COMPLEXITIES OF CONTEMPORARY SEARCH

I mention these fragments of history in the hope that they will give perspective to our contemporary search. It is clear that we have not yet solved the problem of the units of man's nature, though the problem was posed twenty-three centuries ago. It is equally clear that psychology lags far behind chemistry, which has its periodic table of elements; behind physics with its verifiable if elusive quanta; and even far behind biology with its cell. Psychology does not yet know what its "cell" may be. It is partly for this reason that skeptics question psychology's right to be called a science. Its investigators have not yet reached agreement on what units of analysis to employ.

Some of the trouble lies in the fact that psychology could make little use of a "cell," even if it discovered one. (It has given up the "reflex arc," which for a time seemed to serve the purpose.) Psychology's peculiar problem lies in the existence of many different levels of organization whose number and nature are as yet unascertained. Units of structure may be smaller or larger, depending on our interests. If we happen to be concerned with an elementary behavioral problem, such as the alternate extension and flexion of the leg, we may adopt *spinal innervation* as our unit. If we wish to classify forms of motor activity, then *walking* seems a more acceptable unit. Should we be interested in interpersonal behavior, we can conceivably establish a measurable habit of *walking away from people* (thus approaching Karen Horney's conception). If our concern is with the generalized dispositions of personality, we may consider some such unit as a *trait of withdrawal*. Finegrained or coarse-grained—units of both orders have their place. Ultimately, of course, our hope is to be able to reduce molar units to molecular and, conversely, to compound molecular units into molar.

But we are far from this goal. Even at the coarser levels of analysis we are not in agreement on the kinds of units we seek. Shall they be habits or habit systems, needs or sentiments, vectors, factors, trends, or traits? Shall they be drives or dimensions, *Anschauungen* or attitudes, regions, syndromes, personal constructs, or ergs? All have been proposed and empirically defended. The most hopeful note in the confused situation is that for the past thirty years there has been boundless zeal for both measurement and theory. By now the measured aspects of personality cannot fall far short of the 14,000 instinctive units reported by Bernard. When psychologists face up to this orgy of units, let us hope they will not fall into the state of collapse that terminated the earlier search for instincts. There seems to be no immediate danger, for one reads in the *American Psychologist* (1957, p. 51):

A Ford Foundation grant of $238,400 will enable a research team of the University of Minnesota to conduct a five year study aimed at developing a more adequate system of descriptive, diagnostic, and dynamic categories. . . . The team will work toward developing terms or systems of terms maximally descriptive of personality.

I have elected to speak on this bewildering topic, not because I have a secret solution for a two-thousand-year-old problem, nor because I am so clairvoyant that I can prevision the final Minnesota results. I do so because I believe that our present research lacks perspective on its own efforts, and I should like to achieve a balanced view of the efforts of assessors to date. Toward the end of this paper I shall venture one somewhat radical proposal for a shift of direction in our research.

CENTRAL PROPOSITIONS FOR A NEW APPROACH

First, a few central propositions on which I hope we can all agree. It seems clear that the units we seek in personality and in motivation are relatively complex structures, not molecular. They lie in the upper reaches of what Hull called the habit hierarchy, and not at the level of specific habits. We do not seek cells or even cell assemblies; we do not seek reflexes, hedons, traces, or quanta of endocrine discharge, or the gating processes of the nervous system. Ultimately, of course, we should like to translate complex structures into microelements and discover their neurohumoral counterparts. But at present, and for some time to come, we must be satisfied to search out the generalized units that define relatively broad forms of organization.

There is a second proposition on which I hope we can reach equally rapid agreement. Methodologists tell us that we can never observe a motive or a trait or any similar unit directly. We agree. They tell us that any unit we discover is only a "hypothetical construct" or an "intervening variable." Here, too, they are right, though for my part I vote for "hypothetical construct," which, in the usage proposed by MacCorquodale and Meehl (1948), implies that the units we seek, though invisible, are factually existing. Methodologists tell us, furthermore, that we must have sound and repeatable operations for establishing the units we fix upon; we may not bring them into being by merely naming them, as did the addicts of instinct a generation or two ago. Again we agree. In fact, we do well to accept all the cautions and safeguards of modern methodology, save only that excess of zeal which holds all units to be fictional and existing only in the manipulations of the investigator.

A third proposition will detain us longer, for it has to do with the greatest stumbling block of all in our search for objectively existing structures. I refer to the unquestioned variability of a person's behavior from situation to situation. Motivational units discovered under laboratory conditions often seem to evaporate when the subject moves from the laboratory to his office, to his home, to his golf club. Indeed, his behavior in these familiar settings may often seem contradictory. Situational variability has led many social scientists to the conviction that any search for a consistent personality with specifiable motives and traits is doomed to failure.

Recently I attended a conference of psychologists working on the problem of the "perception of persons" (see Tagiuri, 1958). At this conference one heard much about perception but little about persons, the object of perception. The reason, I think, is that the participants were keenly aware of the chameleonlike changes that mark a person as he moves from situation to situation. They much preferred to study the perception-of-a-person-in-a-situation, and thus evade the question of what the person is really like. Not only does the individual vary his behavior, but our perception of him is heavily affected by our subjective sets, by our liking for him, by his uncongeniality, or by his degree of similarity to ourselves. The perceiver himself may, therefore, be the principal source of variance; the situation in which the object-person acts may be the second source of variance; and the fixed traits and motives of the object-person may be only a minor factor.

The hope for an accurate assessment of motives and traits is thus badly bedeviled by the person's variability and by the perceiver's bias. It is also badly bedeviled by the uncertainty of criteria. When are we to know that our assessment is accurate and veridical? Not by comparing our assessment with ratings by others, who may be subject to both common and idiosyncratic errors. Not by the self-report of the subject, who is capable of self-deception. Not by prediction of future behavior, which will depend to a considerable extent on the situation that evokes this behavior. Not by other tests and measurement, for these too are fallible.

SITUATIONAL VARIABLES

Role Theory. All these objections are sound, and their combined force is today, as I say, leading many investigators away from the assessment of motives and persons. One tempting escape is found in the concept of "role." Emanuel Brown, to use one example, is no longer viewed as a single person: he is a colligation of roles. As a teacher he meets certain expectancies; as a father, others; still others as a citizen, or as a Rotarian. In one of his enthusiastic moments William James (1910) took the same way out. "A man," he says, "has as many selves as there are distinct groups of persons about whose opinion he cares." (p. 179)

The extreme version of this situational doctrine is found in Coutu's book, *Emergent Human Nature* (1949), where the author argues that the search for traits of personality and their assessment is chimerical; that the most we can say of any person is that in a given situation he has a specific tendency to respond in a certain limited way. The only acceptable unit, therefore, according to Coutu, is the "tinsit" or "tendency-in-a-situation."

Unless we can successfully refute the extreme forms of role theory and tinsit theory, and James's statement about the social self, our work should cease here and now. What is the use of assessing motivation or personality if behavior is as dependent on the situation as these theories assert? Let us see what may be said on the other side.

Safeguards against Situational Variability. In the first place, some of our assessment methods have built into them a safeguard against situational variability. They explicitly vary the situation. Thus a person's disposition to be ascendant, or his aesthetic value, or his neurotic tendency is tested by a wide range of items depicting a great variety of situations commonly experienced. While some studies show that a trait measured in this way does vary, say, from the academic to the business situation, or from the athletic to the purely social, it is more common to find that the person carries with him, by and large, his typical level of anxiety, a typical amount of aesthetic interest, of ascendance, or a typical aspiration level, or a fairly constant degree of prejudice.

In the second place, it is obviously not true that a man has as many social selves as there are groups whose opinion he prizes. A man who is deferential, ambitious, or compulsive in the office is not likely to shed these characteristics at home or on the golf course. Their intensity may vary and their mode of expression may alter, but true Jekyll and Hyde cases are exceedingly rare. So far as roles are concerned, is it not a fact that characteristic styles run through a person's conduct even when he is playing diverse roles? Is it not also true that a person *seeks* the roles that are most congenial to his personality, avoiding others that cramp his style or put an undue strain upon his internal motivational structure? That some persons are forced into roles they do not like we must admit, just as we must admit that a range of variation marks anyone's behavior according to the circumstances in which he finds himself.

But though these factors greatly complicate our search for structures, they need not discourage us. There is too much consistency, too much dependability, too much sameness in a person's behavior to warrant the surrender of our task.

Two Suggested Solutions for Simplifying the Situational Problem. There are two steps we can take to meet this problem. We can continue to seek methods of assessment that cross over many situational boundaries. Pencil-and-paper techniques can do so more easily than experimental techniques, since the former can ask the subject about his behavior in many daily contexts. But if a technique is limited to a given experimental situation (as is the Rorschach, for example), we can at least insist that our diagnosis be confirmed by additional evidence drawn from ancillary techniques.

Elsewhere I have deplored our reliance on too limited a battery (1953). Projective tests, for example, need the supplement of direct methods, for otherwise we may obtain a picture of certain latent tendencies without ever knowing whether these are separated from or integrated with conscious interests and self-knowledge. It makes a world of difference whether anxiety, or homosexuality, or aggression are repressed tendencies or whether they are fully accepted and known. Projective devices used alone would never answer this question.

Besides using multiple or wider devices to enlarge the coverage of situations, we may often need frankly to admit the limited range covered by our assessment. We can say, for example, that this college student in a series of tests at college displays such and such characteristics. Just what he will do at home or in business we cannot be sure. Or that this patient, manifestly disturbed, shows such propensities, but that, owing to his condition, no wider generalization is allowable at this time.

What I am saying is that situationism is a serious obstacle to overcome. Diagnosticians should be more aware of the problem and strive for broader coverage in their instruments; at the same time they should safeguard their statements about motivation by making clear the conditions covered by the battery.

Relating Intraindividual Structure to Situational Patterns. But let us not join the camp of skeptics who say that an individual's personality is "a mere construct tied together with a name"—that there is nothing outer and objectively structured to be assessed. No scientist, I think, could survive for long if he heeded this siren song of doubt, for it leads to shipwreck. An astronomer spots a star. Like any good realist he assumes that it has properties, elements that compose it, and structure, all of which it is his scientific duty to search out and to study. When a botanist dissects a plant he does not assume that he is dissecting a construct tied together by a name. It is a plant; and its structure and its functioning interest him. Similarly, the psychologist of personality wants to come as close as he can to the veridical structure of the person he studies, and he does so in spite of the extensive and troublesome situational variability, and in spite of his own errors of observation and measurement, which he tries constantly to reduce.

A theoretical task for the future is to relate the intraindividual structure to the recurrent situational patterns which in themselves may be regarded as complex social or cultural structures. In the terms of F. H. Allport, we have to deal both with *trend structures* in the personality and with *tangential collective structures*. Between them exists some degree of *interstructurance*. Analytical research, such as that carried out by Tannenbaum and Allport (1956) should help us to determine the differentials of energy in the individual's pattern of behavior that may be ascribed, on the one hand, to internal-trend structures and, on the other, to tangential collective structures.

UNITS OF MOTIVATION AND UNITS OF PERSONALITY

We move now nearer to the heart of our subject. What is the relation between units of motivation and units of personality? I would suggest that all units of motivation are at the same time units of personality, but that not all units of personality are simultaneously units of motivation. Only a few writers have made this distinction systematically. Murray (1938) does so when he distinguishes motivational needs, or vectors, from the styles or manners of fulfilling needs represented by actones and verbones. Similarly, McClelland (1951, 1956) distinguishes motives from traits and from schemata. *Traits* he limits to recurrent patterns of expressive or stylistic behavior; *schemata*, to attitudinal orientations, cognitive and symbolic habits, and frames of reference. To him *motives* alone are the dynamic or causal forces, and these he finds satisfactorily designated by the term "needs."

We will all agree that some characteristics of personality are of a highly dynamic order, while some are of an instrumental or stylistic order. There is, for example, a distinct difference between a hate-filled complex or a driving ambition, on the one hand, and a style of urbanity or a hesitating manner, on the other. In Lewin's terms, certain regions are capable of greater tension than others. And some regions (the stylistic) are called into play only to guide the individual in the execution of more central motives. Thus a young man who is hungry for friendships goes out in the evening on a quest, but conducts himself according to his own peculiar style of timidity or confidence, reticence or garrulity. His need for affiliation and his style of seeking it are both characteristics of personality, the one being more dynamic (more motivational) than the other.

At the same time, we are not all in agreement about what constitutes a motivational unit. If we were to follow Murray, McClelland, or Freud, we would put on the one side only the inferred forces called needs, instinctual energies, or id impulses. On the other side, we would put the schemata, traits, cathexes, and features of ego structure. The implication here is that there are raw, primary, urgelike forces that alone constitute units of motivation. It is chiefly these, of course, that the projective tests seek to assess. But for my part I cannot believe that motivational units are as abstract as this procedure implies. Let me illustrate my misgiving by reference to a certain man's interests. He is, let us say, profoundly interested in politics. This simple statement tells you a great deal about his motivational structure. Is it helpful, for purposes of assessment, to dissipate this integral structure in some such analysis as follows? He has an aggressive drive, a need for externalization, and a modicum of father fixation—all of which are cathected on politics; he has certain cultural schemata that he has learned, and has a habit of reading the political news in the morning paper, together with a history of reinforcement so far as civic participation is concerned. Or to make the point simpler, shall we say that his need for aggression (which some might hold to be the ultimate motivational unit in his case) is somehow arbitrarily cathected by politics? Or shall we say—I think more accurately—that his aggression and his interest are now all of a piece? His passion for politics is one true structural fact, no matter what his past behavior history may have been. You will recognize that I am here enlisting the principle of functional autonomy.

There is no need to debate this issue now. I want merely to point out that ultimate motivational units may not be only the unconscious urges, ergs, needs, or instinctual energies favored by certain forms of psychodynamic theory; nor are they accessible solely through projective techniques, even though these are certainly legitimate tools to use in a total battery of assessment methods.

Classes of Units in Current Assessment Research. Let us ask now what classes of units we find in current assessment research. No single investigator deals with them all, for each specializes in his own pet dimensions. Our question is what picture emerges if we try to catch a glimpse of all the investigators at work at once.

Tests and scales: The preference of many investigators for multivariate scales makes difficulty at the outset for our attempt at orderly classification. A generation ago we were content with one test for ascendance-submission, with a wholly separate test for extroversion-introversion, and so on. While such single scales are still with us, our hunger for omnibus instruments has grown. Take the field of neuroticism. At first (in 1917), we had the Woodworth Personal Data Sheet, which measured one and only one alleged unit—a neurotic disposition. The Cornell Index developed by Weider in 1945 still yielded a general score for the selection or rejection of armed services personnel, but at the same time differentiated various types of neurotic maladjustment. More widely used today is the MMPI, with its 550 items subdivided into twenty-six unitary tendencies. Most of these relate to pathological trends, but one cannot say that the units sought are conceptually uniform. Thus our multiphasic instruments, our many-faceted inventories, our multiple-factor devices, and our miscellaneous profiles make it hard to sort out the types of units involved. The current vogue is to assess everything all at once, but in the process the possibility of theoretical analysis seems to suffer. I wonder whether this desire is not caused in part by the fact that the Rorschach Test at first claimed to measure "the total personality." Such an intoxicating possibility led us to give up our earlier slingshot scales and adopt the shotgun inventory.

In spite of the shotgun's scatter, let us try to classify the units sought in personality assessment. Without claiming any finality for my listing, I call attention to ten classes of units that seem to me to be widely studied today.

The ten classes of units studied today: 1. INTELLECTUAL CAPACITIES. This area is so large in its own right that we ordinarily segregate it from both motivation and personality assessment. I mention it here only because a complete assessment could not possibly leave it out of account. Some day, I hope, we may be able to relate intellectual functioning more intimately than we now do to motivational and personal functioning.

2. SYNDROMES OF TEMPERAMENT. In this group we note recent progress. One thinks of the work of Sheldon, of Thurstone, Cattell, Guilford, and others. Thanks to their efforts, we can now assess such units as general activity, sense of well-being, restraint, emotional stability, lability, somatotonia. While one could wish for a stricter limitation of the concept of temperament than some of these investigators employ, still they deal constructively with units representing the prevailing "emotional weather" in which personalities develop.

3. UNCONSCIOUS MOTIVES. Without doubt the greatest interest of clinical psychologists is in units of this general class. Sometimes they are called needs (though no one insists that all needs are unconscious); often they involve dimensions with a Freudian flavor, such as anxiety, aggression, oral or anal trends, Oedipal fixation. The theory holds that

such deep and buried motives are somehow more real and basic than
units tapped by other methods. This contention, as I have already indicated, can never be proved unless both direct methods and projective
methods are used for the same variables with the same personalities.

4. SOCIAL ATTITUDES. Here are units of quite a different order. While
they have been evolved chiefly in social psychology, they are part and
parcel of any complete clinical assessment program. We want to know
how our subject views the church, or how he regards Russia. We want
to know his liberal or conservative tendencies, likewise his score on
scales for authoritarianism, ethnocentrism, dogmatism, traditional family ideology. These last-mentioned units illustrate the inevitable arbi-
trariness of our classification, for while they deal with social attitudes
they likewise pretend to disclose deeper aspects of character structure,
and thus overlap with our other categories.

5. IDEATIONAL SCHEMATA. Growing out of the study of social attitudes
we find today considerable concern with generalized thought-forms. One
may cite Klein's efforts to discover general styles or *Anschauungen*
which cut through both motivational and cognitive functions. One may
cite Kelly's proposal to study the constructs a person employs in viewing
the world around him. Witkin (1954) and others establish the syndromes of "field dependence" and "field independence." Though Witkin's diagnostic method is anchored in perceptual measurement, he finds
that the "field dependent" person is characterized also by anxiety, by
fear of his impulses, by poor impulse control, and by a general lack of
awareness of his own inner life.

6. INTERESTS AND VALUES. In contrast to unconscious motivational
units, we find many dimensions that deal with structured motives rather
than with their presumed underlying dynamics. Here we would cite
measures of interest in art, farming, or salesmanship. We would cite the
six Spranger units as measured by the Allport-Vernon-Lindzey *Study of
Values*. Perhaps here, too, we would locate the summary measure of
masculinity-femininity based on a potpourri of conscious choices.

7. EXPRESSIVE TRAITS. A number of units seem to fall halfway between
motivational and stylistic dimensions. For want of a better term, we may
call them expressive. Among them we may include dominance tendencies, extroversion, persistence and empathy, also sociability, self-control,
criticalness, accessibility, and meticulous or "just so" trends.

8. STYLISTIC TRAITS. This group receives least attention, probably because psychologists regard stylistic traits as lying on the surface of personality. One might include here politeness, talkativeness, consistency, hesitancy, and other measurable manners of behaving. Ultimately we may expect that these stylistic characteristics will be related to deeper structural units, but they are also measurable in their own right.

9. PATHOLOGICAL TRENDS. Many investigators prefer to analyze motivation and personality in familiar clinical terms. Hysteric, manic, neurotic, schizoid dispositions are the sort of units we find employed in the assessments of both normal and abnormal personalities. We have spoken of the evolution of these measures from the Woodworth PD sheet to the MMPI. One could mention as equally illustrative of this group the Humm-Wadsworth Test and other derivations from the Kraepelin and Kretschmer classifications.

10. FACTORIAL CLUSTERS. As yet I have not referred to factors. Factorial units in part belong in the classes we have already considered. Clearly, Thurstone's "primary mental abilities" are properly classified under Intellectual Capacities. Most of the factors proposed by Guilford and Zimmerman can be located under temperament syndromes or under expressive traits. Most of Cattell's factors can be similarly sorted. But at the same time many of the factors that result from summarizing mathematically the data from many tests used with many people often defy conceptual analysis in any of the preceding classes. Thus Guilford and Zimmerman (1956) report an "unidentified" factor, called C_2, that represents some baffling blend of impulsiveness, absentmindedness, emotional fluctuation, nervousness, loneliness, ease of emotional expression, and feelings of guilt. When units of this sort appear—and I submit that it happens not infrequently—one wonders what to say about them. To me they resemble sausage meat that has failed to pass the pure food and health inspection.

I am not saying that factorial analysis does not have its place in the search for units. It seems to me that when factor analysts deal with a conceptually defined field to start with, such as extroversion and introversion, they often succeed in improving for us the clarity and accessibility of dimensions. In other words, factors are better when they follow theory than when they create it.

Factors are simply a summary principle of classification of many measures used with (usually) many people. This property does not suddenly endow them with new power. They are not, as some enthusiasts hold, "the cause of all human conduct," nor are they "source" traits as opposed to "surface" traits. Nor are they the "influence" underlying all behavior. They are neither more nor less motivational than other units. Usually they are nothing more than empirically derived descriptions of the average man.

In this respect factors do not differ markedly from the other types of units we have described. All of them presume to offer scalable dimensions; that is to say, they are common units in respect to which all personalities can be compared. None of them corresponds to the cleavages that exist in any single personality unless the single personal structure happens to be like that of the empirically derived average man. Still, scalable dimensions are useful dimensions, and we hope that work will continue until we reach firmer agreement concerning their number and nature.

I cannot claim that the thousands of dimensions proposed to guide our analysis of motivation and personality can all be neatly included in this tenfold scheme; but it may be helpful to our thinking.

As yet investigators have reached little or no agreement; they are not yet able to say, "These are the most useful units to employ." For the guidance of elementary students, Woodworth and Marquis (1947), basing their classification on Cattell (1946), ventured a "List of the most clearly established primary traits":

Easy-going, intelligent, emotionally stable, dominant, placid, sensitive, trained and cultured, conscientious, adventurous, vigorous, hypersensitive, friendly.

But professional psychologists are not yet ready to fix upon this, or any other "primary" list.

Intercorrelation of traits: A word should be said about the intercorrelation of traits. Factor analysis in its earlier years hoped to eliminate this troublesome phenomenon by seeking factors orthogonal to one another. But even factor analysts now admit that this goal is impracticable. A certain tendency to co-exist must be expected among human qualities. Of course, if correlations are very high (as they would certainly be between scales for "dominance" and "ascendance," or for "depression" and "melancholy"), it would be foolish to retain separate scales for synonymous, or nearly synonymous, traits.

One of the most insistent intercorrelations that occur indicates a general soundness, or strength, or dependability of character structure, or the opposite syndrome. Vernon (1953) shows how this pattern—he calls it "dependability"—emerges in factorial studies. The Grant Study at Harvard, working intensively with normal young men, was forced to adopt a general over-all measure of "soundness" (Heath, 1945). In general, it does not seem that a "halo" effect deriving from the bias of raters can account for this finding.

When such persistent intercorrelations occur between any clusters of traits, what shall we call them—types? syndromes? far-reaching dimensions? My own preference would be for "syndrome," since the term clearly indicates co-existence among conceptually distinct variables. The term "type," I fear, would lead us into trouble, since the term has many additional meanings.

Individual Structural Pattern. Now let us turn finally to a somewhat alarming possibility. What shall we do if the cleavages in any single life do not correspond to the empirical cleavages derived from studies of the average man? Can it be that our unending search for common units, now multiplying year by year, is a kind of nomothetic fantasy on our part? Can it be that the structural organization of Joseph Doakes's personality is unique to him alone?

If such a possibility seems too traumatic to face, let us ask the question in a milder way. Suppose we leave our common units unmolested and apply them as seems helpful in our assessment work; what shall we do when a given case seems to be completely by-passed by the common dimensions? A. L. Baldwin (1946), for example, in discussing four nursery school children, writes that the group analysis gave reasonably accurate interpretations of the behavior of three of the four children, but the fourth was not described adequately in terms of the group factors. And he adds, "Even in cases where group factors were approximately accurate, some aspects of the individual's personality were not revealed" (p. 168).

Perhaps what we need is fewer units than we now use, but units more relevant to individual structural patterns.

Pilot exercise: To gain some preliminary insight into this matter I tried a simple pilot exercise with ninety-three students. I asked them "to think of some one individual of your own sex whom you know well"; then "to describe him or her by writing in each space provided, a word, phrase, or a sentence that expresses fairly well what seems to you to be some essential characteristic of this person." The page provided eight spaces, and the students were told to "use as many spaces as you need." The term "essential characteristic" was defined as "any trait, quality, tendency, interest, etc. that you regard as of major importance to a description of the person you select."

After the student had finished with the first page he received a second page that added two additional blank spaces for further characteristics. The question was then asked, "Do you feel the need for more than ten essential characteristics? If so, about how many more do you think you would need?" A further question asked, "Do you feel that some of the characteristics you have named are duplicates (i.e., more or less synonymous), so that really fewer would have sufficed? If so, about how many in all would have been sufficient?"

Faulty though this method may be, the results are not without interest. Only 10 per cent of the subjects felt that they needed more than ten "essential characteristics," and for the most part these were vague regarding the total number that would be required: two said they needed an additional ten, one needed fifty, others did not know.

Ninety per cent of the students, however, found the exercise meaningful and the total of ten spaces provided fully adequate. On the average, they indicated that 7.2 "essential characteristics" would cover their needs, the range being from 3 to 10.

One might object that the method employed had the effect of suggesting a rather small number of "essential characteristics." Perhaps this is so, though I shall in a moment cite independent supporting evidence for the proposition that a relatively small number of structural units covers the major aspects of personality.

From my point of view the weakness of the experiment lies chiefly in the somewhat sketchy definition of "essential characteristic." Many students, though not all, were content with common trait names, such as *friendly, loyal, intelligent,* or *dependable.* I should not expect such terms ordinarily to do justice to the peculiar coherent structure of friendliness, loyalty, intelligence, or dependability that mark the life in question. Here we are confronted with the universal problem in all idiographic research: nouns cut slices *across* people rather than *within* people. It requires more deftness with language than most of us possess to put together a phrase or sentence that will pinpoint *individual* structure. It is precisely here that the gifts of the novelist and biographer exceed those of the psychologist.

In literature: Turning for a moment to the field of biography, we find confirmation of our point in Ralph Barton Perry's (1936) definitive volumes on *The Thought and Character of William James*. Summing up his exhaustive study of this complex and fascinating figure, Perry concludes that in order to understand him one must deal with eight leading "traits" or "ingredients." He first lists four "morbid" or "pathological" traits—tendencies that taken by themselves would have proved to be severe handicaps. These are (1) hypochondria, (2) preoccupation with "exceptional mental states," (3) marked oscillations of mood, and (4) repugnance to the processes of exact thought. Blended with, and redeeming, these morbid trends are four "benign" traits: (5) sensibility, (6) vivacity, (7) humanity, (8) sociability. While, like the students in our exercise, Perry uses common trait names, he proceeds immediately to define them in such a way that the peculiar Jamesian flavor of each ingredient is brought to light. Clinical psychologists need some of the biographer's skill in particularizing terms. Standing alone, such terms are only hollow universals.

It seems to me that George Kelly in his *Psychology of Personal Constructs* (1955) is approaching the same goal from a different direction. He holds that the important thing about any person is the major way in which he construes his life-experiences, including his social contacts. Hence, in order to understand a person, we should adopt what Kelly calls the "credulous approach." Through interviewing or by studying self-characterizations, perhaps with the aid of the Role Construct Repertory Test (REP), we arrive at our diagnosis. The method yields constructs that are unique to the individual as well as constructs he has in common with others. Further, it leads to the discovery of the unique pattern of relations, among the several constructs of a given person. Speaking of widely used scaling and factoring procedures, Kelly rightly observes that while such methods provide a quick and sure exploitation of common constructs (applicable to all people) they prevent us from discovering new and unique constructs and fall into the additional error of assuming that the greatest commonality defines the greatest truth.

In a personal communication Professor Kelly tells me that he is not yet prepared to say how many major constructs the average individual uses, but sometimes, he reports, an individual's responses to REP "can be condensed into one or two major dimensions with two or three rows left over as specific constructs." It is true that people with an intellectual bent often seem to produce a variety of constructs, but their large vocabulary does not entirely obscure the relative simplicity of their patterns. Kelly speaks likewise of a useful therapeutic rule of thumb. "The patient may change the topic in the middle of an interview but he rarely changes the theme." Themes are persistent and recurring. While each person may have certain specific and concrete constructs that apply to limited and special areas of experience, Professor Kelly concludes that the clinician does not ordinarily identify more than "four of five major construct dimensions." We hope that work with the REP Test and with other quantitative clinical instruments will continue until we find a firm answer to our question.

A similar promising lead lies in the technique of "personal cluster analysis" set forth by Alfred Baldwin (1942). Analyzing an extensive written correspondence from an elderly woman, he discovers only four or five major ideational and value-laden themes.

Another related proposal was put forward some years ago by F. H. Allport (1937), who suggested measuring the consistency of an individual's acts in relation to his own principal life purposes or "teleonomic trends." The investigator could from previous acquaintance hypothesize the principal themes or trends (or "constructs" or "clusters") he expects to find in a given life. He could then by observation—with due checks for reliability—order the daily acts of the individual to these hypothesized dimensions. If we used this method systematically we might well find, as do Perry, Kelly, and Baldwin, that a handful of major structures covers the life surprisingly well, even though specific and unrelated minor trends may likewise appear.

Individuality in human nature: The proverbial visitor from Mars would, I think, find it incomprehensible that so little sustained work has been done in this promising direction of individuality. He would say to the earthbound psychologist: "Human nature on your planet is infinitely diverse. No two people are alike. While you give lip service to this proposition, you immediately discard it. What is more, people's internal structural organization—individual by individual—may be far simpler and more accessible than you think. Why not take the cleavages nature offers you and follow them through? Even granted that uniformities run through nature at its lower levels of organization—the chemical elements composing the body are identical—still at the higher levels of organization where the psychologist works the units you seek are not uniform at all. A baby, once started on the road of life, will fashion, out of his unique inheritance and special environment, nodes of accretion, foci of learning, directions of growth, that become increasingly unique as the years roll along. And won't you have a good laugh at yourself when you discover this elementary fact? And then perhaps you'll look for your units where you ought to look for them—in each developing life."

I venture to hope we shall heed the admonition of the visitor from Mars. That we have not done so is due, of course, to the prevailing conviction that science cannot deal with individual cases at all, excepting as they exemplify general laws or display uniform structures. The philosophers of the Middle Ages felt the same way, their dogma being *scientia non est individuorum*. But isn't the definition of science at best an arbitrary matter—at worst, an idol of the den?

SUMMARY

In the interest of perspective, let me summarize my principal points. The search for the units that comprise motivation and compose personality is very ancient. Not until the past generation or two has appreciable progress been made. During recent years, however, we have followed a bewildering array of approaches, many of them fresh and imaginative, and resulting in more measured aspects than anyone can conveniently compute. Broadly speaking, these uncounted thousands of nomothetic units fall into ten classes: intellectual capacities, syndromes of temperament, unconscious motives, social attitudes, ideational schemata, interests and values, expressive traits, stylistic traits, pathological trends, and factorial clusters not readily classifiable in the other nine categories. Some investigators, of course, propose units that combine two or more of these classes. While I suspect there may be some overenthusiasm for certain categories (I would name here the overzealous use of projective tests for tapping unconscious motives and overaddiction to factorial units), still I would not discourage research in any of these ten directions.

We have to accept the fact that up to now relatively little agreement has been achieved. It seems that each assessor has his own pet units and uses a pet battery of diagnostic devices. But it is too early to despair. Instead of discouragement, I hope that our present disagreement will lead to continuous and wholesome experimentation. Essential to continued progress is a firm belief in the "outer reality" of personal and motivational systems. The fact that the units we seek are invisible should not deter us. Nor should we yield to the destructive skepticism of certain extreme methodologists who hold that the whole search is chimerical. Finally, while we must admit the variabilities of the structures we seek, which are caused by changing situations without and continual growth and change within, we should take this fact into our design and theory, not surrendering our belief that reasonably stable personal and motivational structures exist.

Such, in brief, is the present state of affairs with nomothetic assessment, as I see it. But I have argued in addition that we will do well to turn to the fresher possibilities that lie in improved idiographic analysis. Nor should we be deterred by preconceived ideas about what science can and cannot with propriety do. The conquerors of Mt. Everest did not allow themselves to be blocked by the sacred cows they encountered in the streets of Darjeeling. Nor should we. But perhaps the goal ahead may not be as formidable as Mt. Everest. It may turn out to be only as high and as wide and as human as the personality of John Citizen, who is after all our old and familiar friend.

REFERENCES

Allport, F. H. Teleonomic description in the study of personality. *Char. &
Pers.*, 1937, 6, 202-214.

Allport, G. W. *Personality: a psychological interpretation.* Chap. 3. New
York: Holt, 1937.

————. The trend in motivational theory. *Amer. J. Orthopsychiat.*, 1953,
23, 107-119.

American Psychologist, 1957, 12, 51.

Baldwin, A. L. Personal structure analysis: a statistical method for investigating the single personality. *J. abnorm. soc. Psychol.*, 1942, 37, 163-
183.

————. The study of individual personality by means of the intraindividual
correlation. *J. Pers.*, 1946, 14, 151-168.

Bernard, L. L. *Instinct: a study in social psychology.* New York: Holt, 1924.
P. 220.

Cattell, R. B. *Description and measurement of personality.* Yonkers, N.Y.:
World Book, 1946.

Coutu, W. *Emergent human nature.* New York: Knopf, 1949.

Guilford, J. P., and Zimmerman, W. S. Fourteen dimensions of temperament. *Psychol. Monog.*, 1956, No. 417.

Heath, C .W., *What people are.* Cambridge: Harvard University Press,
1945.

Hebb, D. O. *The organization of behavior.* New York: Wiley, 1949.

James, W. *Psychology: briefer course.* New York: Holt, 1910.

Kelly, G. A. *The psychology of personal constructs.* Vol. I. New York: Norton, 1955. P. 34.

McClelland, D. C. *Personality.* New York: Dryden, 1951. See also his
Personality: an integrative view. In J. L. McCary (ed.), *Psychology of
personality.* New York: Logos, 1956.

MacCorquodale, K., and Meehl, P. E. On a distinction between hypothetical constructs and intervening variables. *Psychol. Rev.*, 1948, 55, 95-
107.

Murray, H. A., *et al. Explorations in personality.* New York: Oxford University Press, 1938.

Perry, R. B. *The thought and character of William James.* Vol. II. Chaps.
90-91. Boston: Little, Brown, 1936.

Sherrington, Charles. *Man on his nature,* 2nd ed. Chap. 1. New York:
Doubleday Anchor Books, 1953.

Tagiuri, R., and Petrullo, L. (eds.). *Person perception and interpersonal behavior.* Stanford University Press, 1958.

Tannenbaum, A. S., and Allport, F. H. Personality structure and group structure: an interpretative study of their relationship through an event-structure hypothesis. *J. abnorm. & soc. Psychol.*, 1956, 53, 272-280.

Vernon, P. E. *Personality tests and assessments*. London: Methuen, 1953.

Witkin, H. A., Lewis, H. B., Hertzman, M., Machover, K., Meissner, P., and Wapner, S. *Personality through perception*. New York: Harper, 1954.

Woodworth, R. S., and Marquis, D. G. *Psychology*. New York: Holt, 1947.

INDEX

Index

Heider, F., 116
Hempel, C., 176, 180
Hernandez-Péon, R., 114, 117
Heron, W., 115, 117
Hertzman, M., 260
Hilgard, E. R., 10, 31, 151, 177, 180
Hippocrates, 239
Hobbes, Thomas, 4
Holt, Robert R., 87 n., 112, 117, 122, 145, 146, 147
Holzman, P. S., 87, 106, 109, 110, 113, 117
Horney, Karen, 175, 180
Hull, C. L., 7, 8, 242
Humor, regression in the service of the ego and, 125-126
Humors, the, 239-240

Individual cases, detailed studies of, compared to experimental research, 29-30, 64
Infallibility, half-truths vs., 33-35
Insight, 52
Instincts, 240
Instrumental attitudes, 88
Interview, psychoanalytic, as an observational method, 149-178
Irrationality, reconciling, with rationality, 36-41
Isaacs, Susan, 165, 180

Jacob, P., 92
James, W., 244, 255, 259
Janis, Irving, 15, 17, 20, 22, 24, 25, 27, 30, 84, 86, 149-178, 180
Johansson, G., 106, 117
Jones, E., 158, 180
Jouvet, M., 114, 117

Kelly, George, 15-16, 19-20, 21-22, 23, 24, 25, 26, 28, 31, 33-64, 250, 255-256, 259
King, B. T., 84, 86
Klein, George S., 15, 16, 20, 22, 23, 25, 26, 28, 29, 87-115, 117, 250
Kluckhohn, C., 170, 180
Knight, R., 161, 180
Koch, S., 4, 7, 8, 31
Kohler, Ivo, 94, 98, 103, 117

Motivation (*Continued*)

    construct of, directionality of movement and, 50-56

        implies that man is essentially inert, 49

        redundant in explaining man's activity, 49-50

    contemporary, importance of knowledge of the past in assessment of, 26, 63

    repudiation of notion of, 35-48, 59-60

    as a theoretical concept, 66, 68

    unconscious, 5, 249-250

        importance of, 19-20, 62

Motivational assessment, direct vs. indirect techniques for, 20-22, 62-63

    interest in, 3-6

    major issues in, 18-31, 62-64

    status of, 3-6

Motivational structure, preconditions for the study of, 199-201

Motivational units, 18, 239-258

    classes of, in current assessment research, 248-253

    contemporary search for, 240-244

    early inadequate, 239-240

Motivational variables, appraisal of small number of, vs. wide array of, 27, 64

    assessing, absence of adequate measuring devices for, 13

    conceptual nature of, 4

    importance of, 3-4

    importance of developing measures of, 26-27, 64

    new, importance of identifying, 26-27, 64

    single, measurement, 201-208

Mowrer, O. H., 54, 64

Murphy, Gardner, 87 *n*., 117

Murray, E., 162, 178

Murray, H. A., 6, 18, 20, 22, 25, 26, 27, 28, 29, 31, 32, 117, 183-196, 211, 217, 238, 247, 259

Needs, variety of, involved in a single course of action, 185-186

Neurotic paradox, 54-55

Newburg, A. S., 188, 196

Objective thinking, 41, 42

    pitfall of, 55

Olden, C., 129, 130, 147

Operationalism, 55

Osgood, C. E., 107, 118